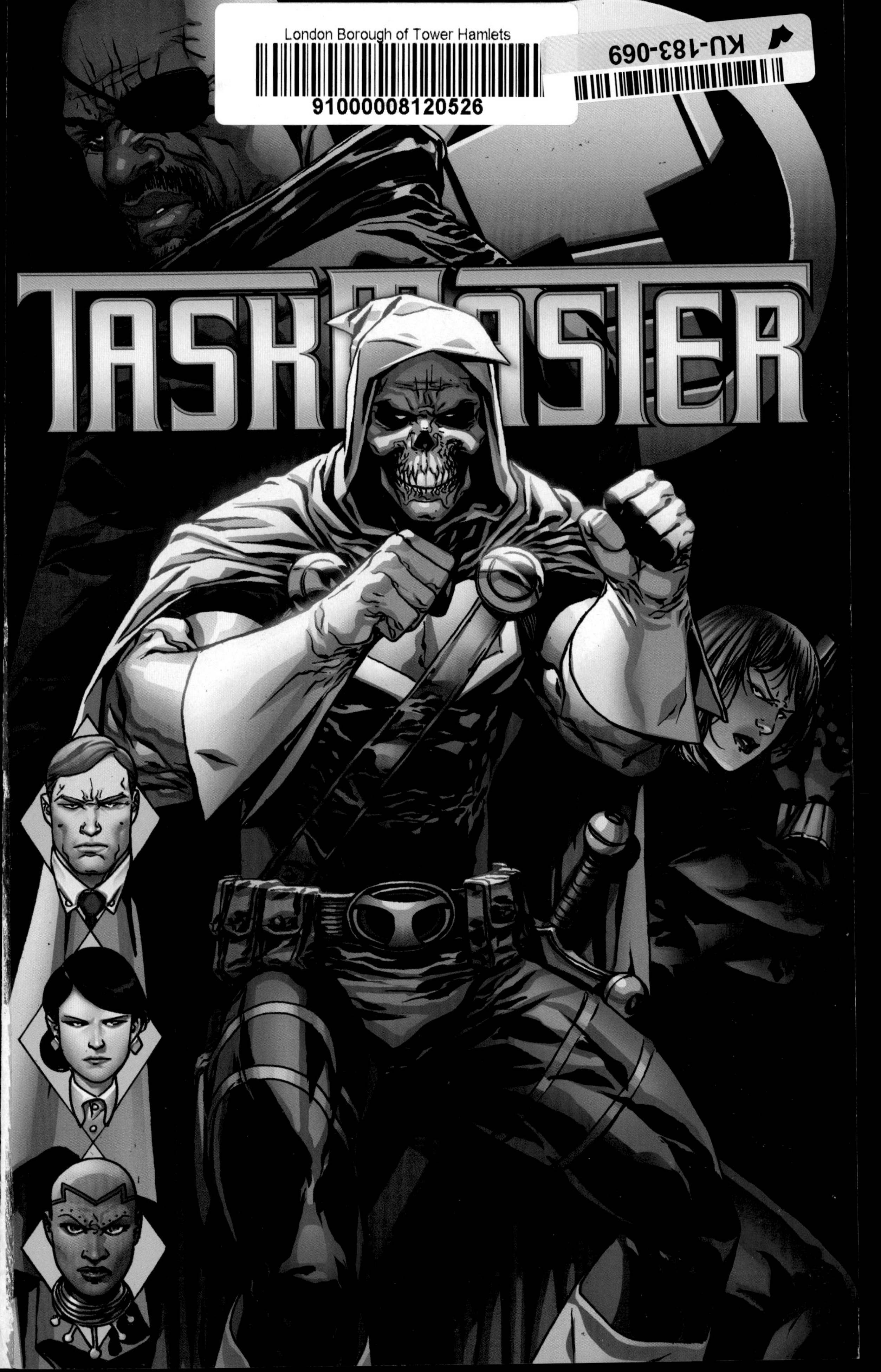
TASKMASTER

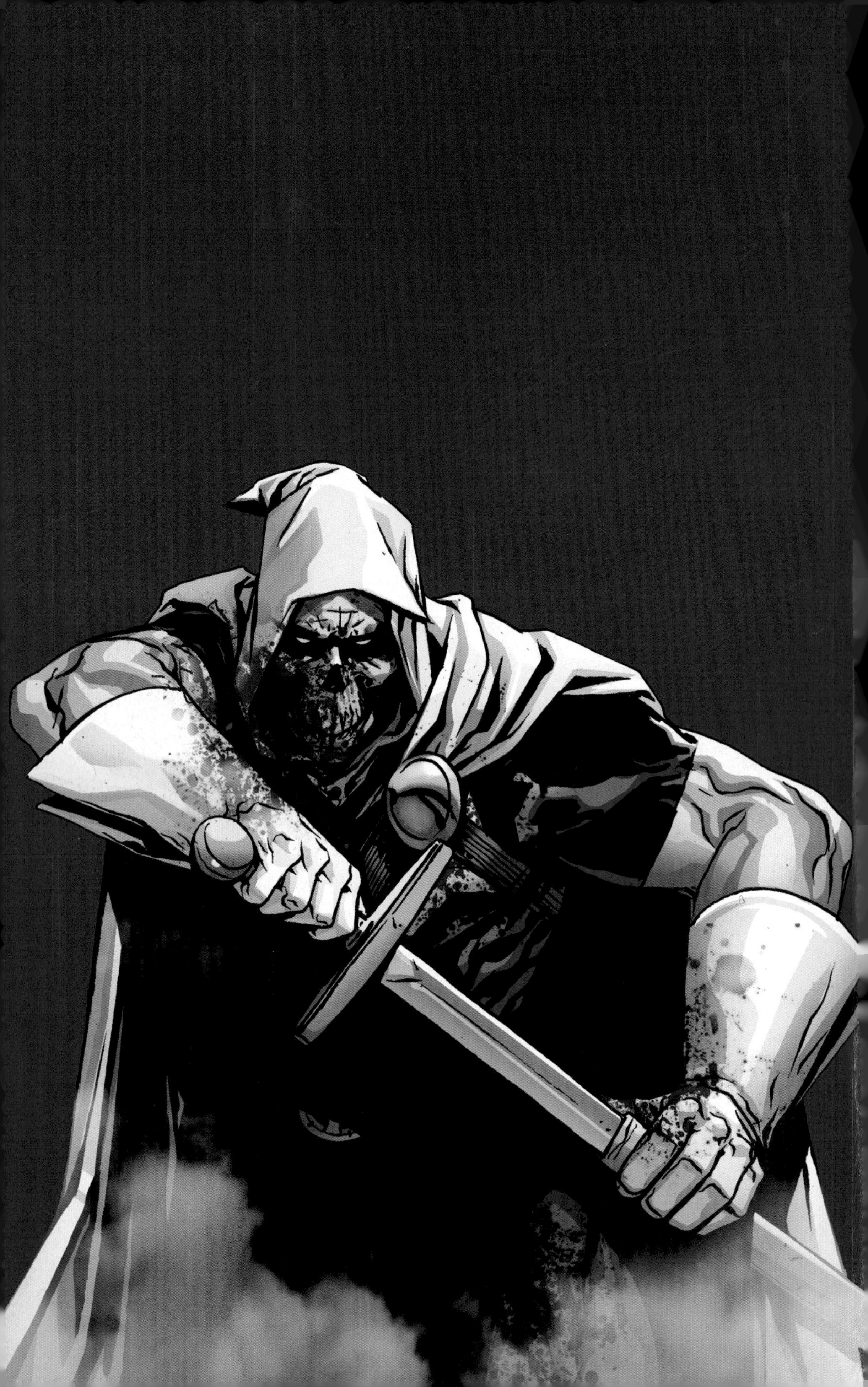

# TASKMASTER
## THE RUBICON TRIGGER

WRITER
### Jed MacKay

ARTIST
### Alessandro Vitti

COLOR ARTIST
### Guru-eFX

LETTERER
### VC's Joe Caramagna

COVER ART
### Valerio Giangiordano & Arif Prianto

EDITOR
### Chris Robinson

SENIOR EDITOR
### Jordan D. White

SPECIAL THANKS TO
### Sarah Brunstad, Jeongkeon Kim & Yujin Lee

COLLECTION EDITOR
JENNIFER GRÜNWALD

ASSISTANT EDITOR
DANIEL KIRCHHOFFER

ASSISTANT MANAGING EDITOR
MAIA LOY

ASSISTANT MANAGING EDITOR
LISA MONTALBANO

VP PRODUCTION & SPECIAL PROJECTS
JEFF YOUNGQUIST

BOOK DESIGNER
ADAM DEL RE

SVP PRINT, SALES & MARKETING
DAVID GABRIEL

EDITOR IN CHIEF
C.B. CEBULSKI

TASKMASTER: THE RUBICON TRIGGER. Contains material originally published in magazine form as TASKMASTER (2020) #1-5. First printing 2021. ISBN 978-1-302-92171-2. Published by MARVEL WORLDWIDE, INC., a subsidiary of MARVEL ENTERTAINMENT, LLC. OFFICE OF PUBLICATION: 1290 Avenue of the Americas, New York, NY 10104. © 2021 MARVEL No similarity between any of the names, characters, persons, and/or institutions in this magazine with those of any living or dead person or institution is intended, and any such similarity which may exist is purely coincidental. Printed in Canada. KEVIN FEIGE, Chief Creative Officer; DAN BUCKLEY, President, Marvel Entertainment; JOE QUESADA, EVP & Creative Director; DAVID BOGART, Associate Publisher & SVP of Talent Affairs; TOM BREVOORT, VP, Executive Editor; NICK LOWE, Executive Editor, VP of Content, Digital Publishing; DAVID GABRIEL, VP of Print & Digital Publishing; JEFF YOUNGQUIST, VP of Production & Special Projects; ALEX MORALES, Director of Publishing Operations; DAN EDINGTON, Managing Editor; RICKEY PURDIN, Director of Talent Relations; JENNIFER GRÜNWALD, Senior Editor, Special Projects; SUSAN CRESPI, Production Manager; STAN LEE, Chairman Emeritus. For information regarding advertising in Marvel Comics or on Marvel.com, please contact Vit DeBellis, Custom Solutions & Integrated Advertising Manager, at vdebellis@marvel.com. For Marvel subscription inquiries, please call 888-511-5480. Manufactured between 5/21/2021 and 6/22/2021 by SOLISCO PRINTERS, SCOTT, QC, CANADA.

10 9 8 7 6 5 4 3 2 1

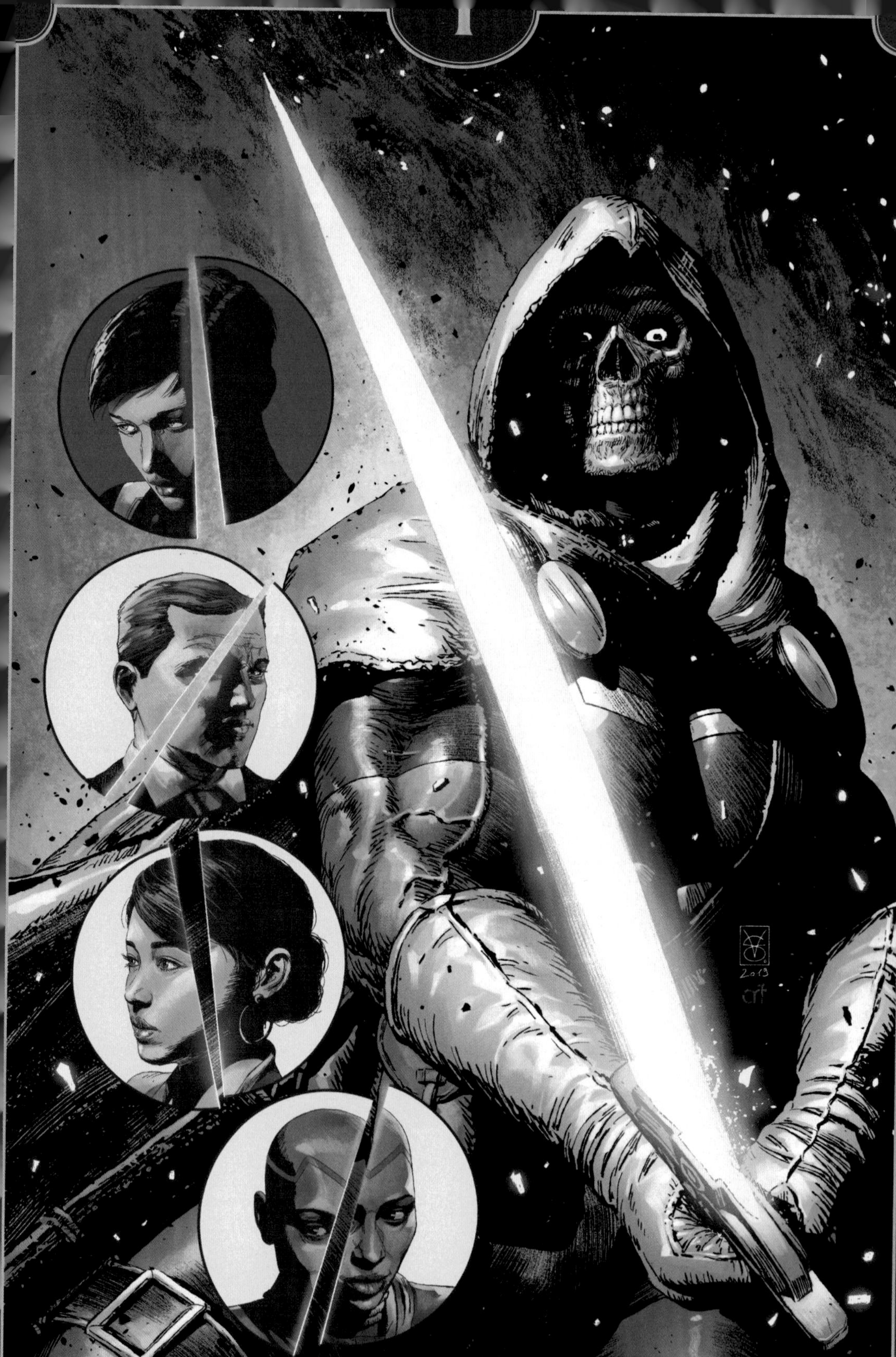

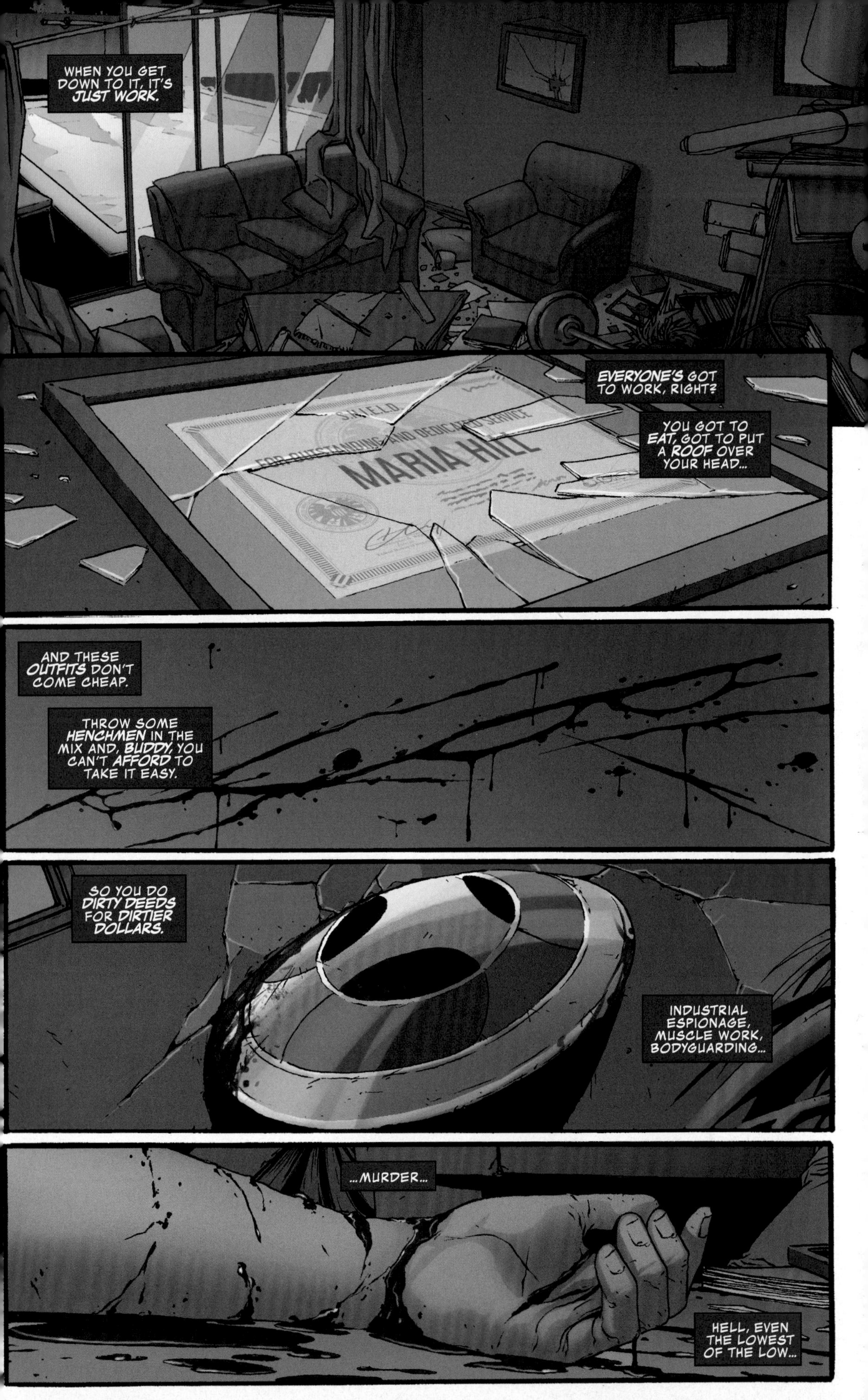
WHEN YOU GET DOWN TO IT, IT'S JUST WORK.
S.H.I.E.L.D.
FOR OUTSTANDING AND DEDICATED SERVICE
MARIA HILL
EVERYONE'S GOT TO WORK, RIGHT?
YOU GOT TO EAT, GOT TO PUT A ROOF OVER YOUR HEAD...
AND THESE OUTFITS DON'T COME CHEAP.
THROW SOME HENCHMEN IN THE MIX AND, BUDDY, YOU CAN'T AFFORD TO TAKE IT EASY.
SO YOU DO DIRTY DEEDS FOR DIRTIER DOLLARS.
INDUSTRIAL ESPIONAGE, MUSCLE WORK, BODYGUARDING...
...MURDER...
HELL, EVEN THE LOWEST OF THE LOW...

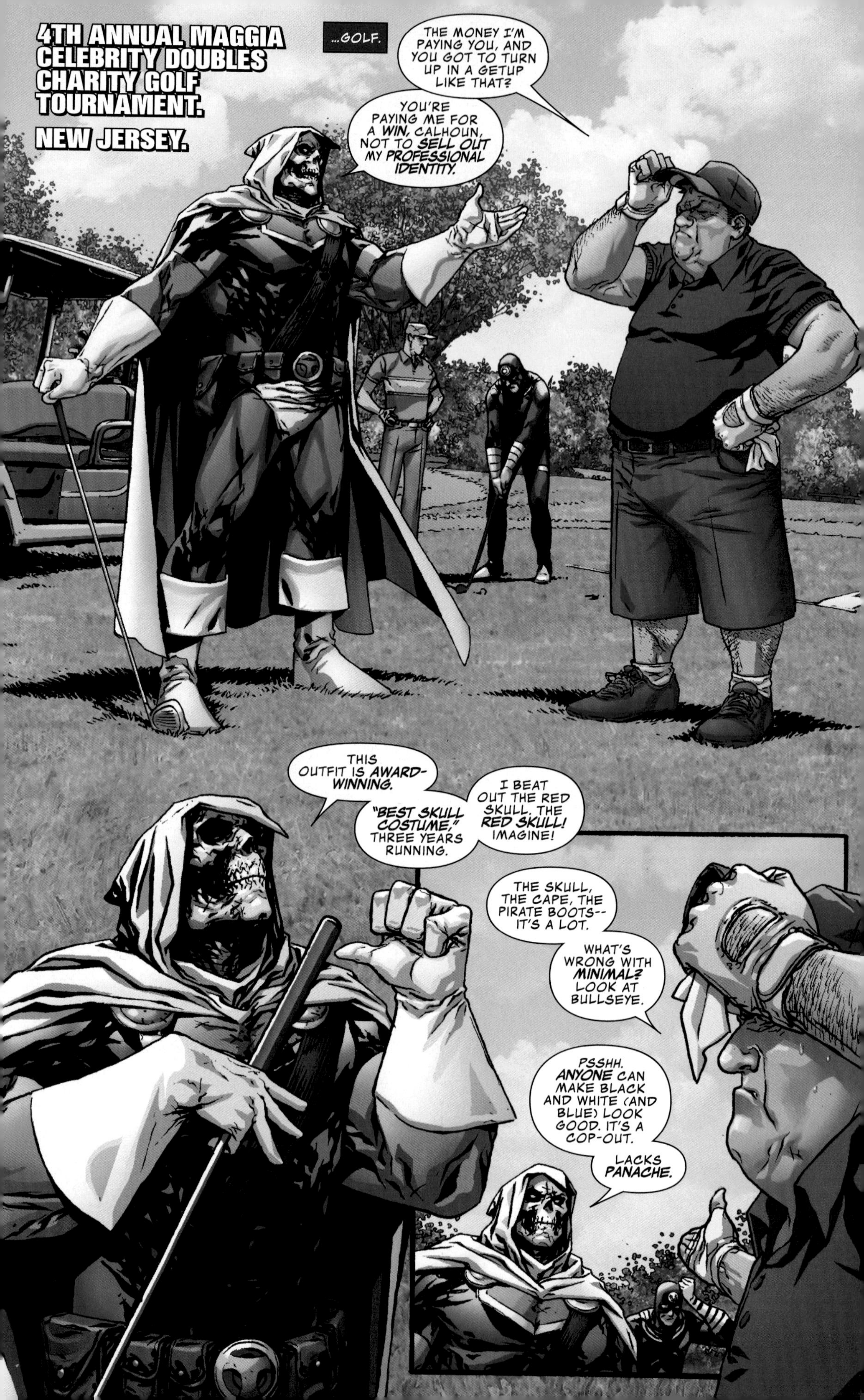
4TH ANNUAL MAGGIA CELEBRITY DOUBLES CHARITY GOLF TOURNAMENT.
NEW JERSEY.
...GOLF.
THE MONEY I'M PAYING YOU, AND YOU GOT TO TURN UP IN A GETUP LIKE THAT?
YOU'RE PAYING ME FOR A WIN, CALHOUN, NOT TO SELL OUT MY PROFESSIONAL IDENTITY.
THIS OUTFIT IS AWARD-WINNING.
"BEST SKULL COSTUME," THREE YEARS RUNNING.
I BEAT OUT THE RED SKULL. THE RED SKULL! IMAGINE!
THE SKULL, THE CAPE, THE PIRATE BOOTS--IT'S A LOT.
WHAT'S WRONG WITH MINIMAL? LOOK AT BULLSEYE.
PSSHH. ANYONE CAN MAKE BLACK AND WHITE (AND BLUE) LOOK GOOD. IT'S A COP-OUT.
LACKS PANACHE.

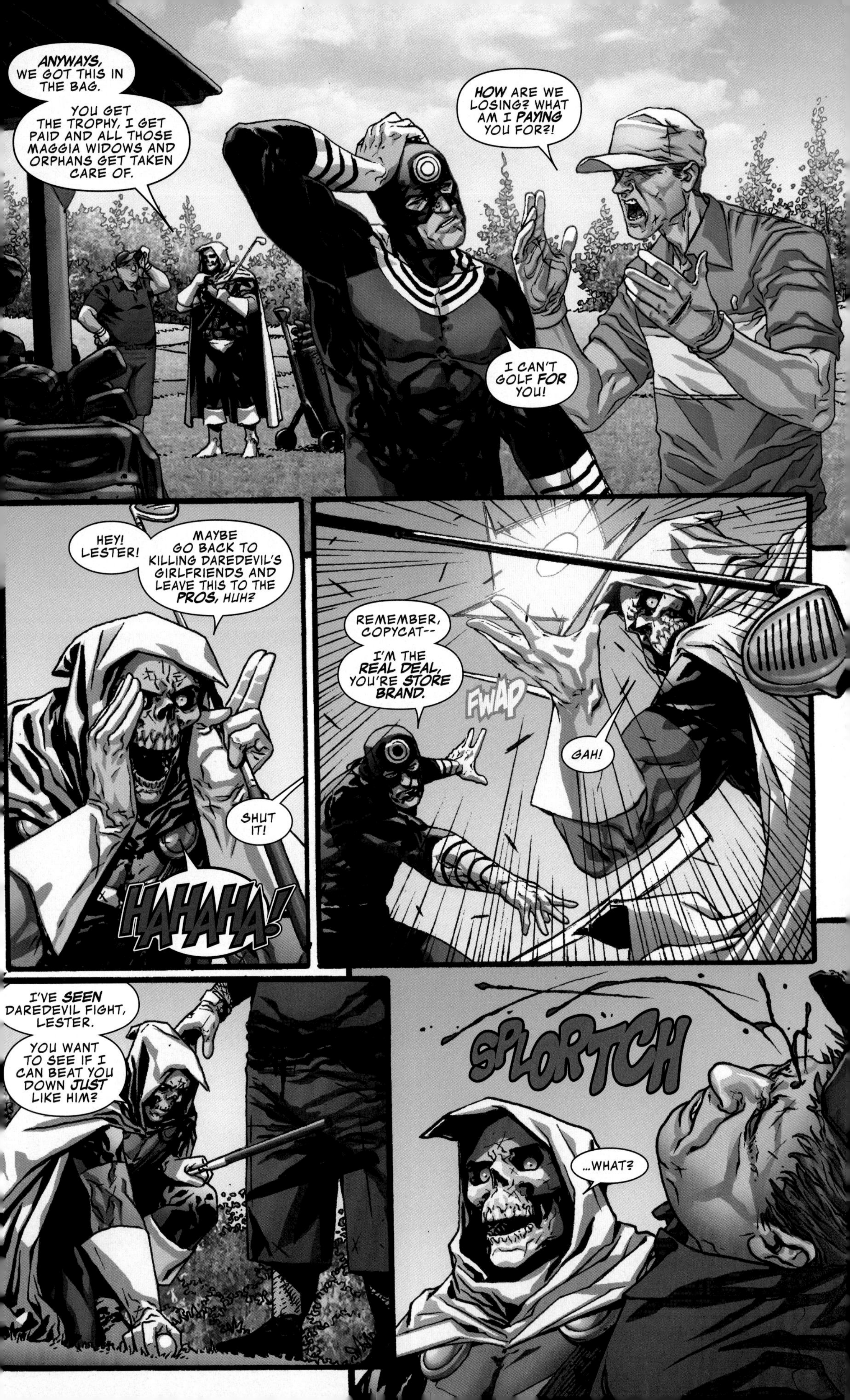
ANYWAYS, WE GOT THIS IN THE BAG.
YOU GET THE TROPHY, I GET PAID AND ALL THOSE MAGGIA WIDOWS AND ORPHANS GET TAKEN CARE OF.
HOW ARE WE LOSING? WHAT AM I PAYING YOU FOR?!
I CAN'T GOLF FOR YOU!
HEY! LESTER!
MAYBE GO BACK TO KILLING DAREDEVIL'S GIRLFRIENDS AND LEAVE THIS TO THE PROS, HUH?
SHUT IT!
HAHAHA!
REMEMBER, COPYCAT--
I'M THE REAL DEAL, YOU'RE STORE BRAND.
FWAP
GAH!
I'VE SEEN DAREDEVIL FIGHT, LESTER.
YOU WANT TO SEE IF I CAN BEAT YOU DOWN JUST LIKE HIM?
SPLORTCH
...WHAT?

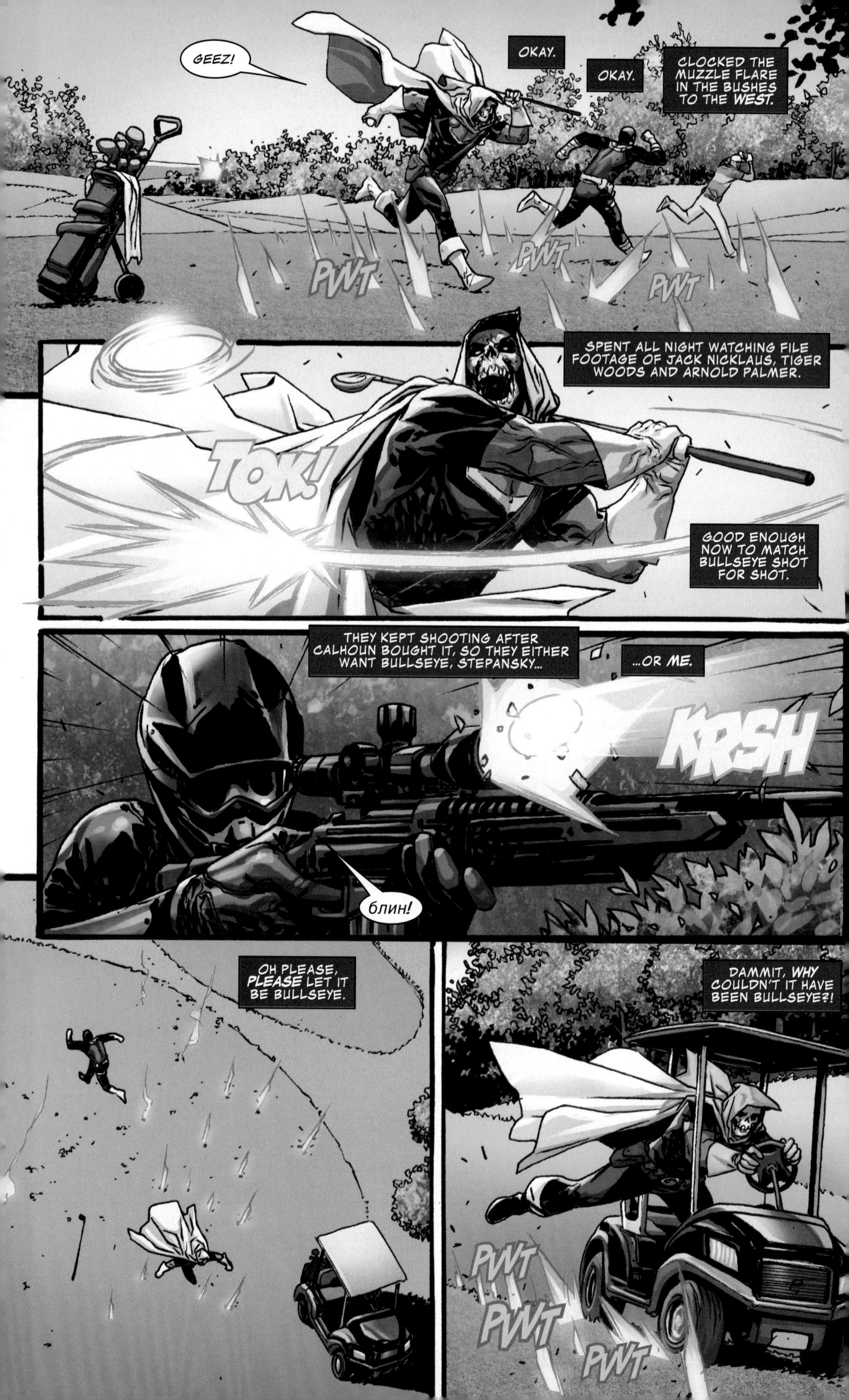
GEEZ!
OKAY.
OKAY.
CLOCKED THE MUZZLE FLARE IN THE BUSHES TO THE WEST.
PWT
PWT
PWT
SPENT ALL NIGHT WATCHING FILE FOOTAGE OF JACK NICKLAUS, TIGER WOODS AND ARNOLD PALMER.
TOK!
GOOD ENOUGH NOW TO MATCH BULLSEYE SHOT FOR SHOT.
THEY KEPT SHOOTING AFTER CALHOUN BOUGHT IT, SO THEY EITHER WANT BULLSEYE, STEPANSKY...
...OR ME.
KRSH
блин!
OH PLEASE, PLEASE LET IT BE BULLSEYE.
DAMMIT, WHY COULDN'T IT HAVE BEEN BULLSEYE?!
PWT
PWT
PWT

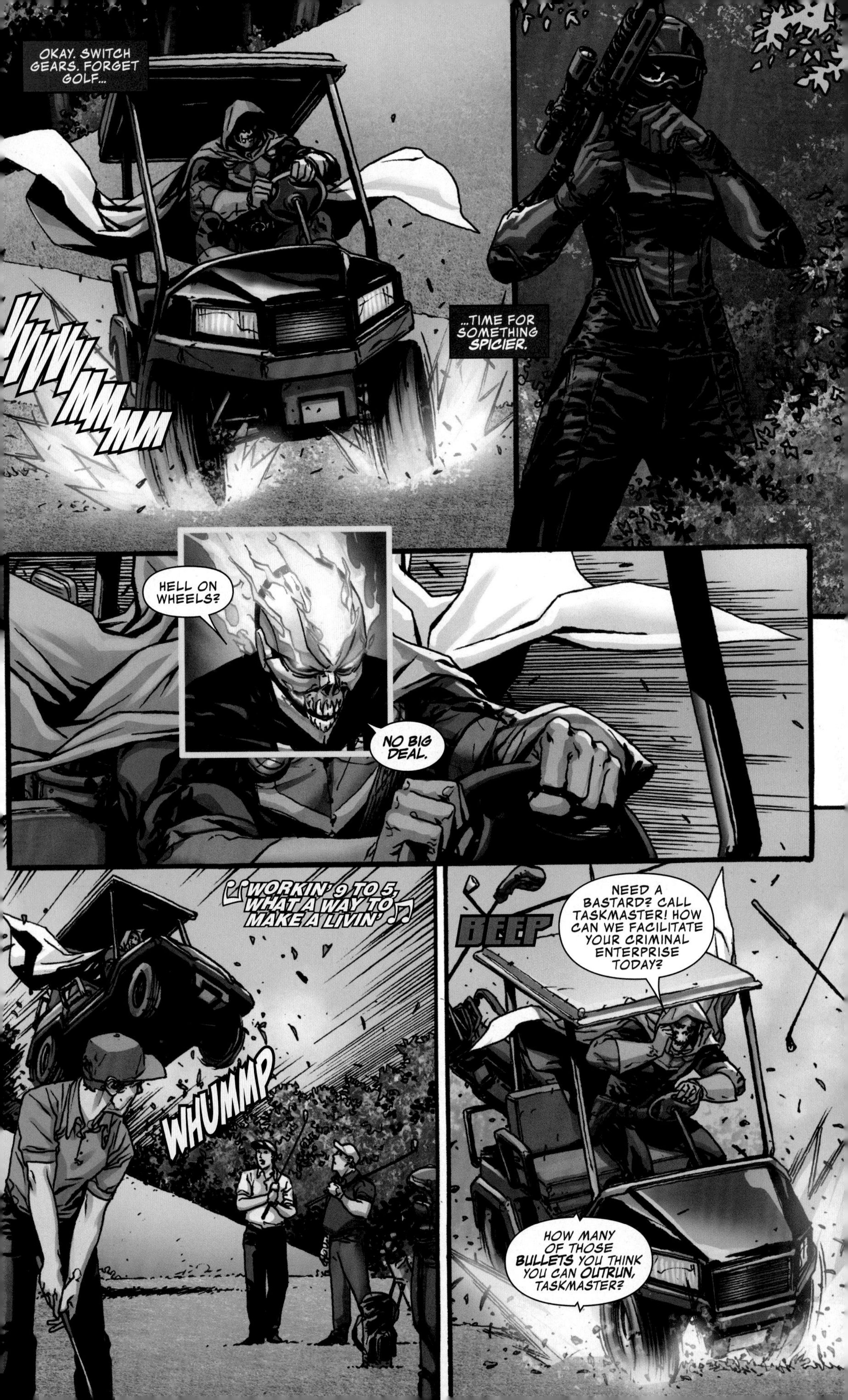
OKAY. SWITCH GEARS. FORGET GOLF...
VVVVVMMMMM
...TIME FOR SOMETHING SPICIER.
HELL ON WHEELS?
NO BIG DEAL.
♪WORKIN' 9 TO 5, WHAT A WAY TO MAKE A LIVIN'♪
WHUMMP
BEEP
NEED A BASTARD? CALL TASKMASTER! HOW CAN WE FACILITATE YOUR CRIMINAL ENTERPRISE TODAY?
HOW MANY OF THOSE BULLETS YOU THINK YOU CAN OUTRUN, TASKMASTER?

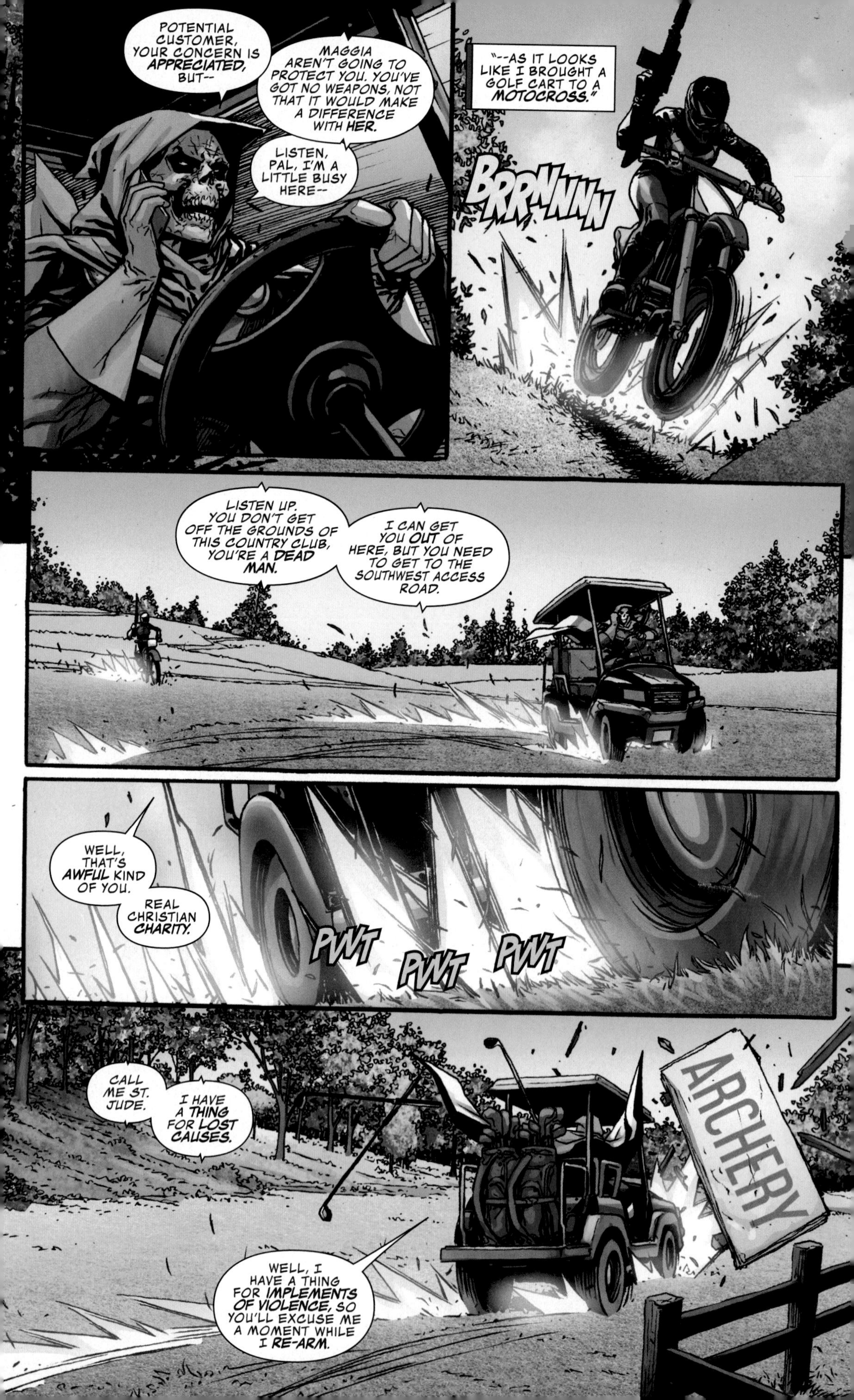
POTENTIAL CUSTOMER, YOUR CONCERN IS APPRECIATED, BUT--
MAGGIA AREN'T GOING TO PROTECT YOU. YOU'VE GOT NO WEAPONS, NOT THAT IT WOULD MAKE A DIFFERENCE WITH HER.
LISTEN, PAL, I'M A LITTLE BUSY HERE--
"--AS IT LOOKS LIKE I BROUGHT A GOLF CART TO A MOTOCROSS."
BRRNNNN
LISTEN UP. YOU DON'T GET OFF THE GROUNDS OF THIS COUNTRY CLUB, YOU'RE A DEAD MAN.
I CAN GET YOU OUT OF HERE, BUT YOU NEED TO GET TO THE SOUTHWEST ACCESS ROAD.
WELL, THAT'S AWFUL KIND OF YOU.
REAL CHRISTIAN CHARITY.
PWT
PWT
PWT
CALL ME ST. JUDE.
I HAVE A THING FOR LOST CAUSES.
ARCHERY
WELL, I HAVE A THING FOR IMPLEMENTS OF VIOLENCE, SO YOU'LL EXCUSE ME A MOMENT WHILE I RE-ARM.

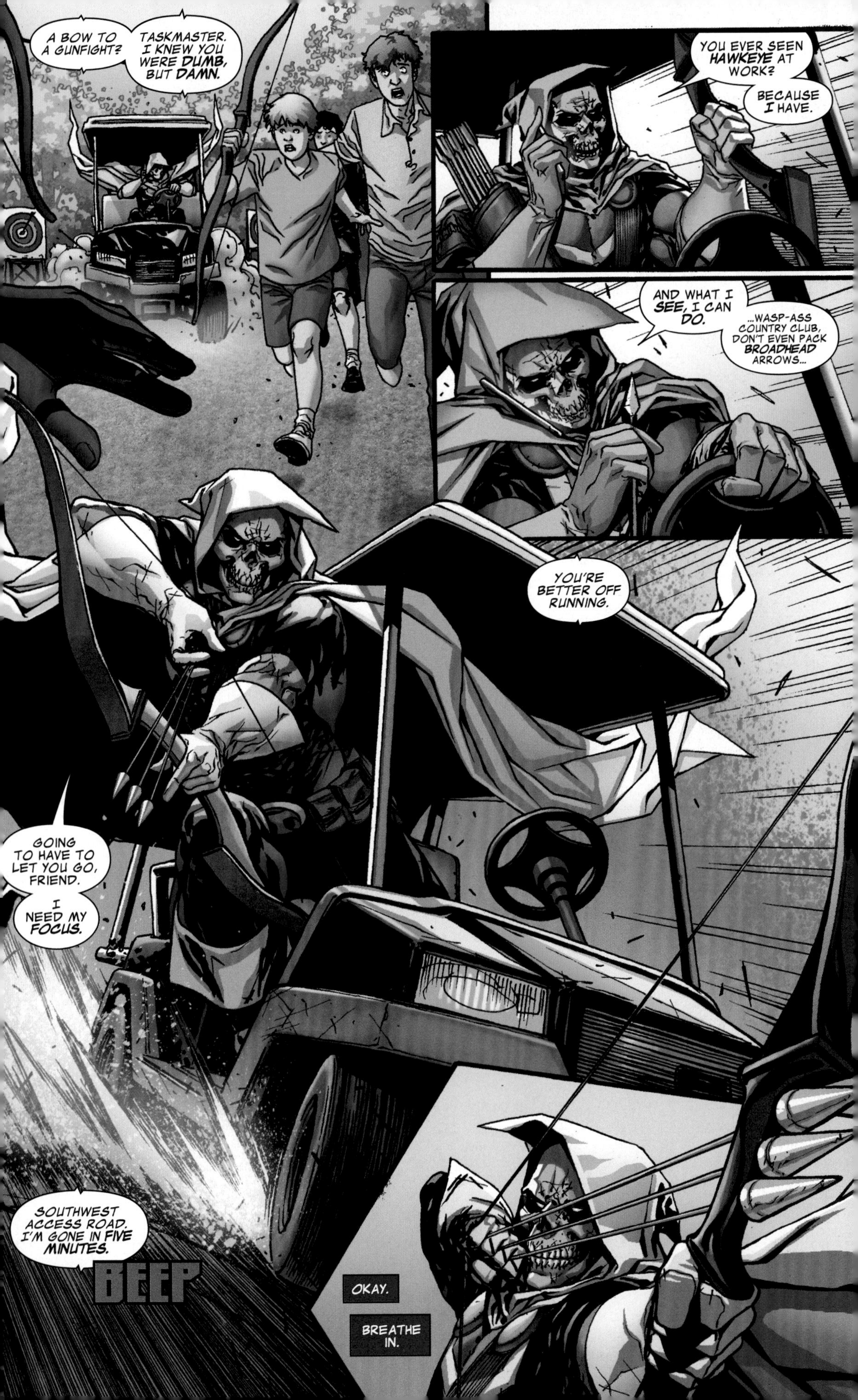
A BOW TO A GUNFIGHT?
TASKMASTER. I KNEW YOU WERE DUMB, BUT DAMN.
YOU EVER SEEN HAWKEYE AT WORK?
BECAUSE I HAVE.
AND WHAT I SEE, I CAN DO.
...WASP-ASS COUNTRY CLUB, DON'T EVEN PACK BROADHEAD ARROWS...
YOU'RE BETTER OFF RUNNING.
GOING TO HAVE TO LET YOU GO, FRIEND.
I NEED MY FOCUS.
SOUTHWEST ACCESS ROAD. I'M GONE IN FIVE MINUTES.
BEEP
OKAY.
BREATHE IN.

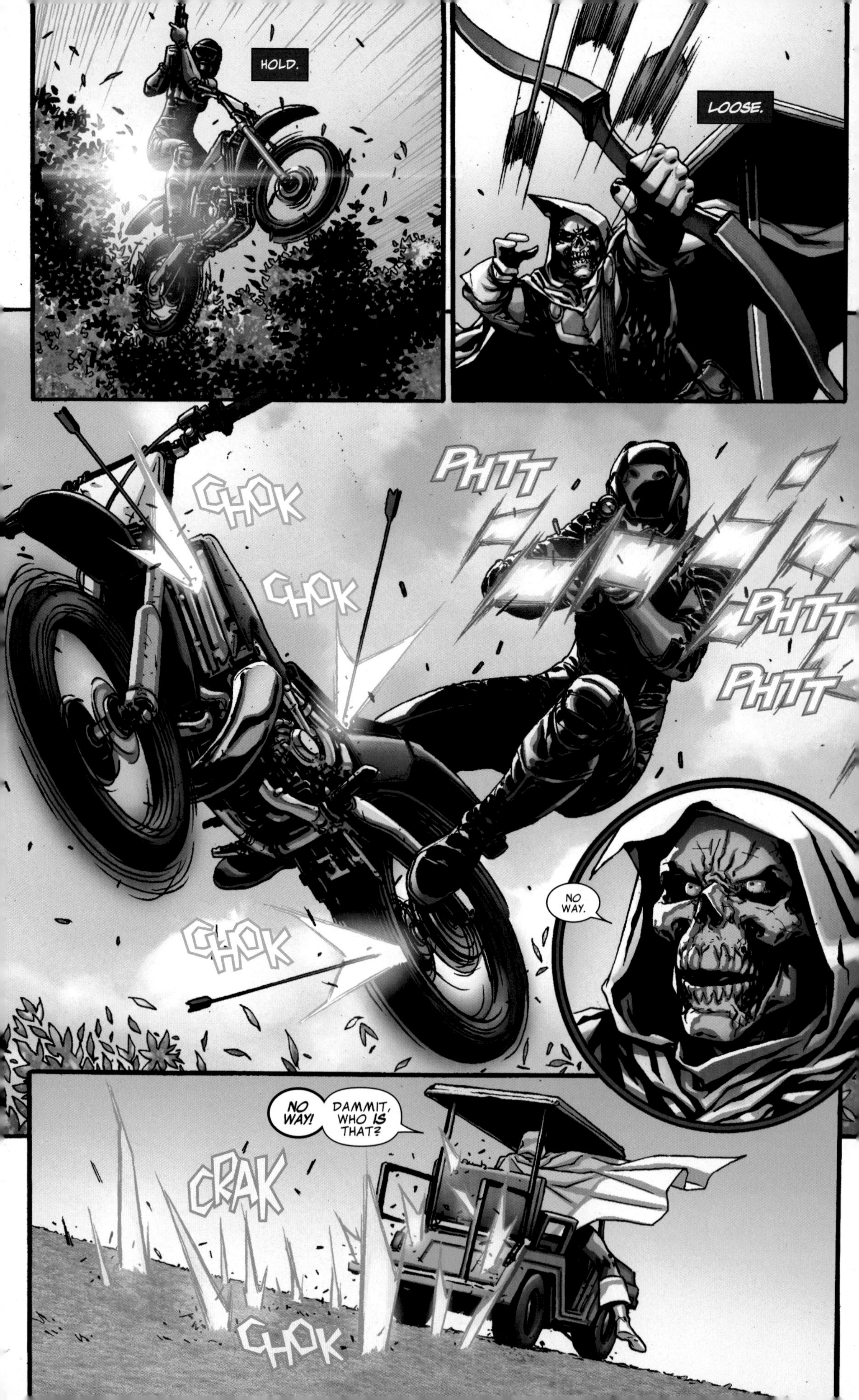
HOLD.
LOOSE.
CHOK
CHOK
PHTT
PHTT
PHTT
NO WAY.
CHOK
NO WAY!
DAMMIT, WHO IS THAT?
CRAK
CHOK

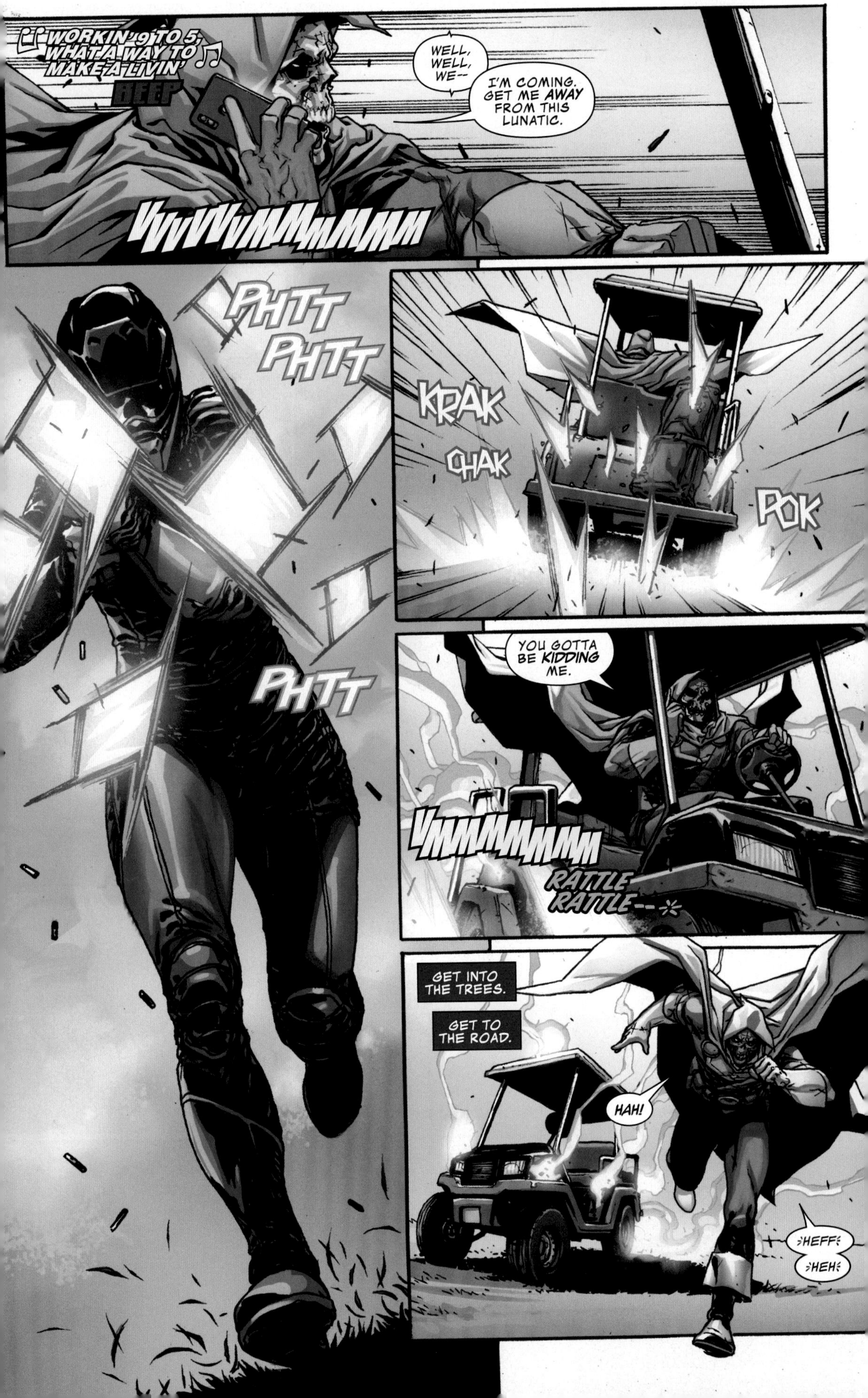

WORKIN' 9 TO 5, WHAT A WAY TO MAKE A LIVIN'
BEEP
WELL, WELL, WE--
I'M COMING. GET ME AWAY FROM THIS LUNATIC.
VVVVVVVMMMMMMMMM
PHTT
PHTT
KRAK
CHAK
POK
PHTT
YOU GOTTA BE KIDDING ME.
VMMMMMMMMM
RATTLE RATTLE--
GET INTO THE TREES.
GET TO THE ROAD.
HAH!
HEFF
HEH

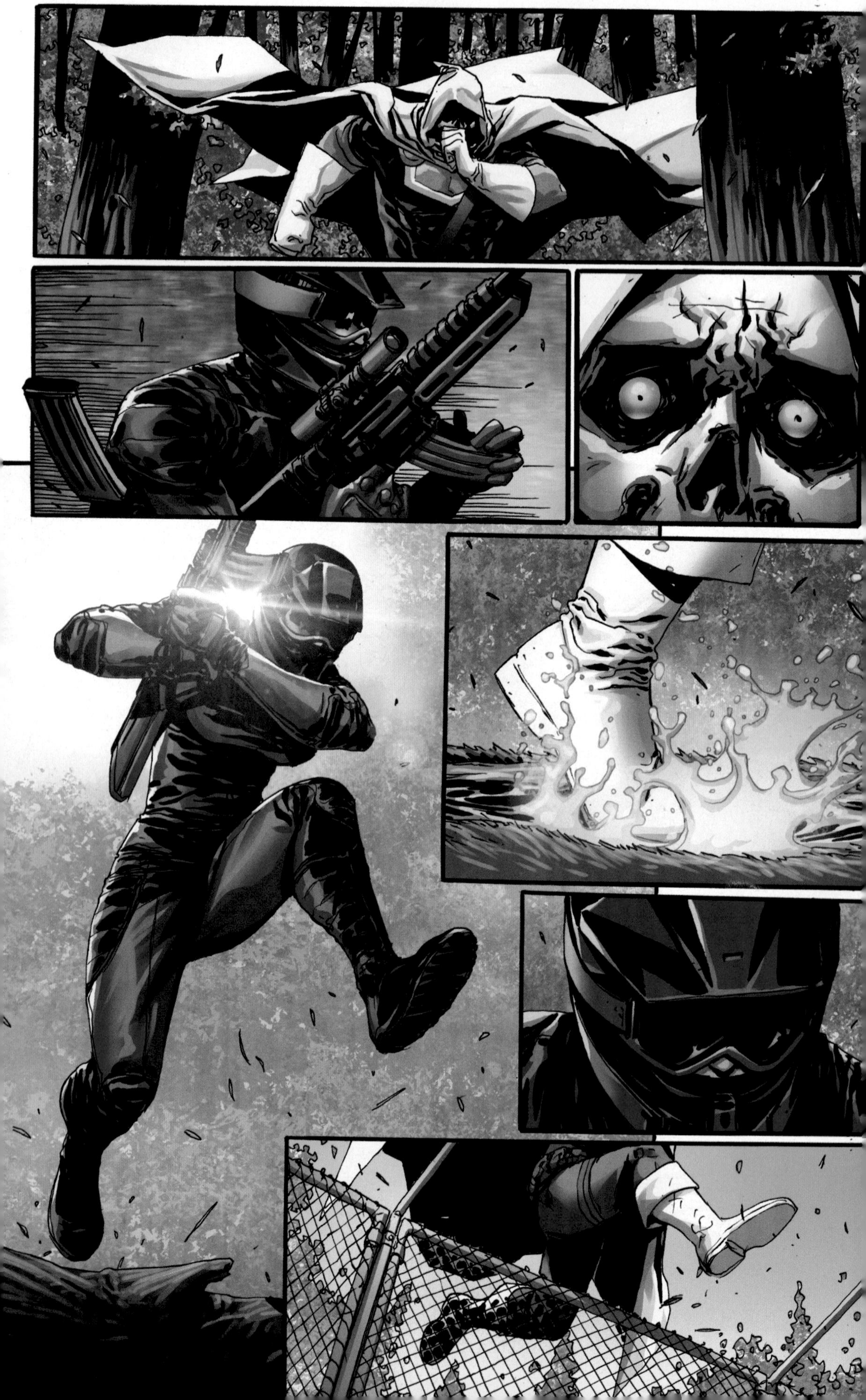

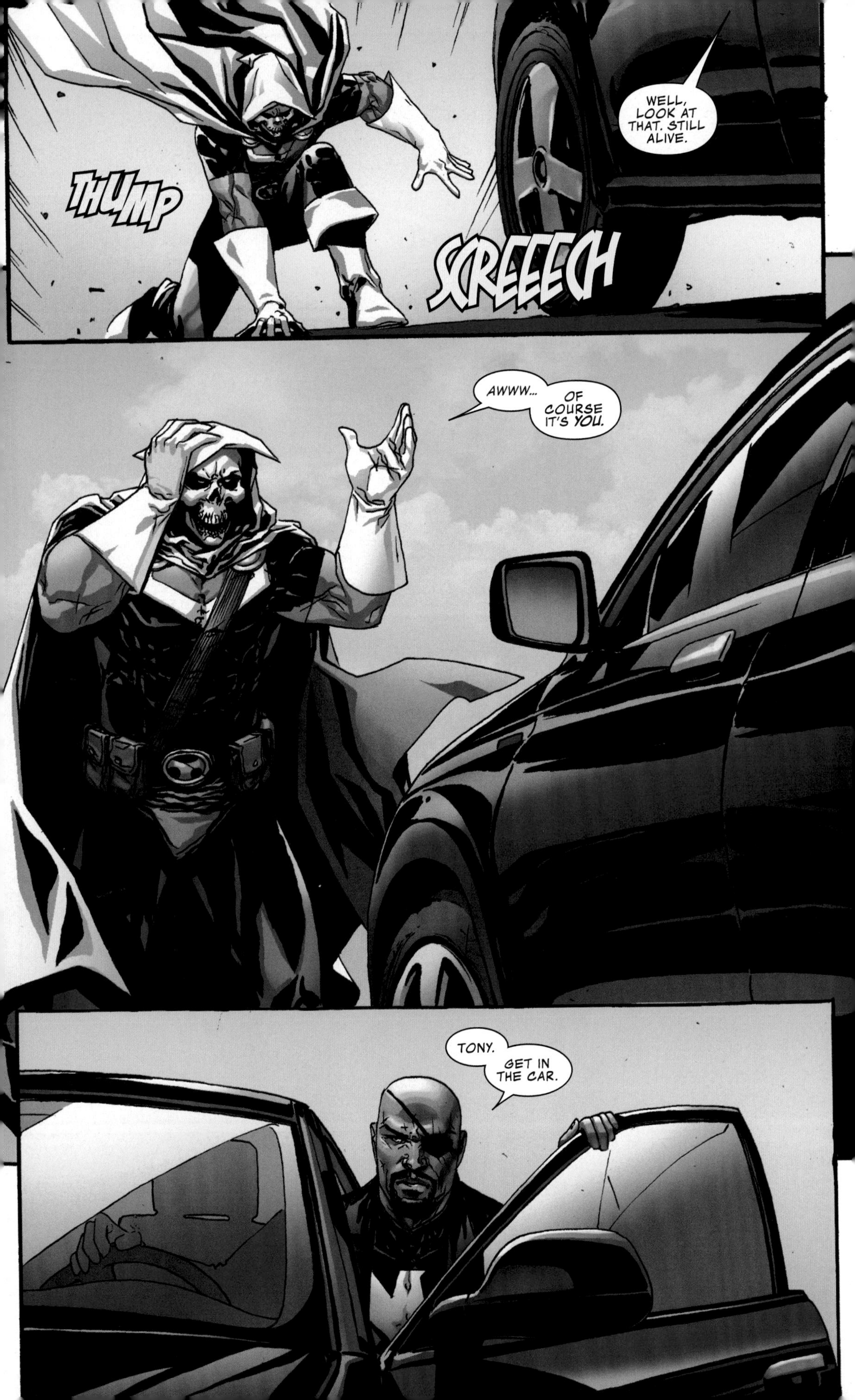

THUMP
WELL, LOOK AT THAT. STILL ALIVE.
SCREEECH
AWWW... OF COURSE IT'S YOU.
TONY. GET IN THE CAR.

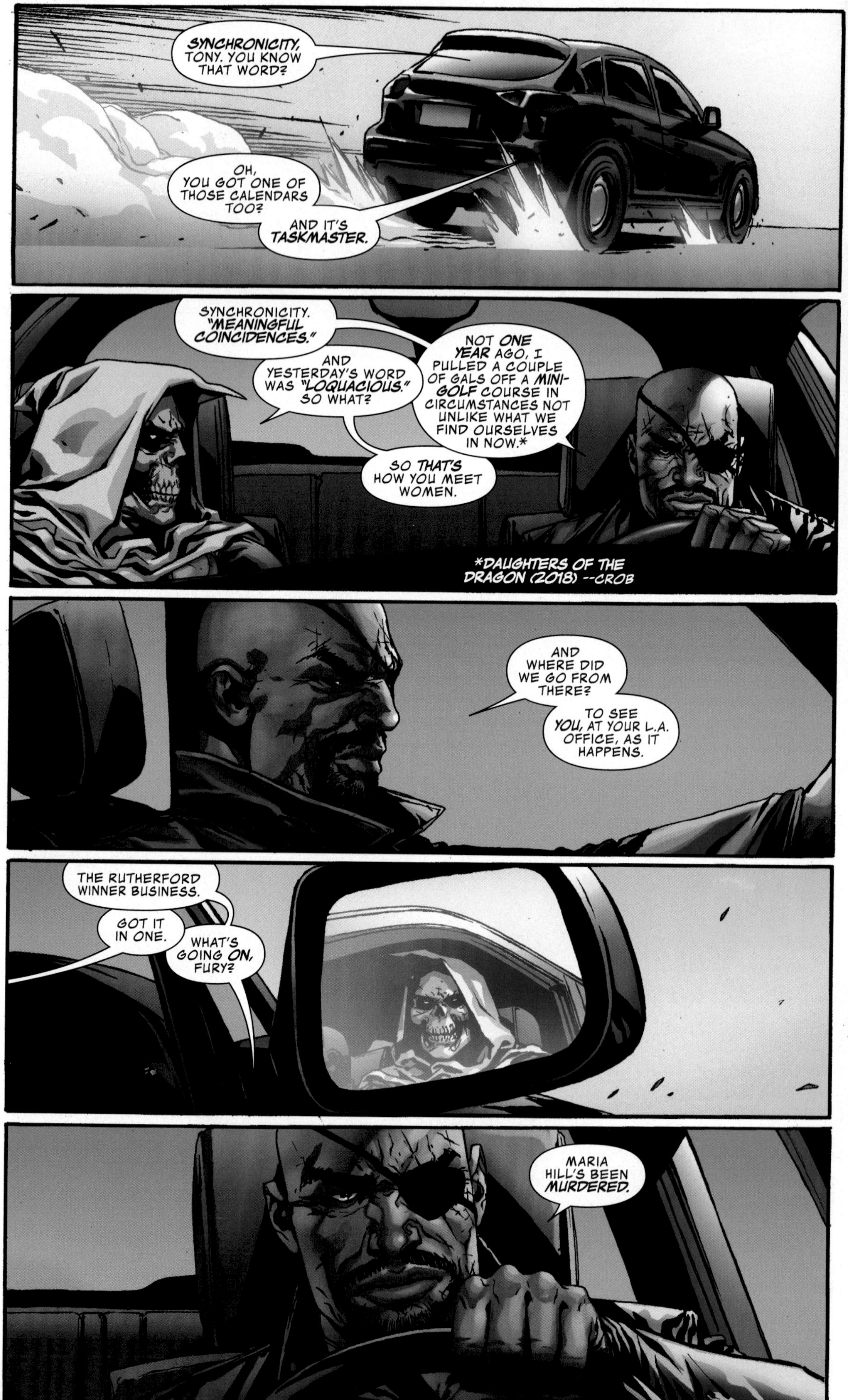
SYNCHRONICITY, TONY. YOU KNOW THAT WORD?
OH, YOU GOT ONE OF THOSE CALENDARS TOO?
AND IT'S TASKMASTER.
SYNCHRONICITY. "MEANINGFUL COINCIDENCES."
AND YESTERDAY'S WORD WAS "LOQUACIOUS." SO WHAT?
NOT ONE YEAR AGO, I PULLED A COUPLE OF GALS OFF A MINI-GOLF COURSE IN CIRCUMSTANCES NOT UNLIKE WHAT WE FIND OURSELVES IN NOW.*
SO THAT'S HOW YOU MEET WOMEN.
*DAUGHTERS OF THE DRAGON (2018) --CROB
AND WHERE DID WE GO FROM THERE?
TO SEE YOU, AT YOUR L.A. OFFICE, AS IT HAPPENS.
THE RUTHERFORD WINNER BUSINESS.
GOT IT IN ONE.
WHAT'S GOING ON, FURY?
MARIA HILL'S BEEN MURDERED.

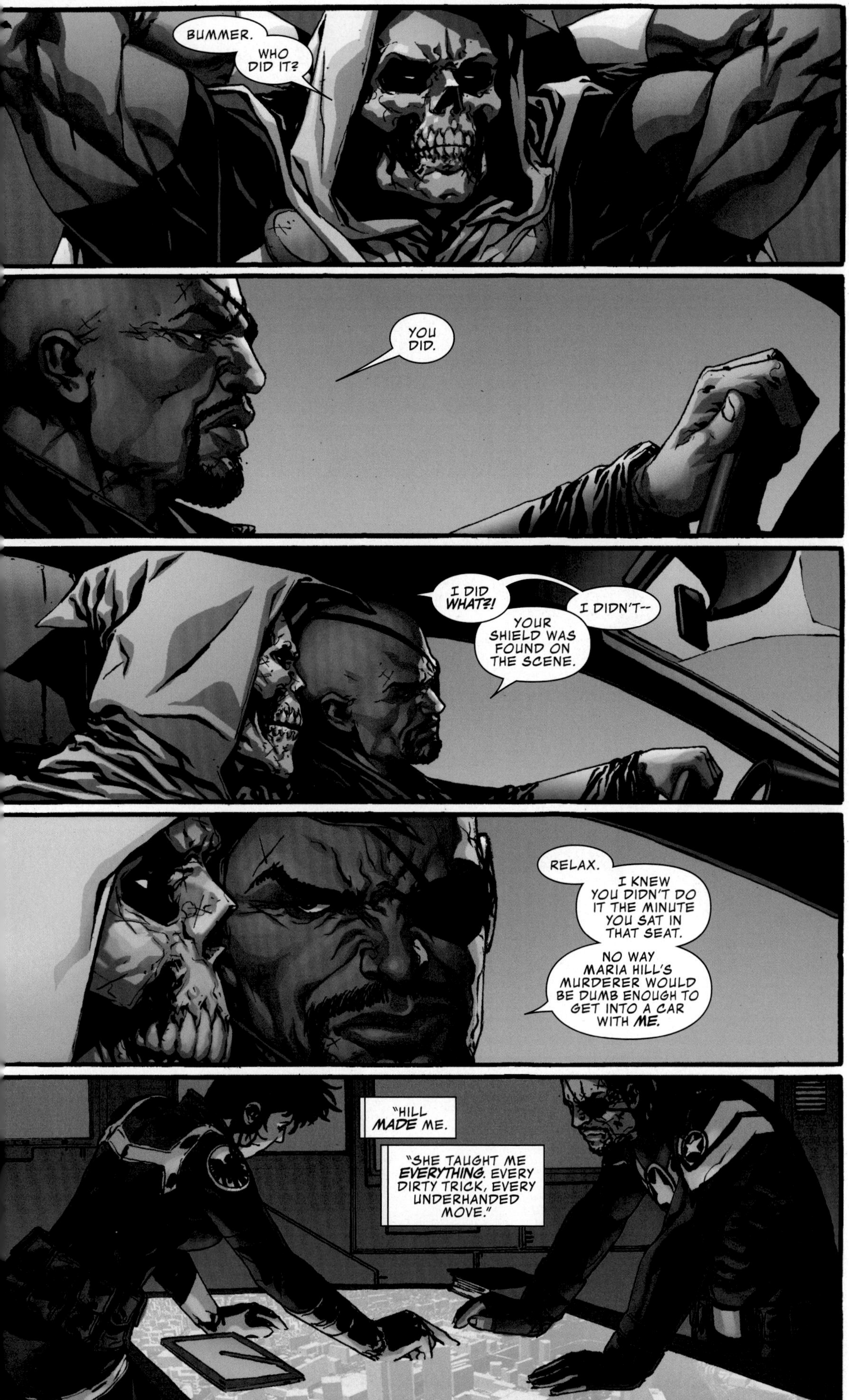

BUMMER.
WHO DID IT?
YOU DID.
I DID WHAT?!
I DIDN'T--
YOUR SHIELD WAS FOUND ON THE SCENE.
RELAX.
I KNEW YOU DIDN'T DO IT THE MINUTE YOU SAT IN THAT SEAT.
NO WAY MARIA HILL'S MURDERER WOULD BE DUMB ENOUGH TO GET INTO A CAR WITH ME.
"HILL MADE ME.
"SHE TAUGHT ME EVERYTHING. EVERY DIRTY TRICK, EVERY UNDERHANDED MOVE."

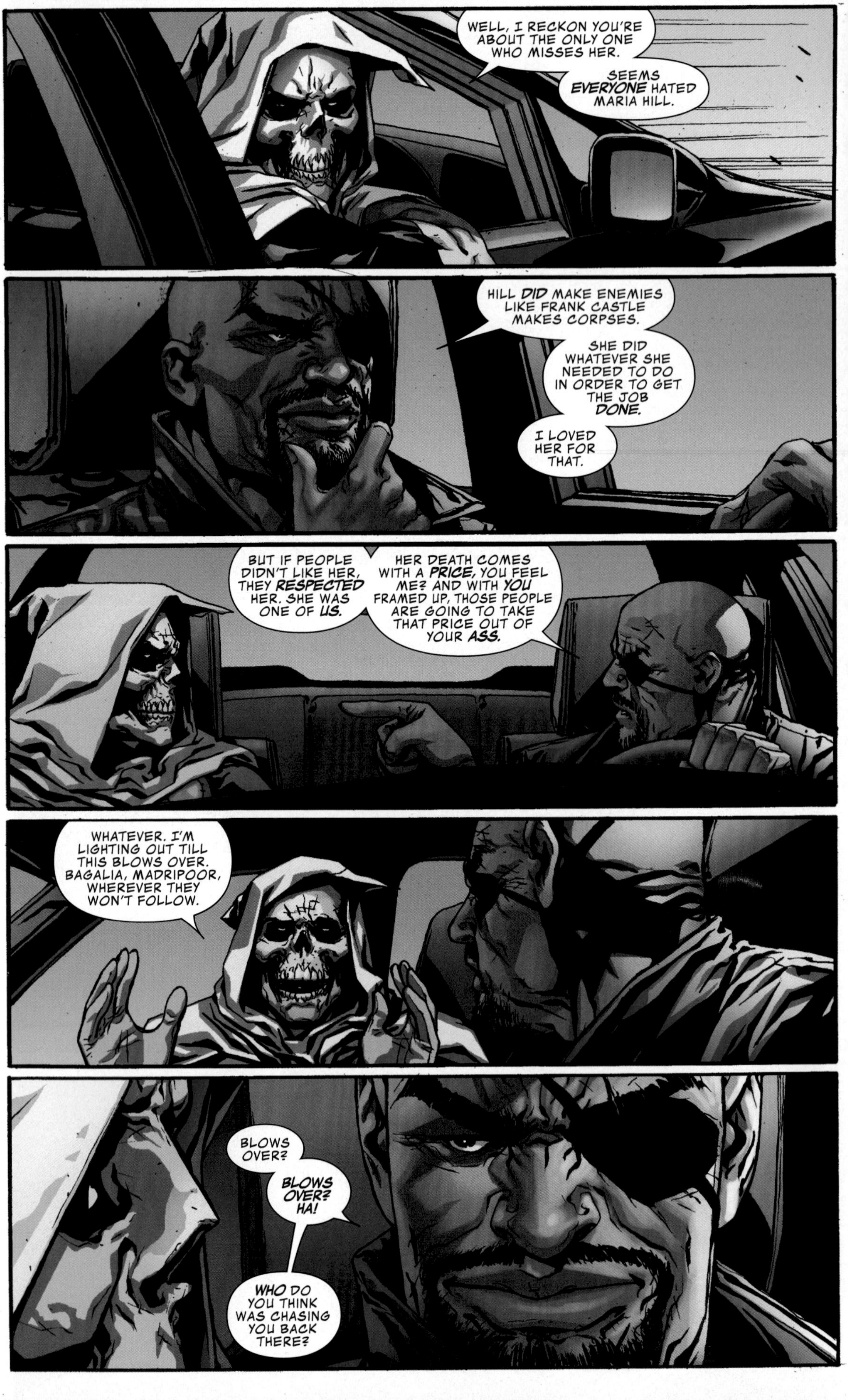
WELL, I RECKON YOU'RE ABOUT THE ONLY ONE WHO MISSES HER.
SEEMS EVERYONE HATED MARIA HILL.
HILL DID MAKE ENEMIES LIKE FRANK CASTLE MAKES CORPSES.
SHE DID WHATEVER SHE NEEDED TO DO IN ORDER TO GET THE JOB DONE.
I LOVED HER FOR THAT.
BUT IF PEOPLE DIDN'T LIKE HER, THEY RESPECTED HER. SHE WAS ONE OF US.
HER DEATH COMES WITH A PRICE, YOU FEEL ME? AND WITH YOU FRAMED UP, THOSE PEOPLE ARE GOING TO TAKE THAT PRICE OUT OF YOUR ASS.
WHATEVER. I'M LIGHTING OUT TILL THIS BLOWS OVER. BAGALIA, MADRIPOOR, WHEREVER THEY WON'T FOLLOW.
BLOWS OVER?
BLOWS OVER? HA!
WHO DO YOU THINK WAS CHASING YOU BACK THERE?

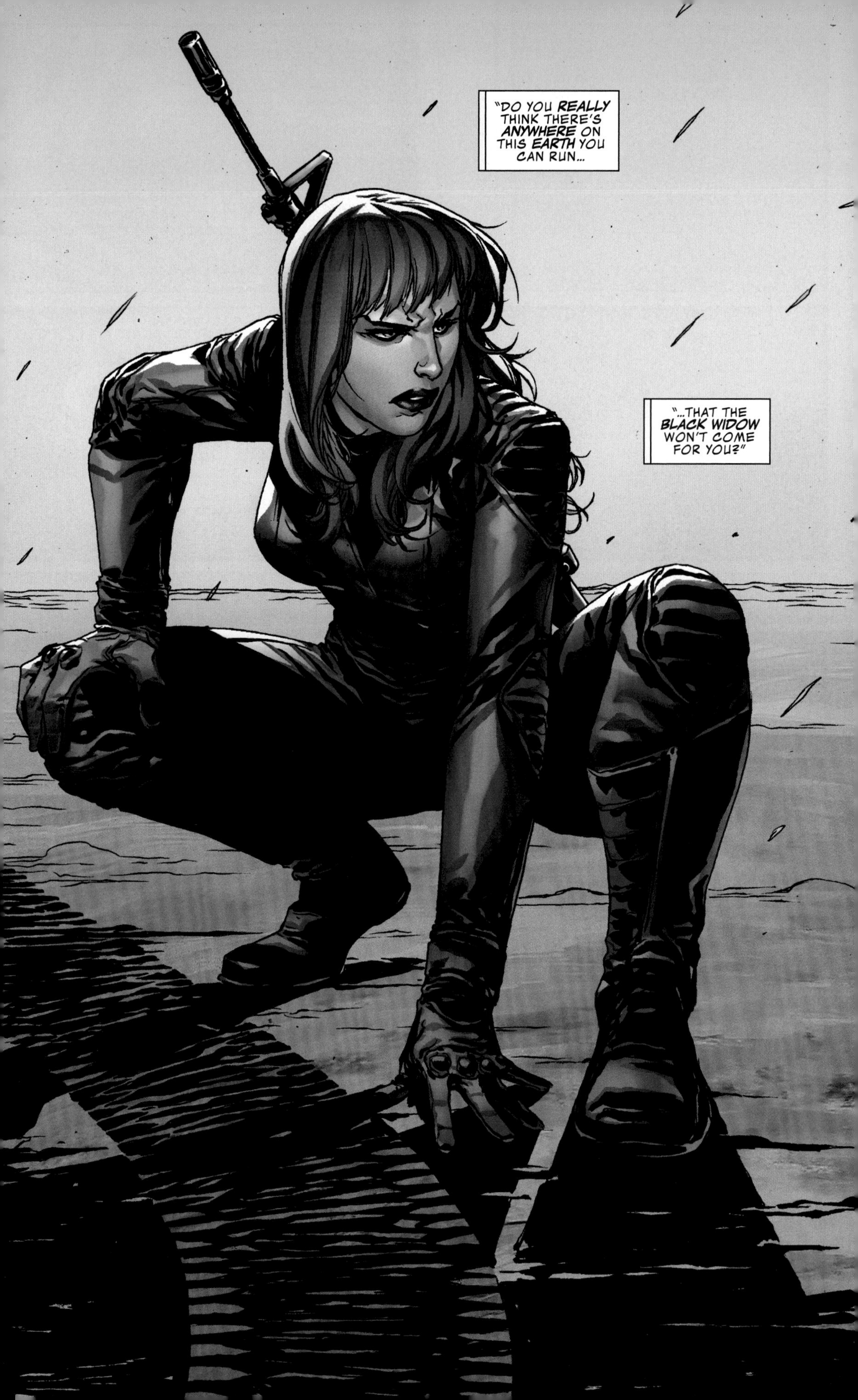
"DO YOU REALLY THINK THERE'S ANYWHERE ON THIS EARTH YOU CAN RUN...
"...THAT THE BLACK WIDOW WON'T COME FOR YOU?"

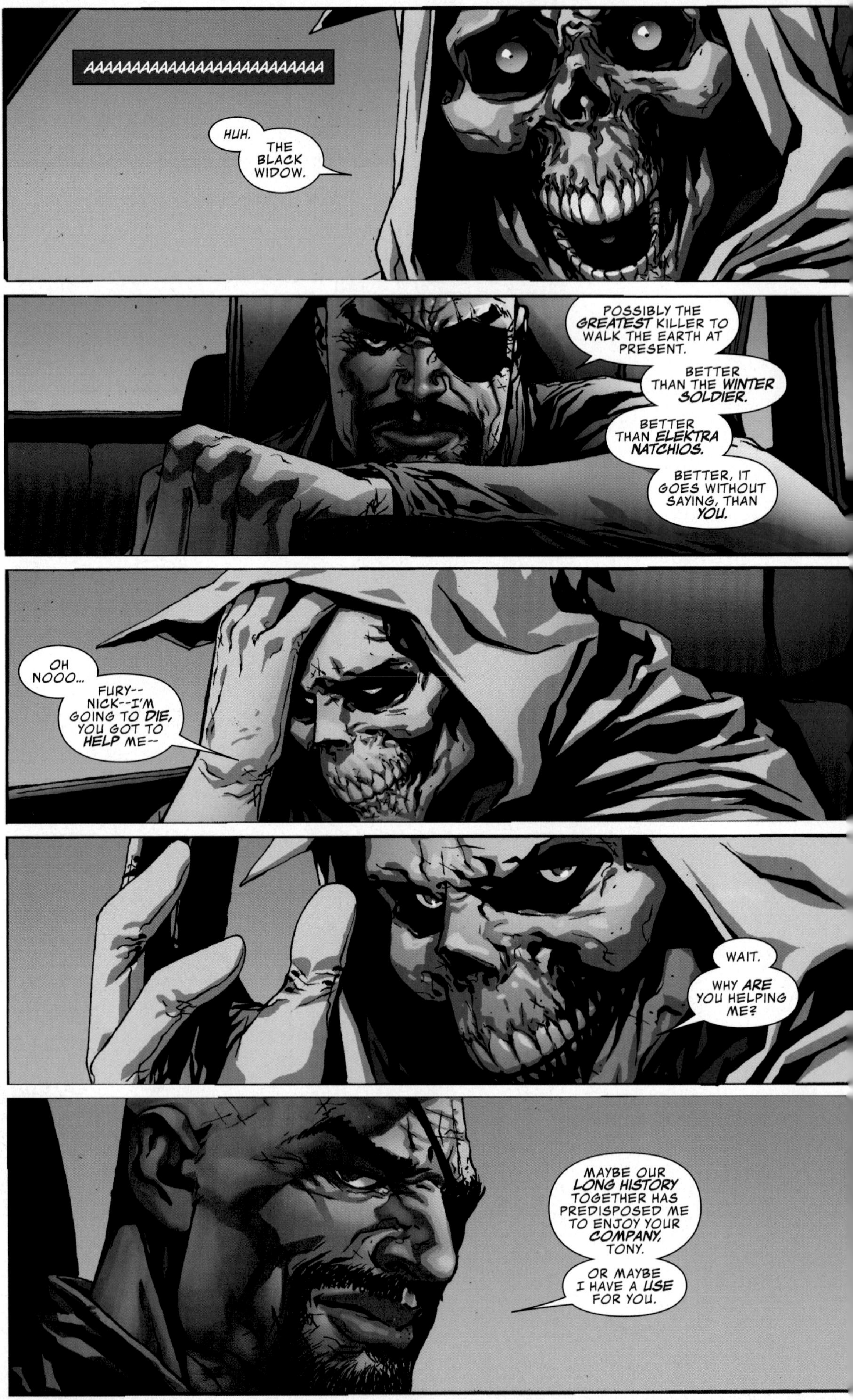
AAAAAAAAAAAAAAAAAAAAAAAAAAAA
HUH. THE BLACK WIDOW.
POSSIBLY THE GREATEST KILLER TO WALK THE EARTH AT PRESENT.
BETTER THAN THE WINTER SOLDIER.
BETTER THAN ELEKTRA NATCHIOS.
BETTER, IT GOES WITHOUT SAYING, THAN YOU.
OH NOOO...
FURY-- NICK--I'M GOING TO DIE, YOU GOT TO HELP ME--
WAIT.
WHY ARE YOU HELPING ME?
MAYBE OUR LONG HISTORY TOGETHER HAS PREDISPOSED ME TO ENJOY YOUR COMPANY, TONY.
OR MAYBE I HAVE A USE FOR YOU.

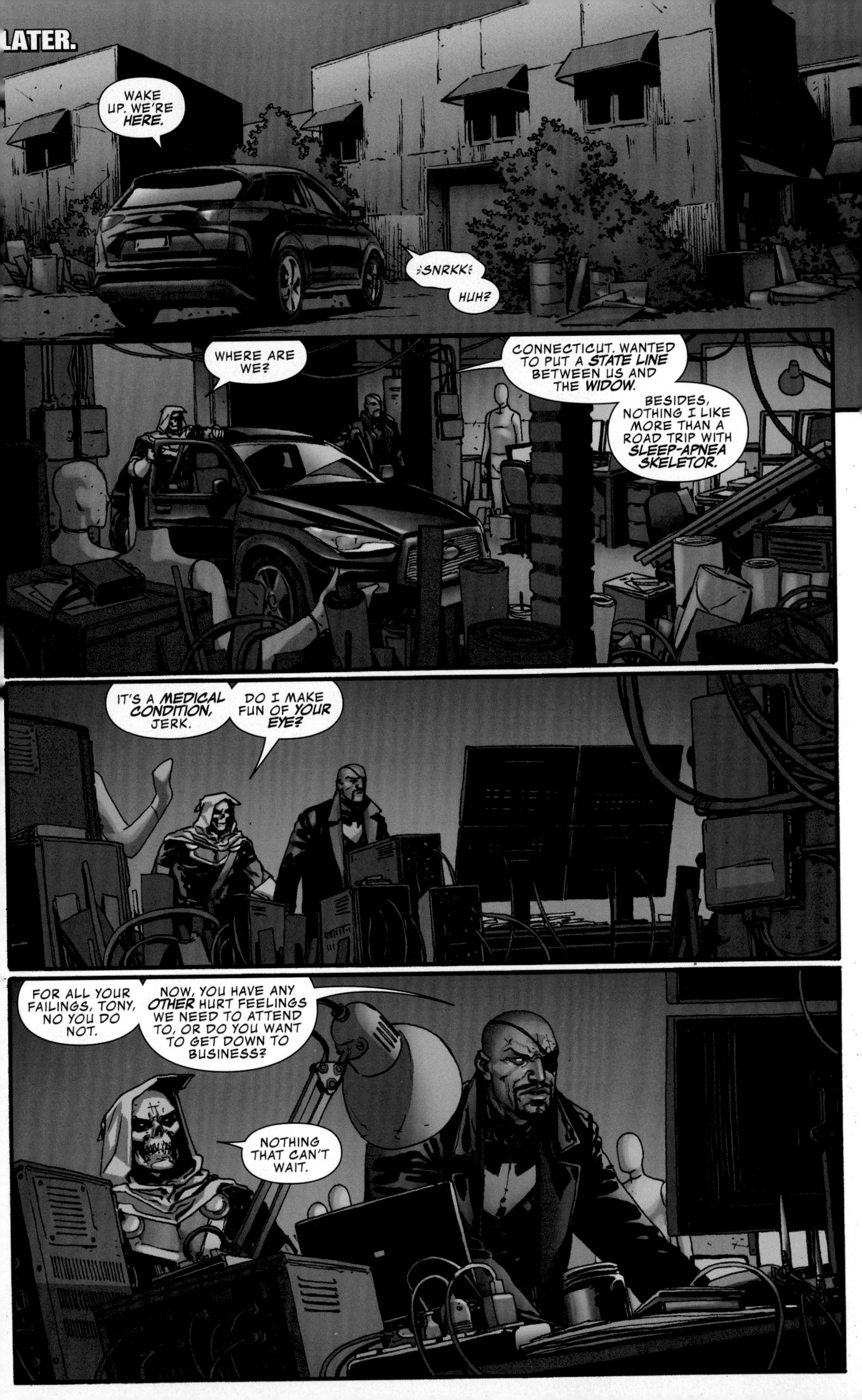
LATER.
WAKE UP. WE'RE HERE.
SNRKK
HUH?
WHERE ARE WE?
CONNECTICUT. WANTED TO PUT A STATE LINE BETWEEN US AND THE WIDOW.
BESIDES, NOTHING I LIKE MORE THAN A ROAD TRIP WITH SLEEP-APNEA SKELETOR.
IT'S A MEDICAL CONDITION, JERK.
DO I MAKE FUN OF YOUR EYE?
FOR ALL YOUR FAILINGS, TONY, NO YOU DO NOT.
NOW, YOU HAVE ANY OTHER HURT FEELINGS WE NEED TO ATTEND TO, OR DO YOU WANT TO GET DOWN TO BUSINESS?
NOTHING THAT CAN'T WAIT.

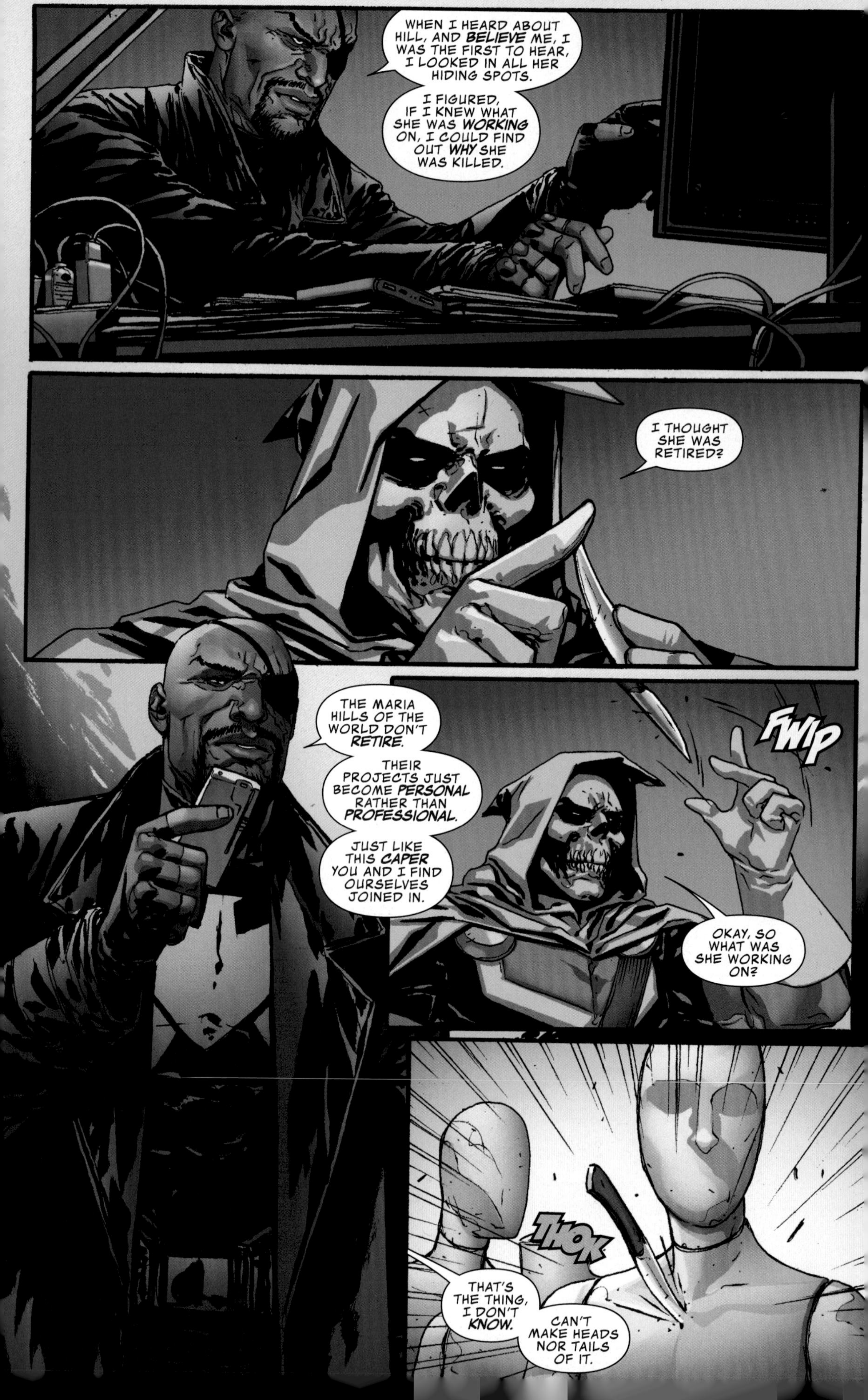
WHEN I HEARD ABOUT HILL, AND BELIEVE ME, I WAS THE FIRST TO HEAR, I LOOKED IN ALL HER HIDING SPOTS.
I FIGURED, IF I KNEW WHAT SHE WAS WORKING ON, I COULD FIND OUT WHY SHE WAS KILLED.
I THOUGHT SHE WAS RETIRED?
THE MARIA HILLS OF THE WORLD DON'T RETIRE.
THEIR PROJECTS JUST BECOME PERSONAL RATHER THAN PROFESSIONAL.
JUST LIKE THIS CAPER YOU AND I FIND OURSELVES JOINED IN.
FWIP
OKAY, SO WHAT WAS SHE WORKING ON?
THOK
THAT'S THE THING, I DON'T KNOW.
CAN'T MAKE HEADS NOR TAILS OF IT.

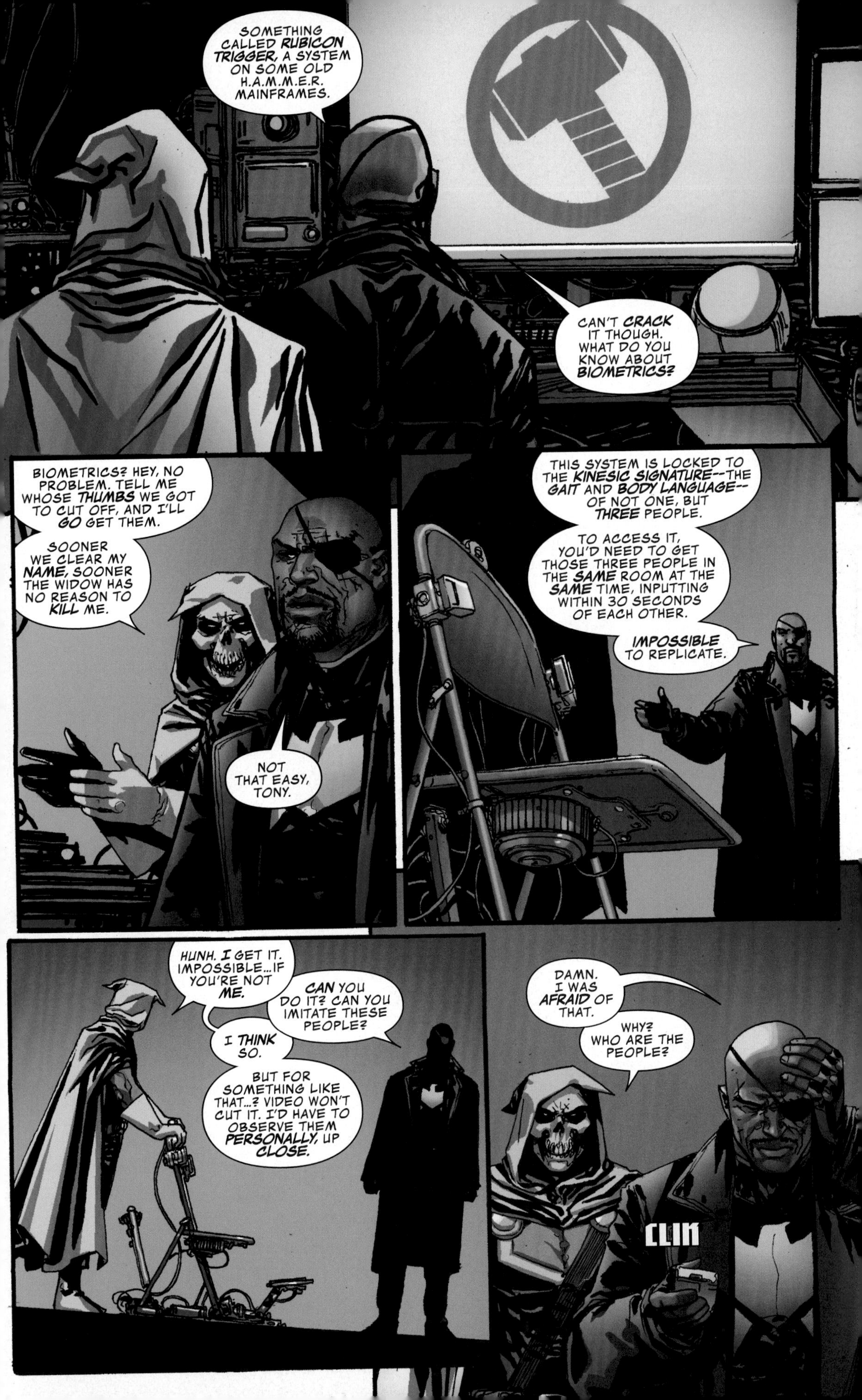

SOMETHING CALLED RUBICON TRIGGER, A SYSTEM ON SOME OLD H.A.M.M.E.R. MAINFRAMES.
CAN'T CRACK IT THOUGH. WHAT DO YOU KNOW ABOUT BIOMETRICS?
BIOMETRICS? HEY, NO PROBLEM. TELL ME WHOSE THUMBS WE GOT TO CUT OFF, AND I'LL GO GET THEM.
SOONER WE CLEAR MY NAME, SOONER THE WIDOW HAS NO REASON TO KILL ME.
NOT THAT EASY, TONY.
THIS SYSTEM IS LOCKED TO THE KINESIC SIGNATURE--THE GAIT AND BODY LANGUAGE--OF NOT ONE, BUT THREE PEOPLE.
TO ACCESS IT, YOU'D NEED TO GET THOSE THREE PEOPLE IN THE SAME ROOM AT THE SAME TIME, INPUTTING WITHIN 30 SECONDS OF EACH OTHER.
IMPOSSIBLE TO REPLICATE.
HUNH. I GET IT. IMPOSSIBLE...IF YOU'RE NOT ME.
CAN YOU DO IT? CAN YOU IMITATE THESE PEOPLE?
I THINK SO.
BUT FOR SOMETHING LIKE THAT...? VIDEO WON'T CUT IT. I'D HAVE TO OBSERVE THEM PERSONALLY, UP CLOSE.
DAMN. I WAS AFRAID OF THAT.
WHY? WHO ARE THE PEOPLE?
CLIN

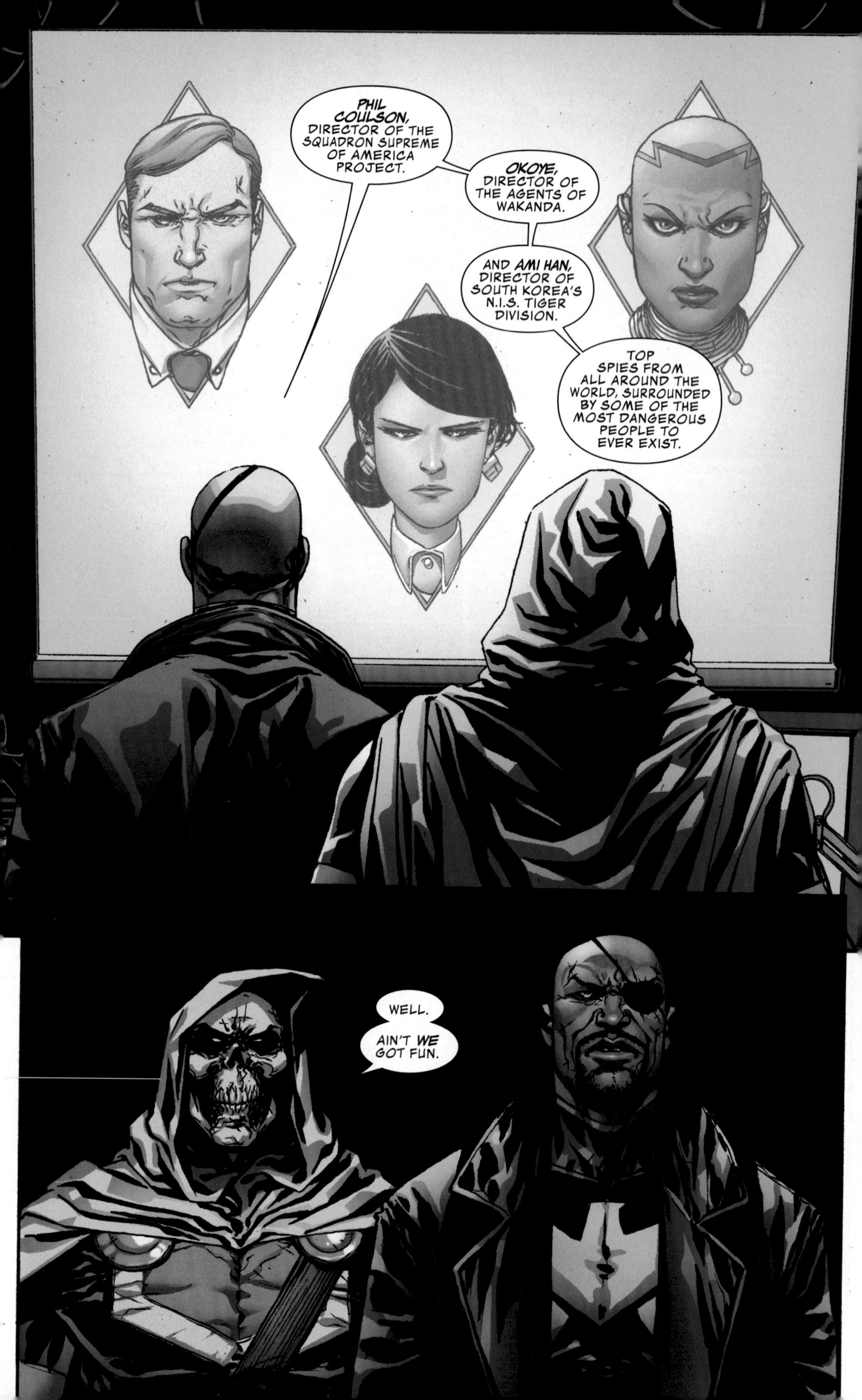
PHIL COULSON, DIRECTOR OF THE SQUADRON SUPREME OF AMERICA PROJECT.
OKOYE, DIRECTOR OF THE AGENTS OF WAKANDA.
AND AMI HAN, DIRECTOR OF SOUTH KOREA'S N.I.S. TIGER DIVISION.
TOP SPIES FROM ALL AROUND THE WORLD, SURROUNDED BY SOME OF THE MOST DANGEROUS PEOPLE TO EVER EXIST.
WELL.
AIN'T WE GOT FUN.

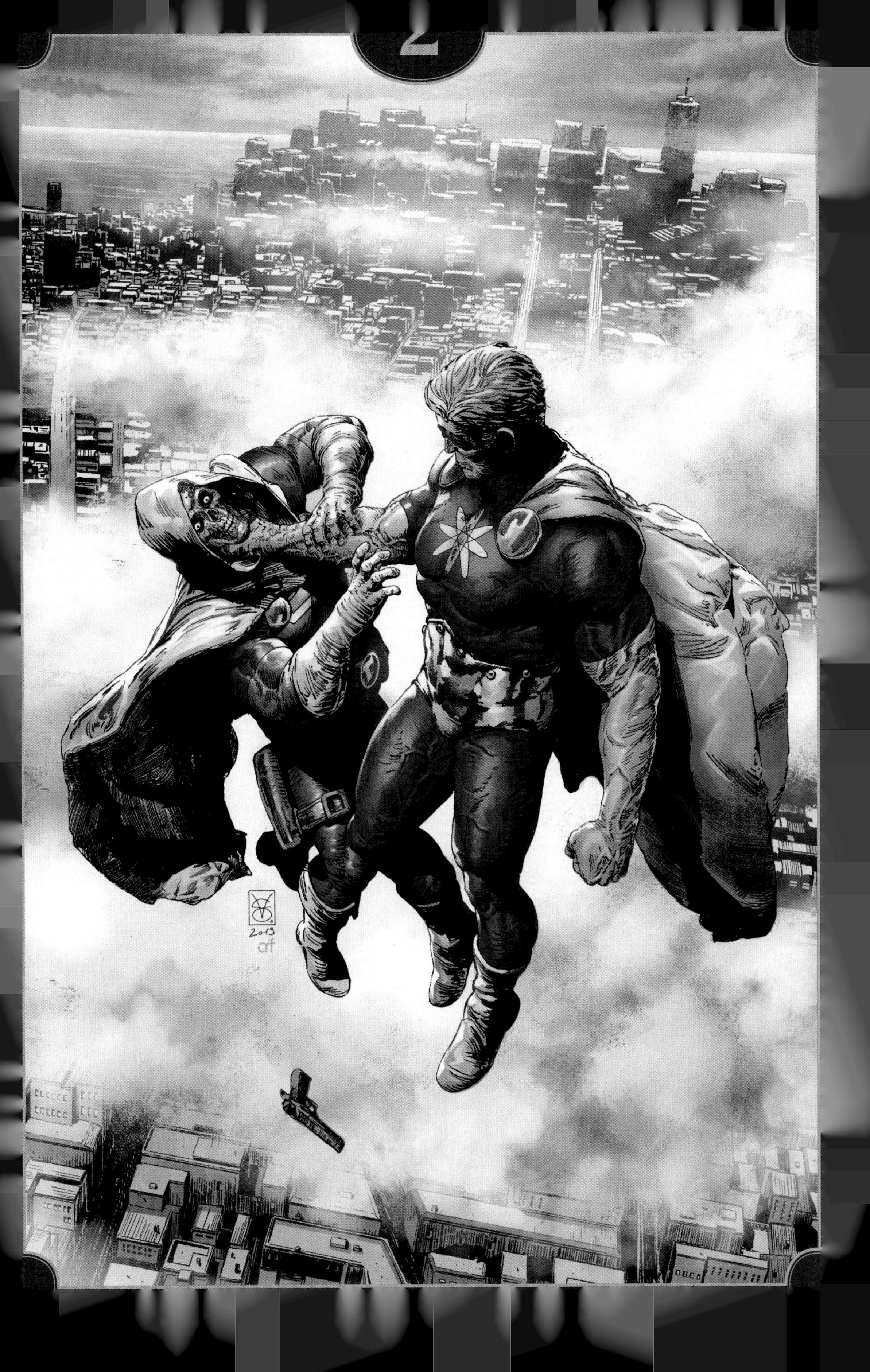
2

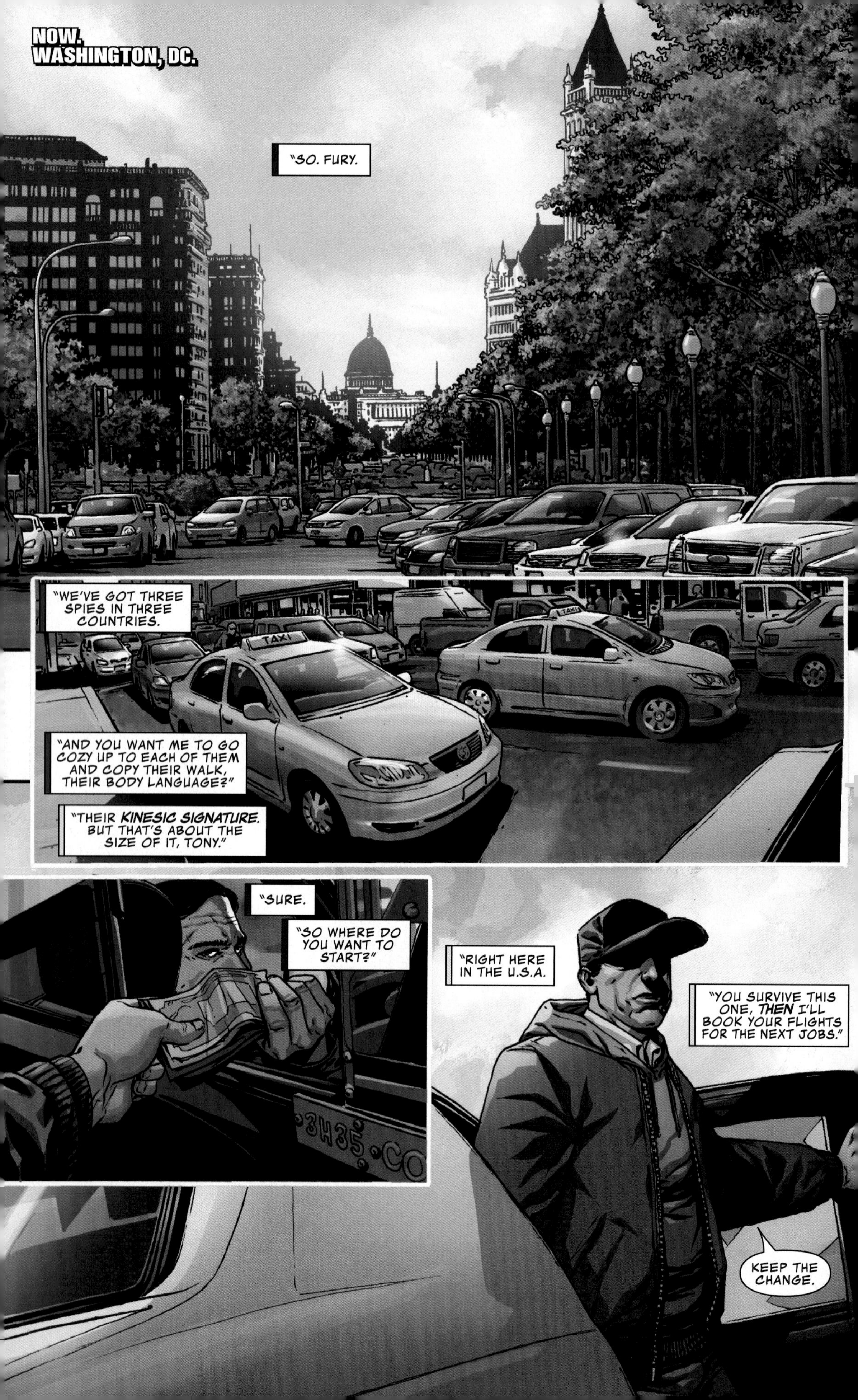
NOW.
WASHINGTON, DC.
"SO. FURY.
"WE'VE GOT THREE SPIES IN THREE COUNTRIES.
"AND YOU WANT ME TO GO COZY UP TO EACH OF THEM AND COPY THEIR WALK, THEIR BODY LANGUAGE?"
"THEIR KINESIC SIGNATURE. BUT THAT'S ABOUT THE SIZE OF IT, TONY."
"SURE.
"SO WHERE DO YOU WANT TO START?"
"RIGHT HERE IN THE U.S.A.
"YOU SURVIVE THIS ONE, THEN I'LL BOOK YOUR FLIGHTS FOR THE NEXT JOBS."
KEEP THE CHANGE.

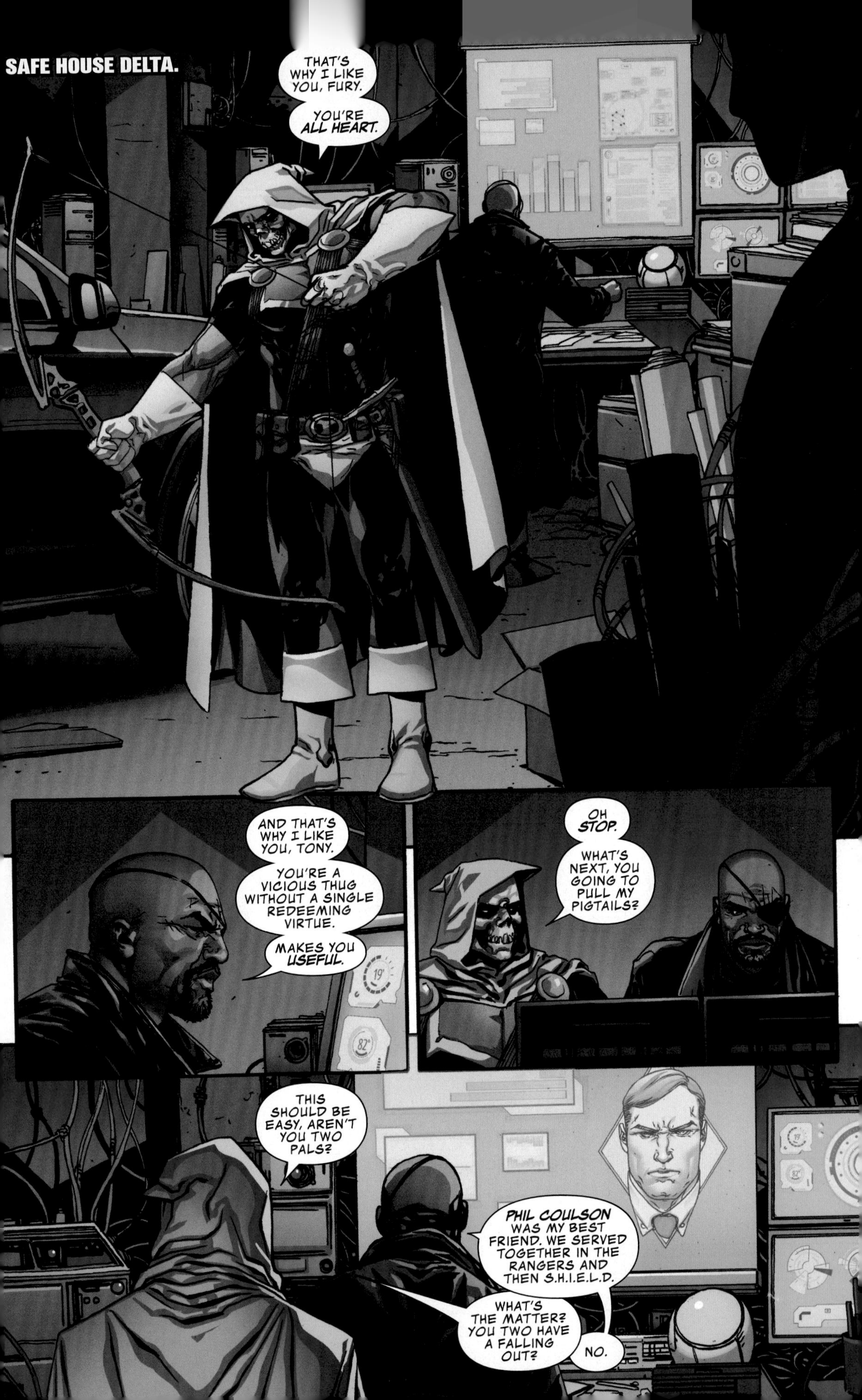
SAFE HOUSE DELTA.
THAT'S WHY I LIKE YOU, FURY.
YOU'RE ALL HEART.
AND THAT'S WHY I LIKE YOU, TONY.
YOU'RE A VICIOUS THUG WITHOUT A SINGLE REDEEMING VIRTUE.
MAKES YOU USEFUL.
OH STOP.
WHAT'S NEXT, YOU GOING TO PULL MY PIGTAILS?
THIS SHOULD BE EASY, AREN'T YOU TWO PALS?
PHIL COULSON WAS MY BEST FRIEND. WE SERVED TOGETHER IN THE RANGERS AND THEN S.H.I.E.L.D.
WHAT'S THE MATTER? YOU TWO HAVE A FALLING OUT?
NO.

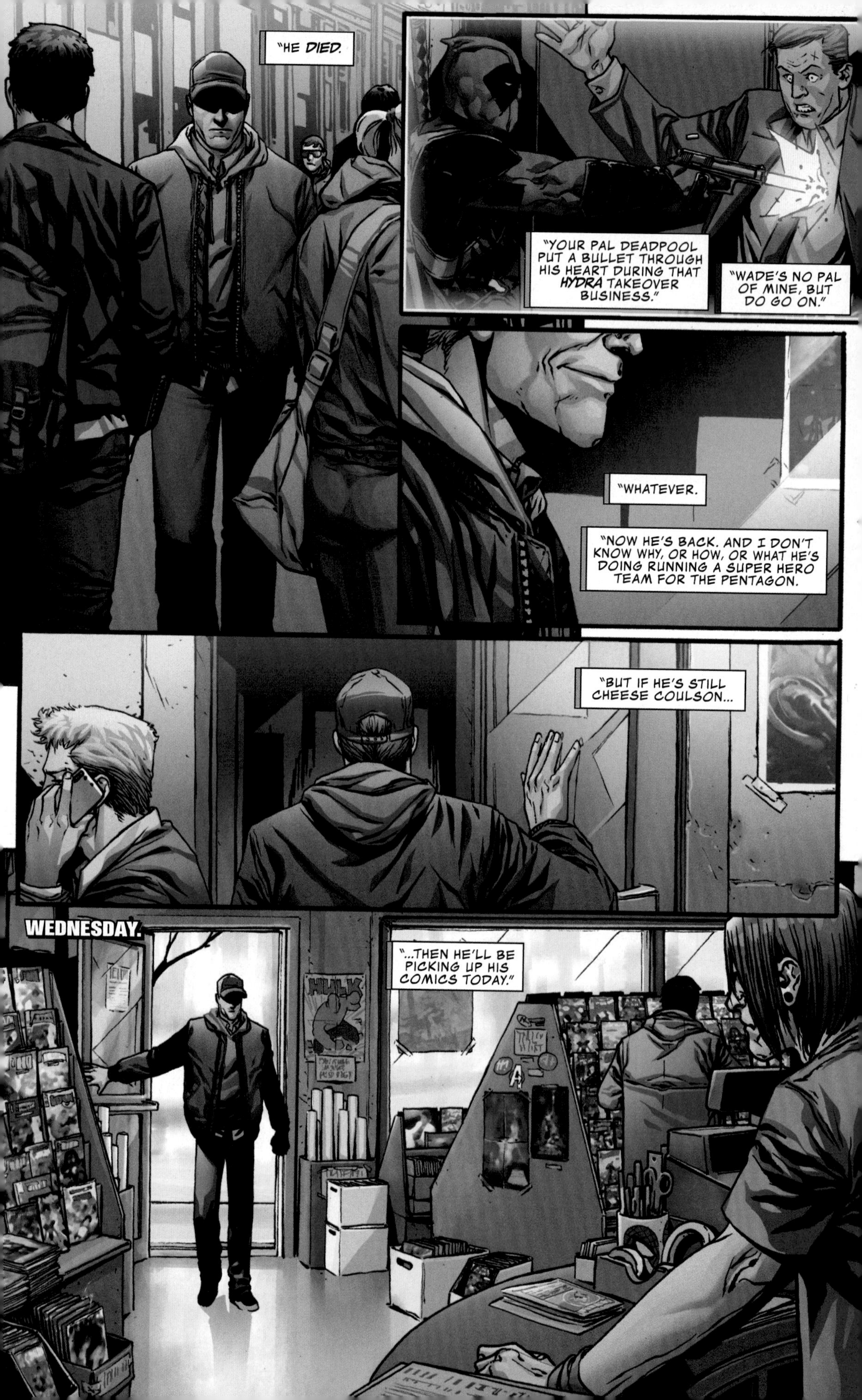
"HE DIED.
"YOUR PAL DEADPOOL PUT A BULLET THROUGH HIS HEART DURING THAT HYDRA TAKEOVER BUSINESS."
"WADE'S NO PAL OF MINE, BUT DO GO ON."
"WHATEVER.
"NOW HE'S BACK. AND I DON'T KNOW WHY, OR HOW, OR WHAT HE'S DOING RUNNING A SUPER HERO TEAM FOR THE PENTAGON.
"BUT IF HE'S STILL CHEESE COULSON...
WEDNESDAY.
"...THEN HE'LL BE PICKING UP HIS COMICS TODAY."
HULK

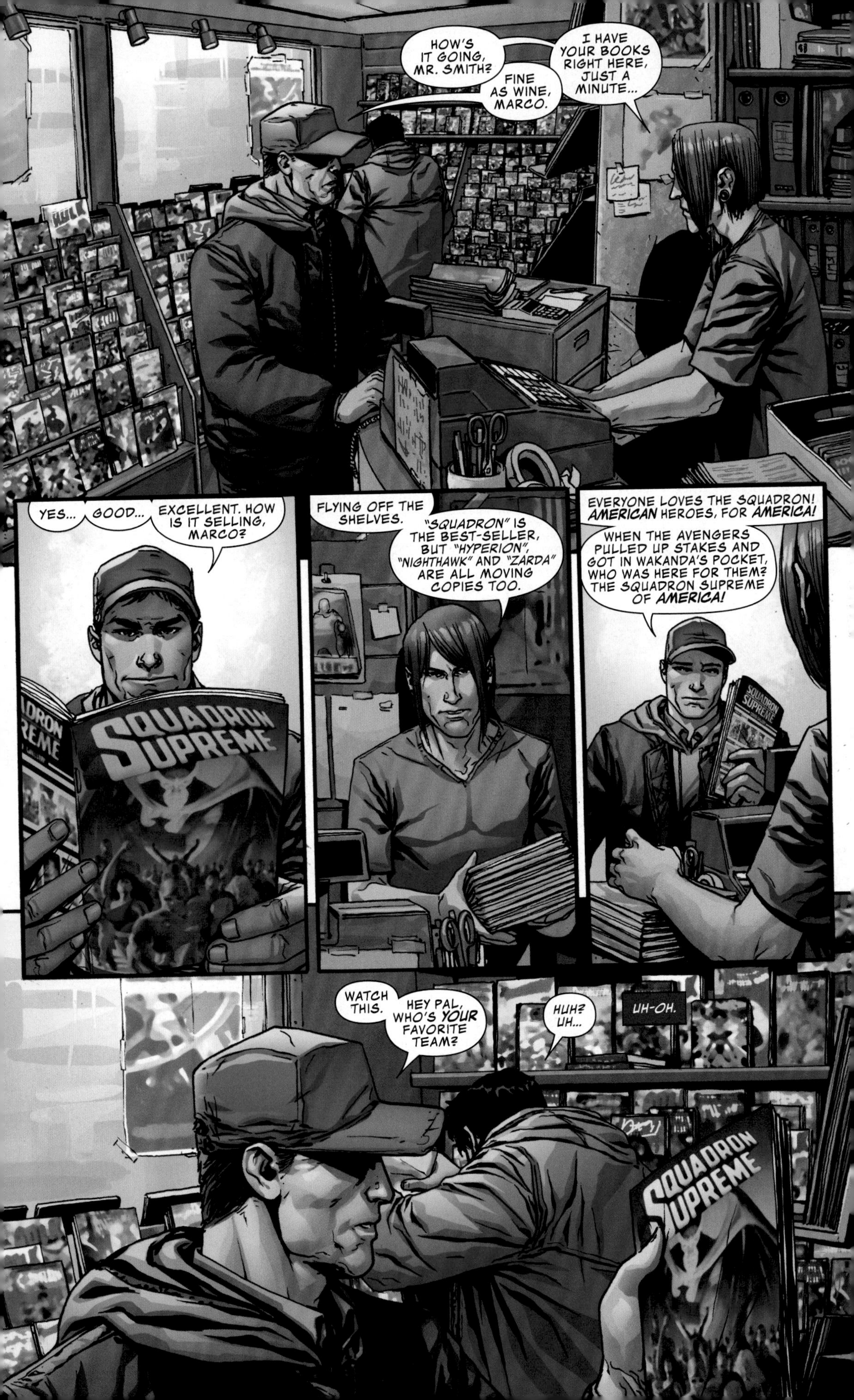
HOW'S IT GOING, MR. SMITH?
FINE AS WINE, MARCO.
I HAVE YOUR BOOKS RIGHT HERE, JUST A MINUTE...
YES...
GOOD...
EXCELLENT. HOW IS IT SELLING, MARCO?
SQUADRON SUPREME
FLYING OFF THE SHELVES.
"SQUADRON" IS THE BEST-SELLER, BUT "HYPERION", "NIGHTHAWK" AND "ZARDA" ARE ALL MOVING COPIES TOO.
EVERYONE LOVES THE SQUADRON! AMERICAN HEROES, FOR AMERICA!
WHEN THE AVENGERS PULLED UP STAKES AND GOT IN WAKANDA'S POCKET, WHO WAS HERE FOR THEM? THE SQUADRON SUPREME OF AMERICA!
SQUADRON SUPREME
WATCH THIS.
HEY PAL, WHO'S YOUR FAVORITE TEAM?
HUH? UH...
UH-OH.
SQUADRON SUPREME

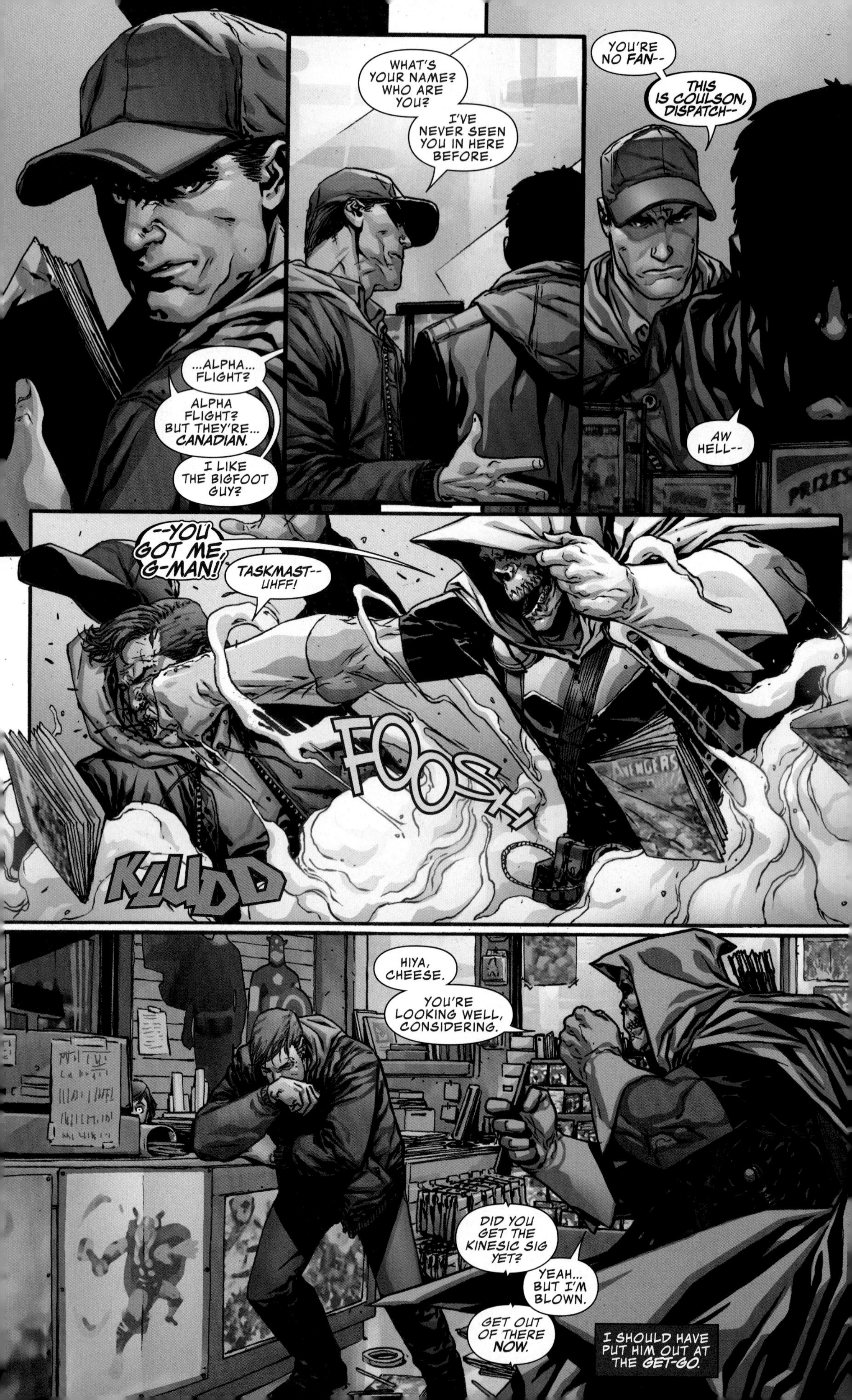

WHAT'S YOUR NAME? WHO ARE YOU?
I'VE NEVER SEEN YOU IN HERE BEFORE.
...ALPHA... FLIGHT?
ALPHA FLIGHT? BUT THEY'RE... CANADIAN.
I LIKE THE BIGFOOT GUY?
YOU'RE NO FAN--
THIS IS COULSON, DISPATCH--
AW HELL--
--YOU GOT ME, G-MAN!
TASKMAST-- UHFF!
FOOSH
KLUDD
HIYA, CHEESE.
YOU'RE LOOKING WELL, CONSIDERING.
DID YOU GET THE KINESIC SIG YET?
YEAH... BUT I'M BLOWN.
GET OUT OF THERE NOW.
I SHOULD HAVE PUT HIM OUT AT THE GET-GO.

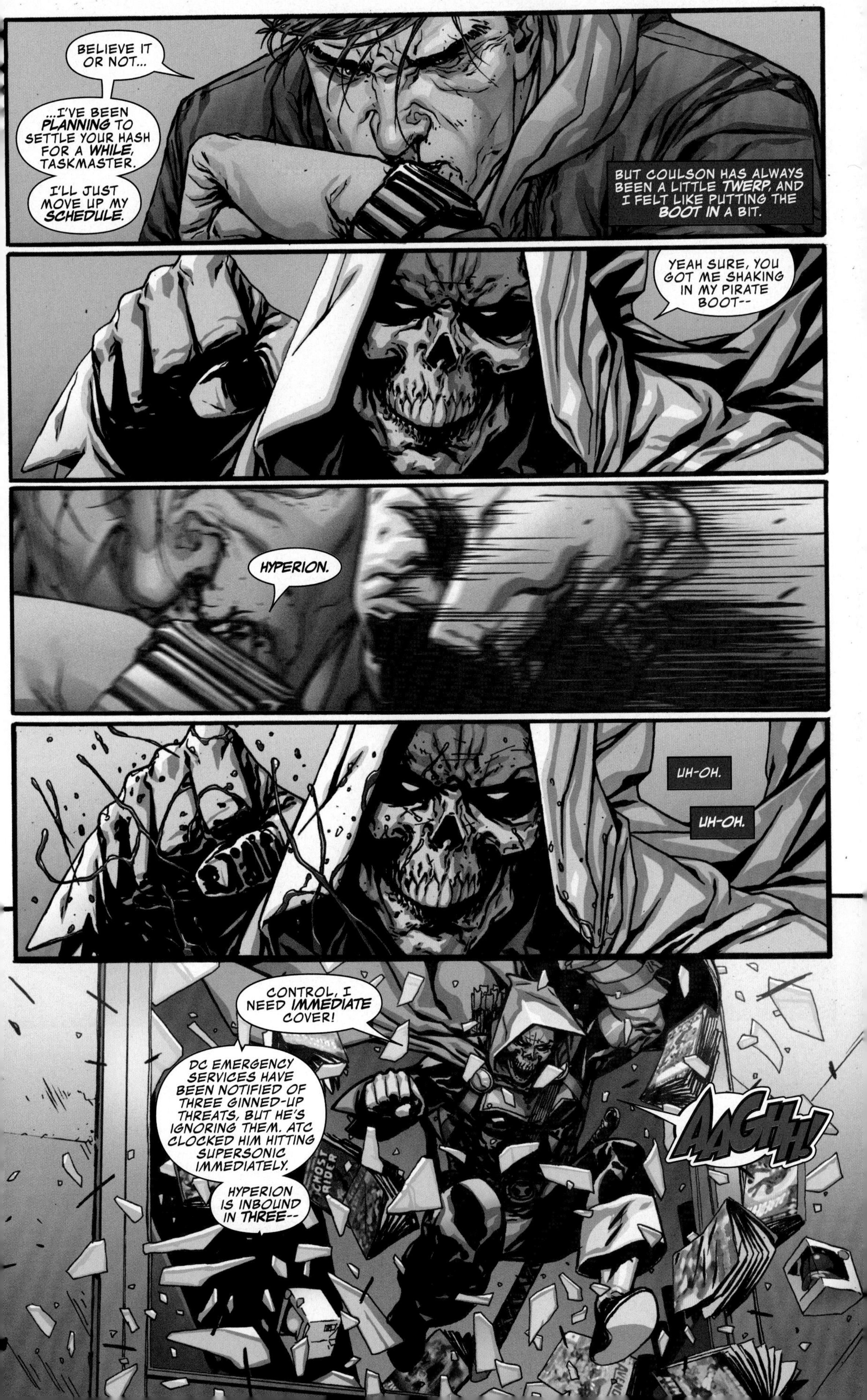
BELIEVE IT OR NOT...
...I'VE BEEN PLANNING TO SETTLE YOUR HASH FOR A WHILE, TASKMASTER.
I'LL JUST MOVE UP MY SCHEDULE.
BUT COULSON HAS ALWAYS BEEN A LITTLE TWERP, AND I FELT LIKE PUTTING THE BOOT IN A BIT.
YEAH SURE, YOU GOT ME SHAKING IN MY PIRATE BOOT--
HYPERION.
UH-OH.
UH-OH.
CONTROL, I NEED IMMEDIATE COVER!
DC EMERGENCY SERVICES HAVE BEEN NOTIFIED OF THREE GINNED-UP THREATS, BUT HE'S IGNORING THEM. ATC CLOCKED HIM HITTING SUPERSONIC IMMEDIATELY.
HYPERION IS INBOUND IN THREE--
AAGHH!

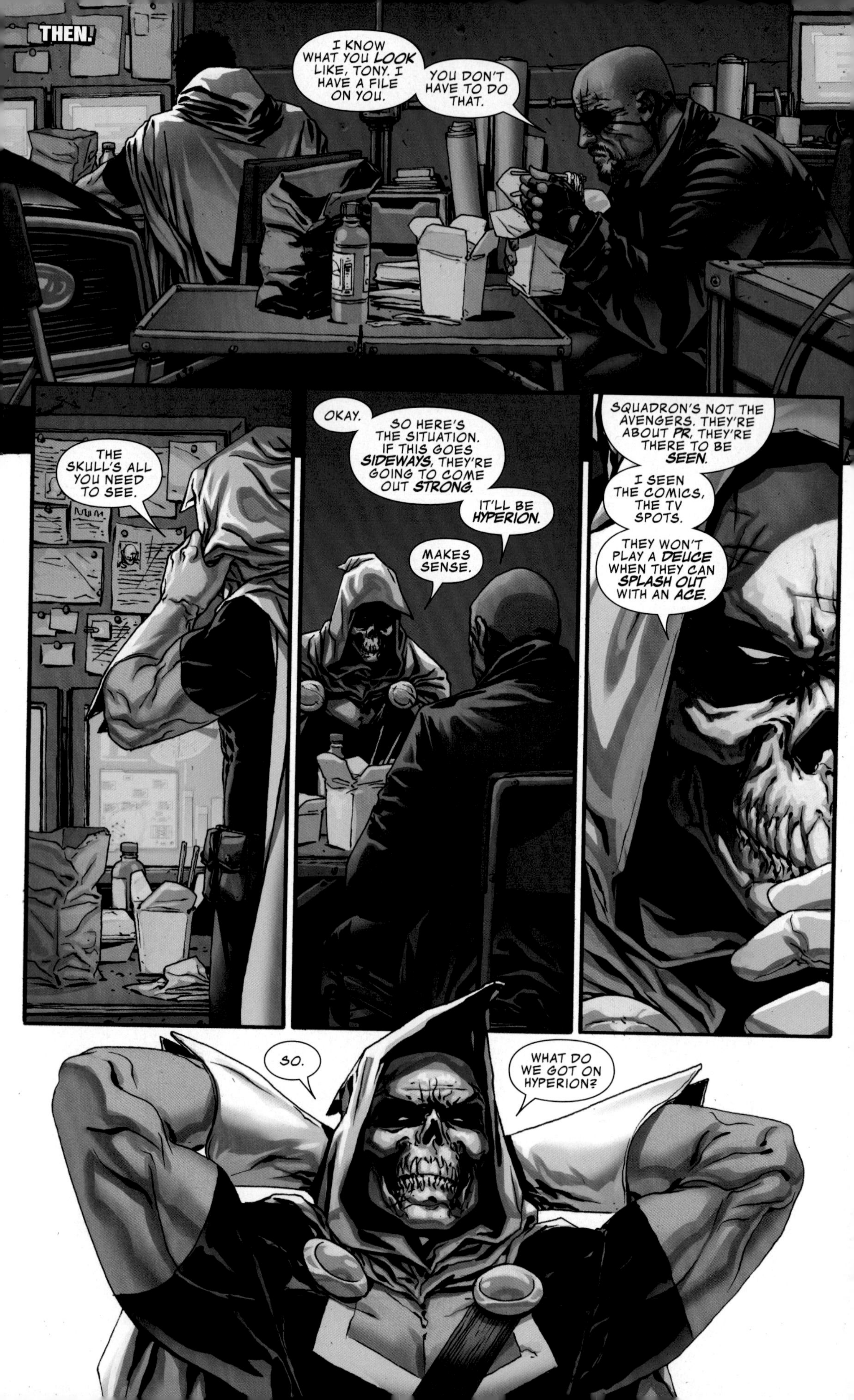
THEN.
I KNOW WHAT YOU LOOK LIKE, TONY. I HAVE A FILE ON YOU.
YOU DON'T HAVE TO DO THAT.
THE SKULL'S ALL YOU NEED TO SEE.
OKAY.
SO HERE'S THE SITUATION. IF THIS GOES SIDEWAYS, THEY'RE GOING TO COME OUT STRONG.
IT'LL BE HYPERION.
MAKES SENSE.
SQUADRON'S NOT THE AVENGERS. THEY'RE ABOUT PR, THEY'RE THERE TO BE SEEN.
I SEEN THE COMICS, THE TV SPOTS.
THEY WON'T PLAY A DEUCE WHEN THEY CAN SPLASH OUT WITH AN ACE.
SO.
WHAT DO WE GOT ON HYPERION?

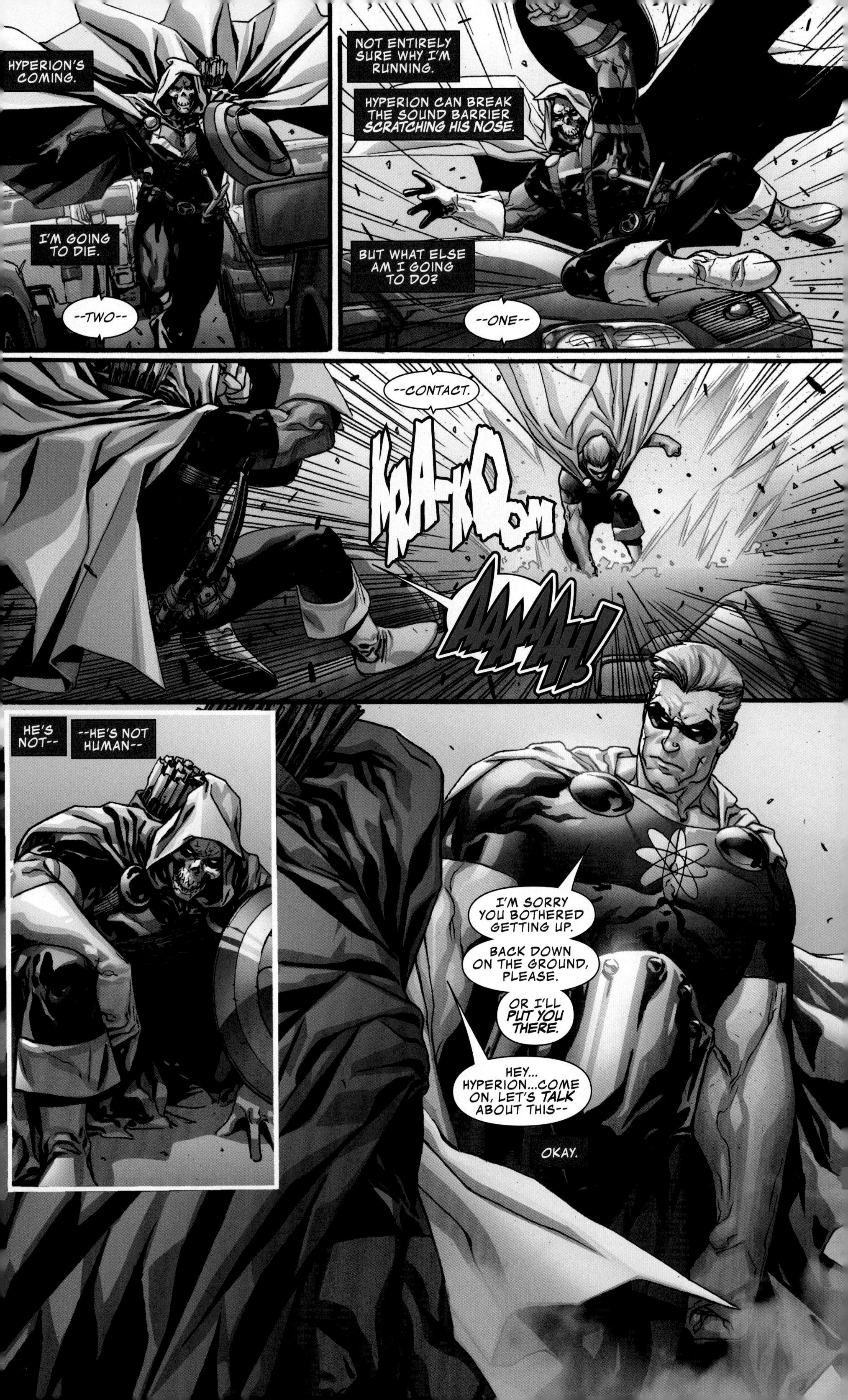
HYPERION'S COMING.
I'M GOING TO DIE.
--TWO--
NOT ENTIRELY SURE WHY I'M RUNNING.
HYPERION CAN BREAK THE SOUND BARRIER SCRATCHING HIS NOSE.
BUT WHAT ELSE AM I GOING TO DO?
--ONE--
--CONTACT.
KRAA-KOOOM
AAAAAAH!
HE'S NOT--
--HE'S NOT HUMAN--
I'M SORRY YOU BOTHERED GETTING UP.
BACK DOWN ON THE GROUND, PLEASE.
OR I'LL PUT YOU THERE.
HEY... HYPERION...COME ON, LET'S TALK ABOUT THIS--
OKAY.

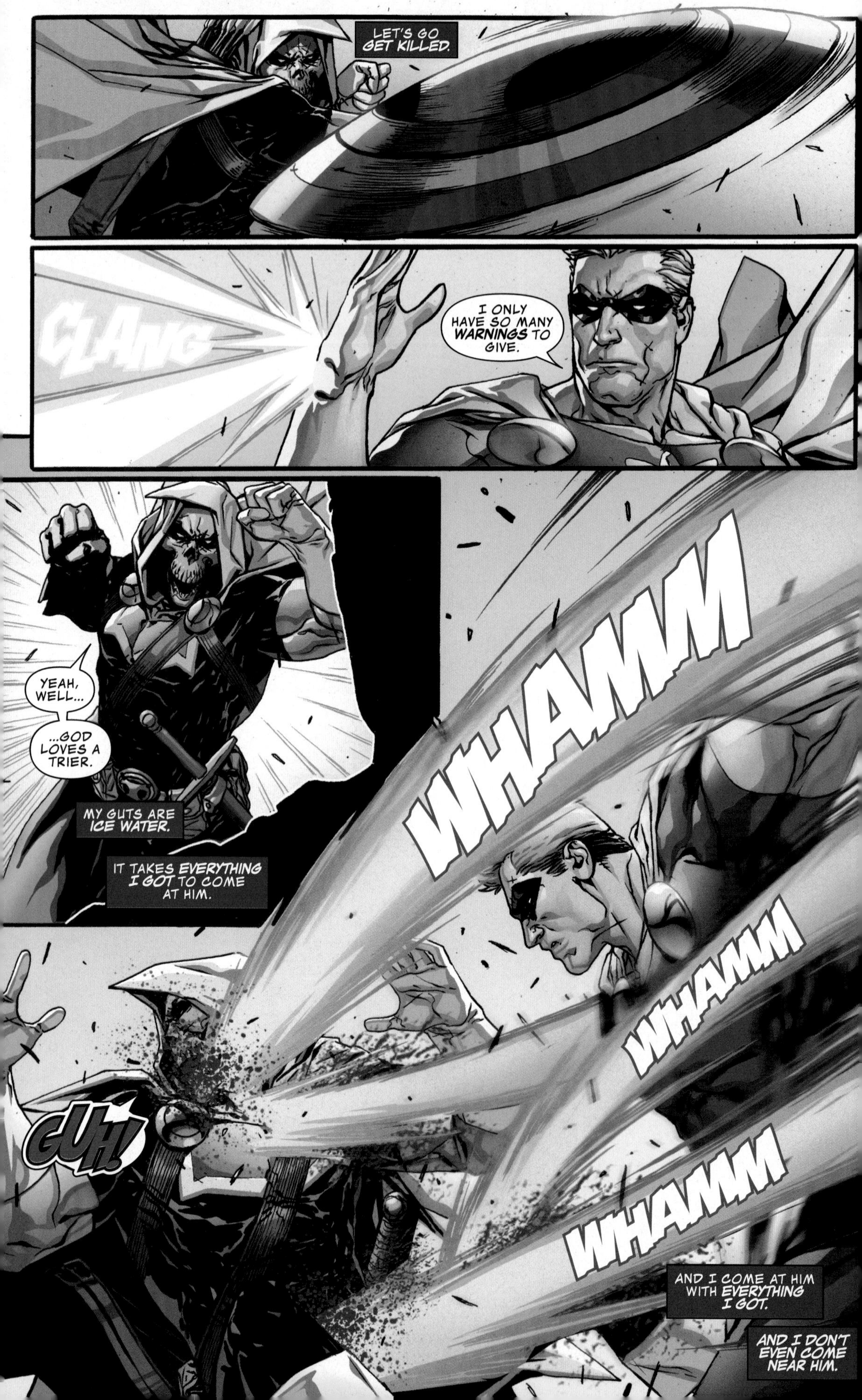
LET'S GO GET KILLED.
CLANG
I ONLY HAVE SO MANY WARNINGS TO GIVE.
YEAH, WELL...
...GOD LOVES A TRIER.
MY GUTS ARE ICE WATER.
IT TAKES EVERYTHING I GOT TO COME AT HIM.
WHAMM
WHAMM
GUH!
WHAMM
AND I COME AT HIM WITH EVERYTHING I GOT.
AND I DON'T EVEN COME NEAR HIM.

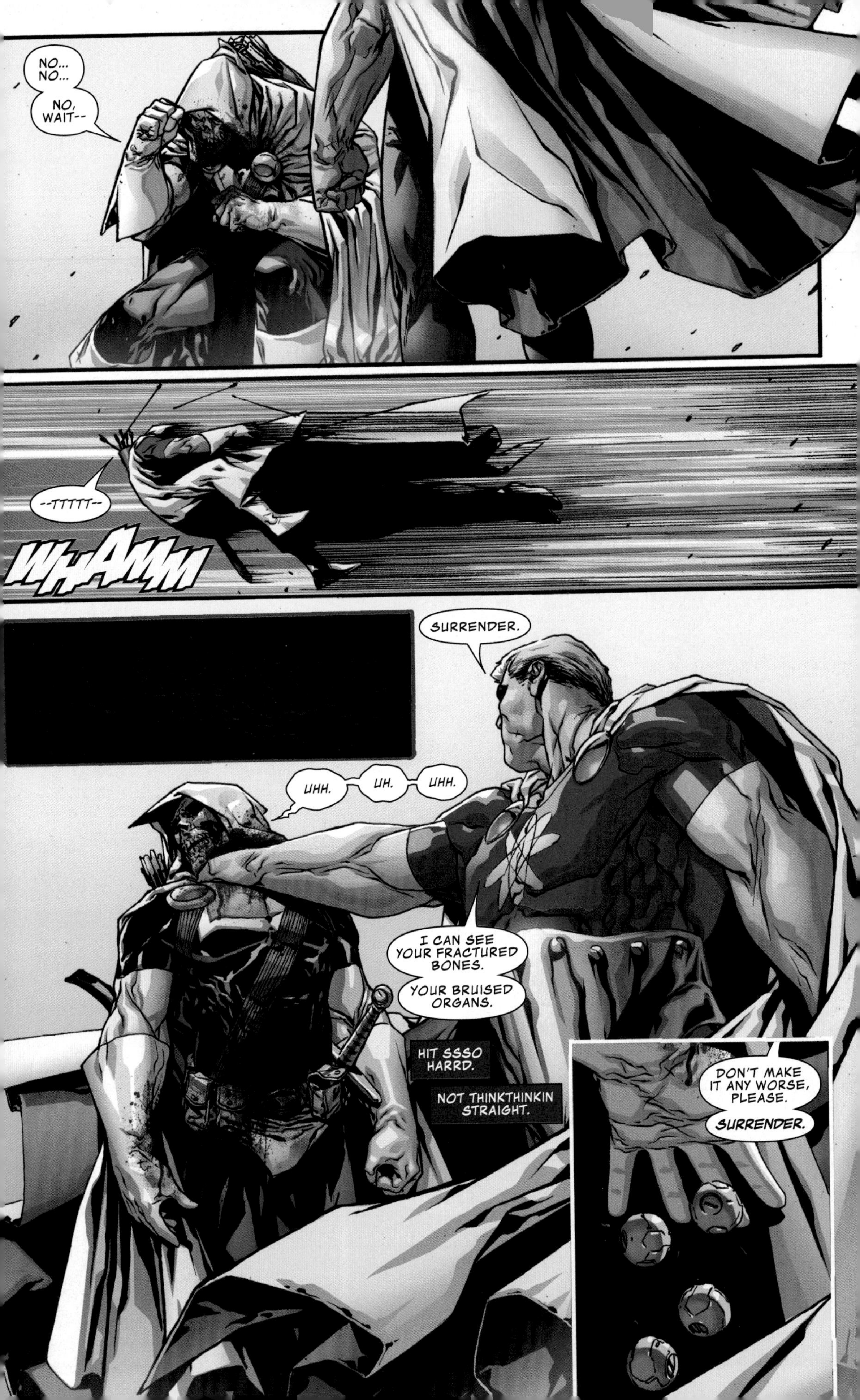
NO... NO...
NO, WAIT--
--TTTTT--
WHAMM
SURRENDER.
UHH.
UH.
UHH.
I CAN SEE YOUR FRACTURED BONES.
YOUR BRUISED ORGANS.
HIT SSSO HARRD.
NOT THINKTHINKIN STRAIGHT.
DON'T MAKE IT ANY WORSE, PLEASE.
SURRENDER.

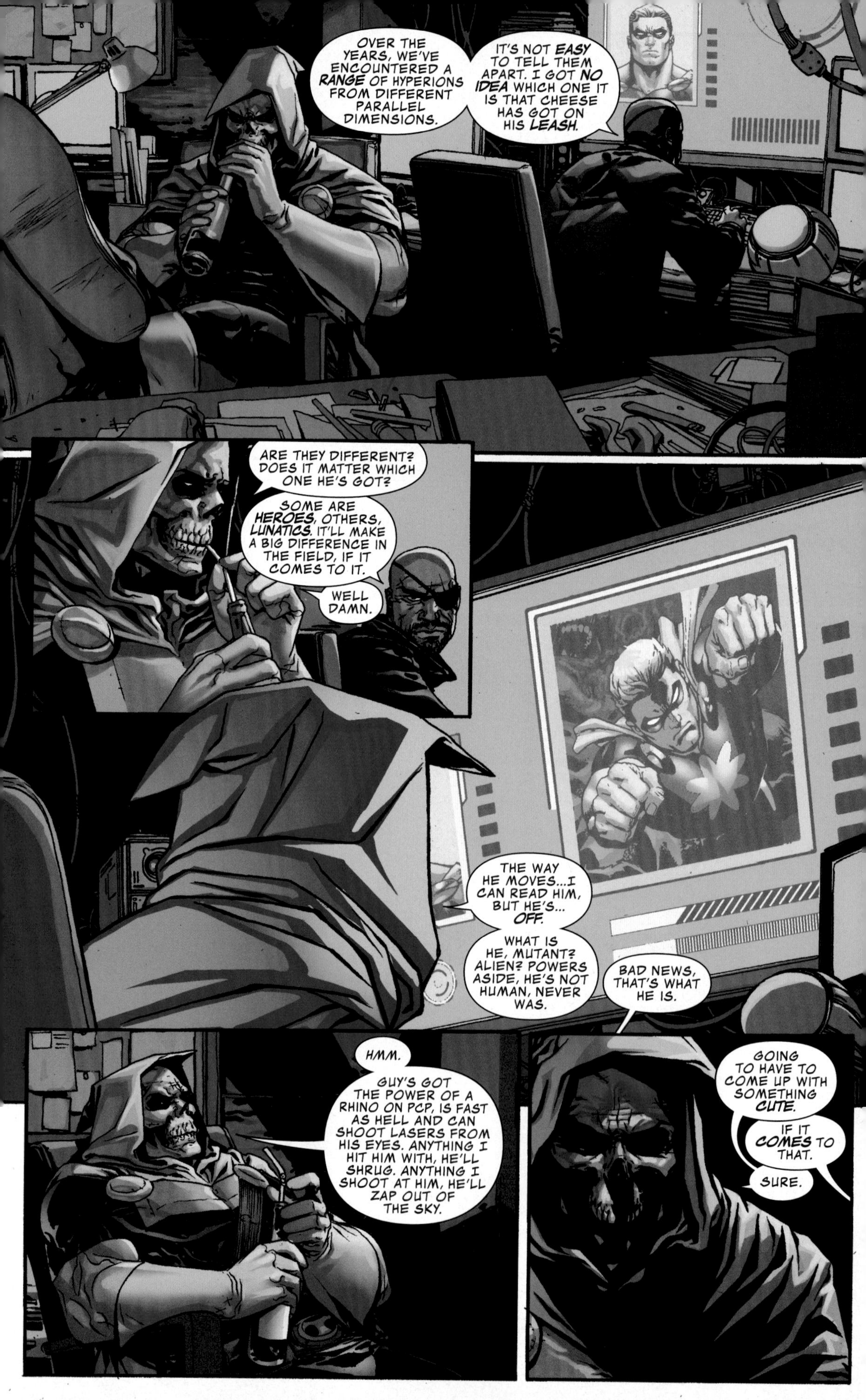
OVER THE YEARS, WE'VE ENCOUNTERED A RANGE OF HYPERIONS FROM DIFFERENT PARALLEL DIMENSIONS.
IT'S NOT EASY TO TELL THEM APART. I GOT NO IDEA WHICH ONE IT IS THAT CHEESE HAS GOT ON HIS LEASH.
ARE THEY DIFFERENT? DOES IT MATTER WHICH ONE HE'S GOT?
SOME ARE HEROES, OTHERS, LUNATICS. IT'LL MAKE A BIG DIFFERENCE IN THE FIELD, IF IT COMES TO IT.
WELL DAMN.
THE WAY HE MOVES...I CAN READ HIM, BUT HE'S... OFF.
WHAT IS HE, MUTANT? ALIEN? POWERS ASIDE, HE'S NOT HUMAN, NEVER WAS.
BAD NEWS, THAT'S WHAT HE IS.
HMM.
GUY'S GOT THE POWER OF A RHINO ON PCP, IS FAST AS HELL AND CAN SHOOT LASERS FROM HIS EYES. ANYTHING I HIT HIM WITH, HE'LL SHRUG. ANYTHING I SHOOT AT HIM, HE'LL ZAP OUT OF THE SKY.
GOING TO HAVE TO COME UP WITH SOMETHING CUTE.
IF IT COMES TO THAT.
SURE.

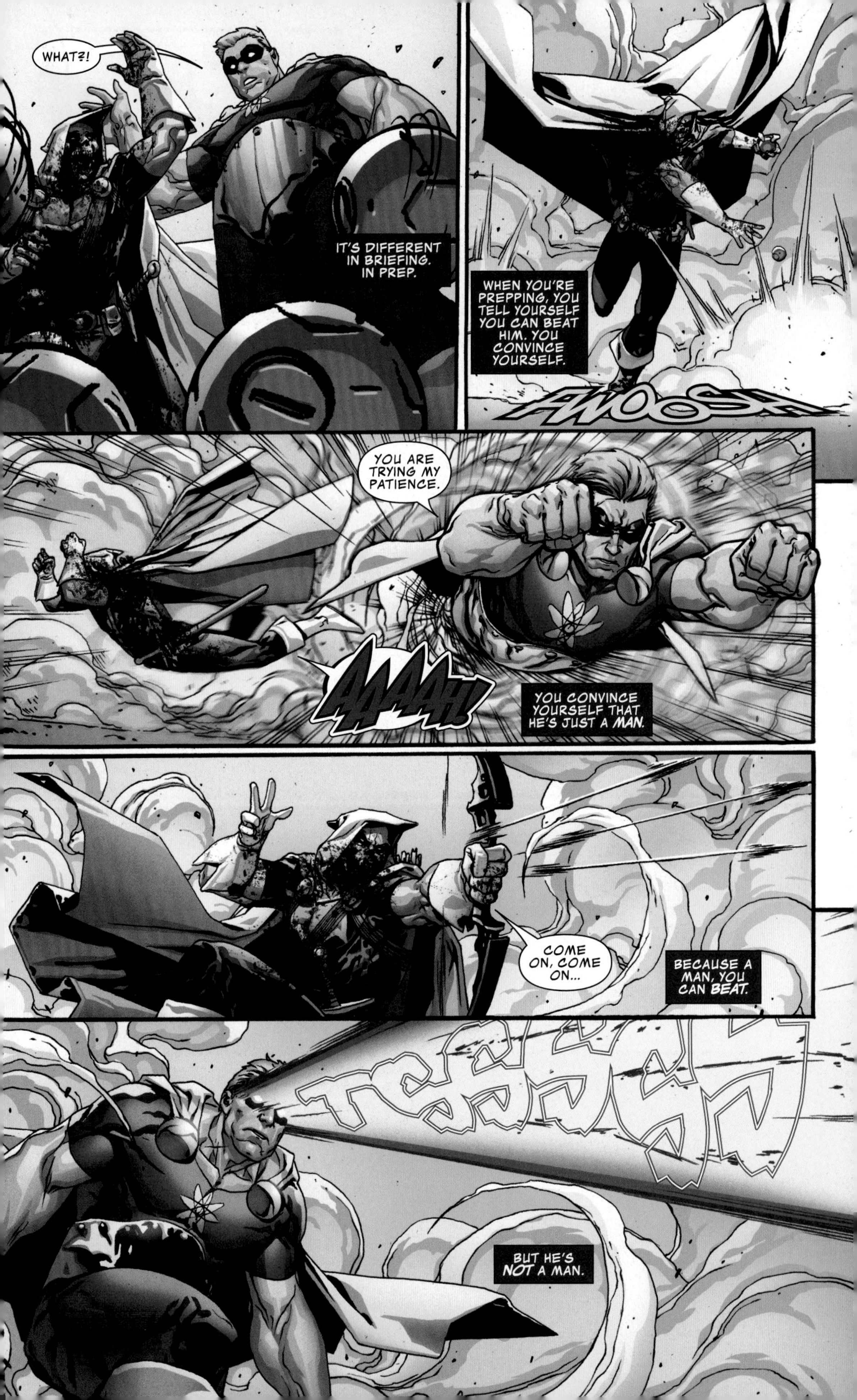
WHAT?!
IT'S DIFFERENT IN BRIEFING. IN PREP.
WHEN YOU'RE PREPPING, YOU TELL YOURSELF YOU CAN BEAT HIM. YOU CONVINCE YOURSELF.
FWOOSH
YOU ARE TRYING MY PATIENCE.
AAAAH!
YOU CONVINCE YOURSELF THAT HE'S JUST A MAN.
COME ON, COME ON...
BECAUSE A MAN, YOU CAN BEAT.
TCHSSSH
BUT HE'S NOT A MAN.

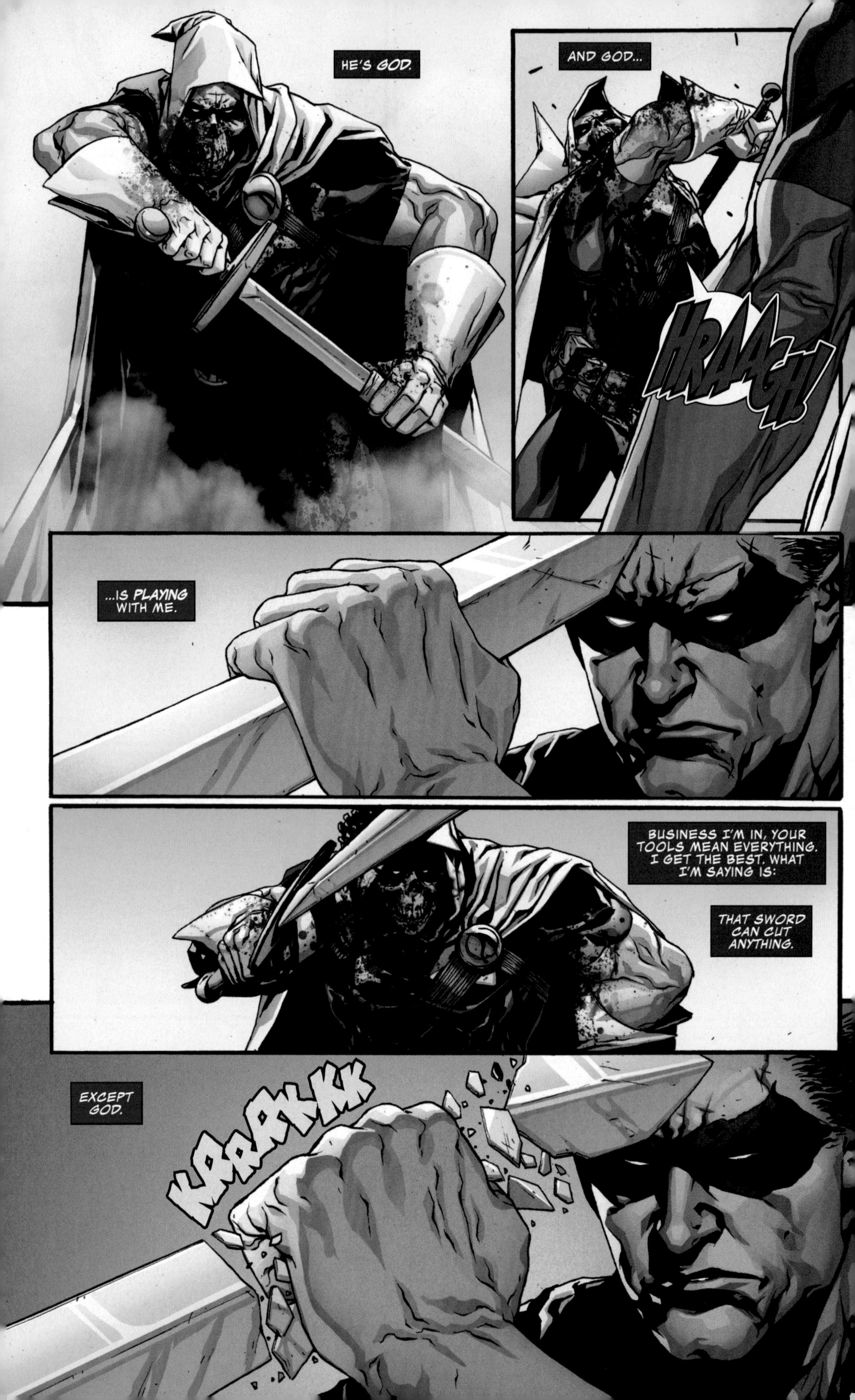
HE'S GOD.
AND GOD...
HRAAGH!
...IS PLAYING WITH ME.
BUSINESS I'M IN, YOUR TOOLS MEAN EVERYTHING. I GET THE BEST. WHAT I'M SAYING IS:
THAT SWORD CAN CUT ANYTHING.
EXCEPT GOD.
KRRAKKK

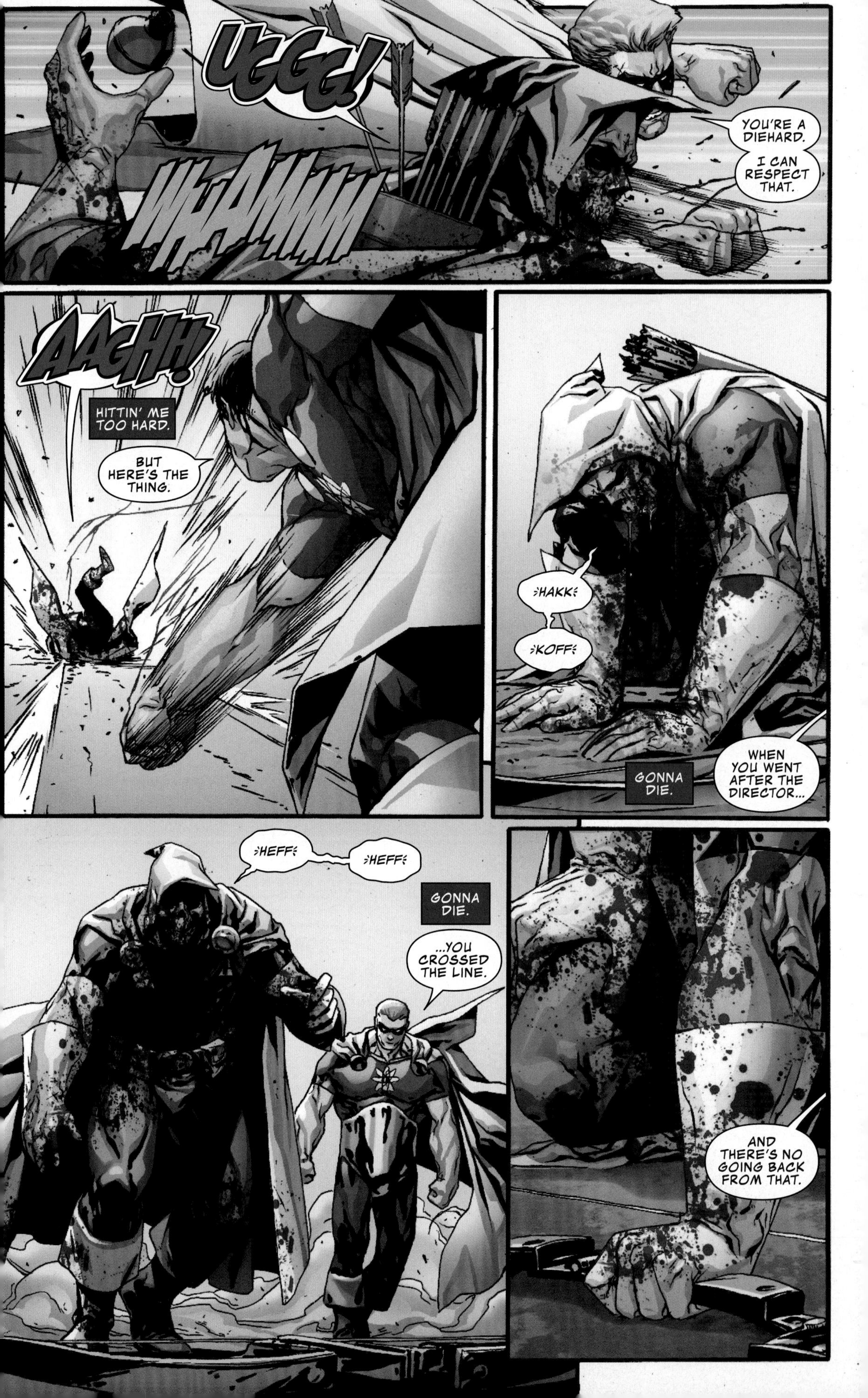
UGGG!
WHAMMM
YOU'RE A DIEHARD.
I CAN RESPECT THAT.
AAGHH!
HITTIN' ME TOO HARD.
BUT HERE'S THE THING.
HAKK
KOFF
GONNA DIE.
WHEN YOU WENT AFTER THE DIRECTOR...
HEFF
HEFF
GONNA DIE.
...YOU CROSSED THE LINE.
AND THERE'S NO GOING BACK FROM THAT.

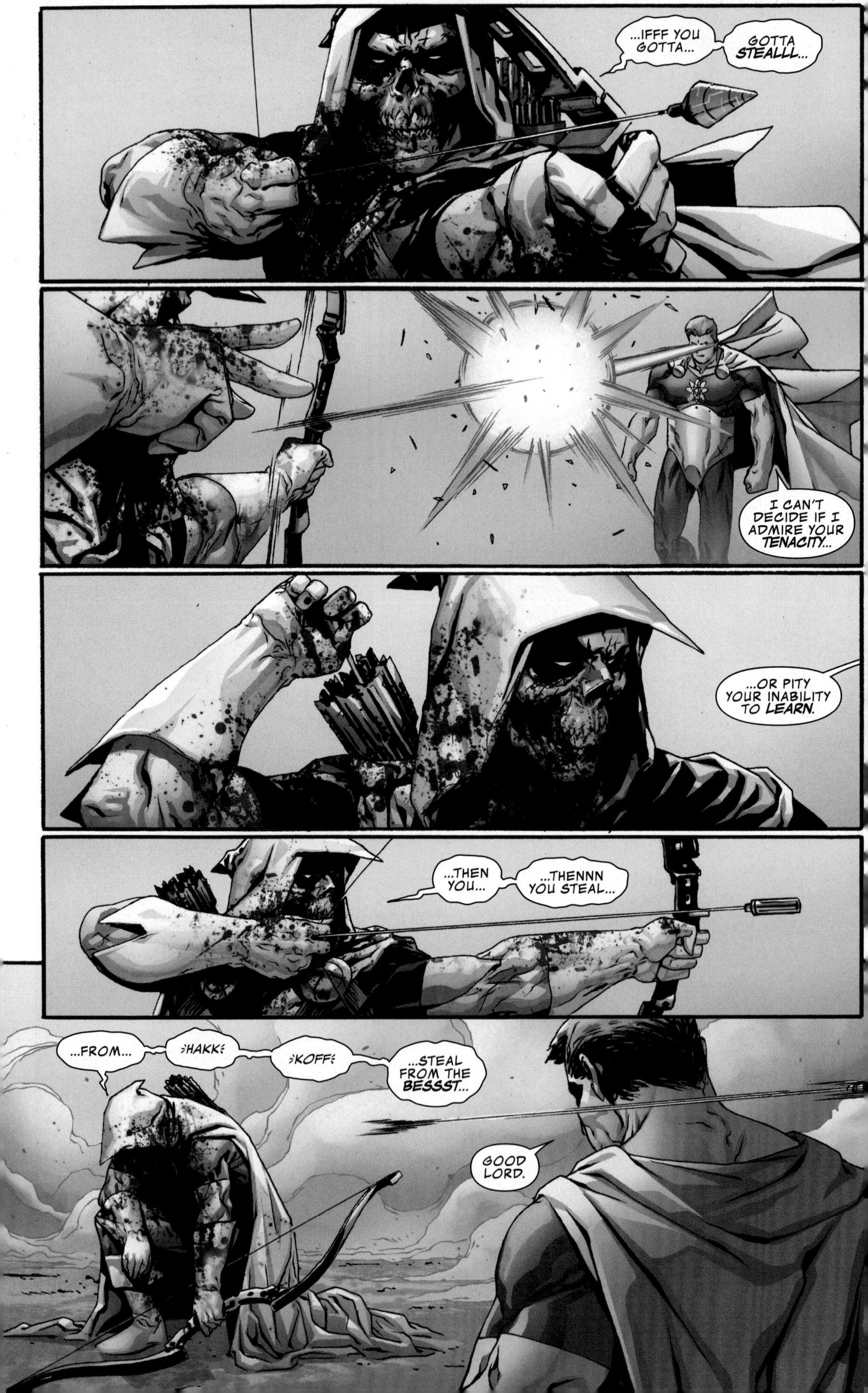

...IFFF YOU GOTTA...
GOTTA STEALLL...
I CAN'T DECIDE IF I ADMIRE YOUR TENACITY...
...OR PITY YOUR INABILITY TO LEARN.
...THEN YOU...
...THENNN YOU STEAL...
...FROM...
HAKK
KOFF
...STEAL FROM THE BESSST...
GOOD LORD.

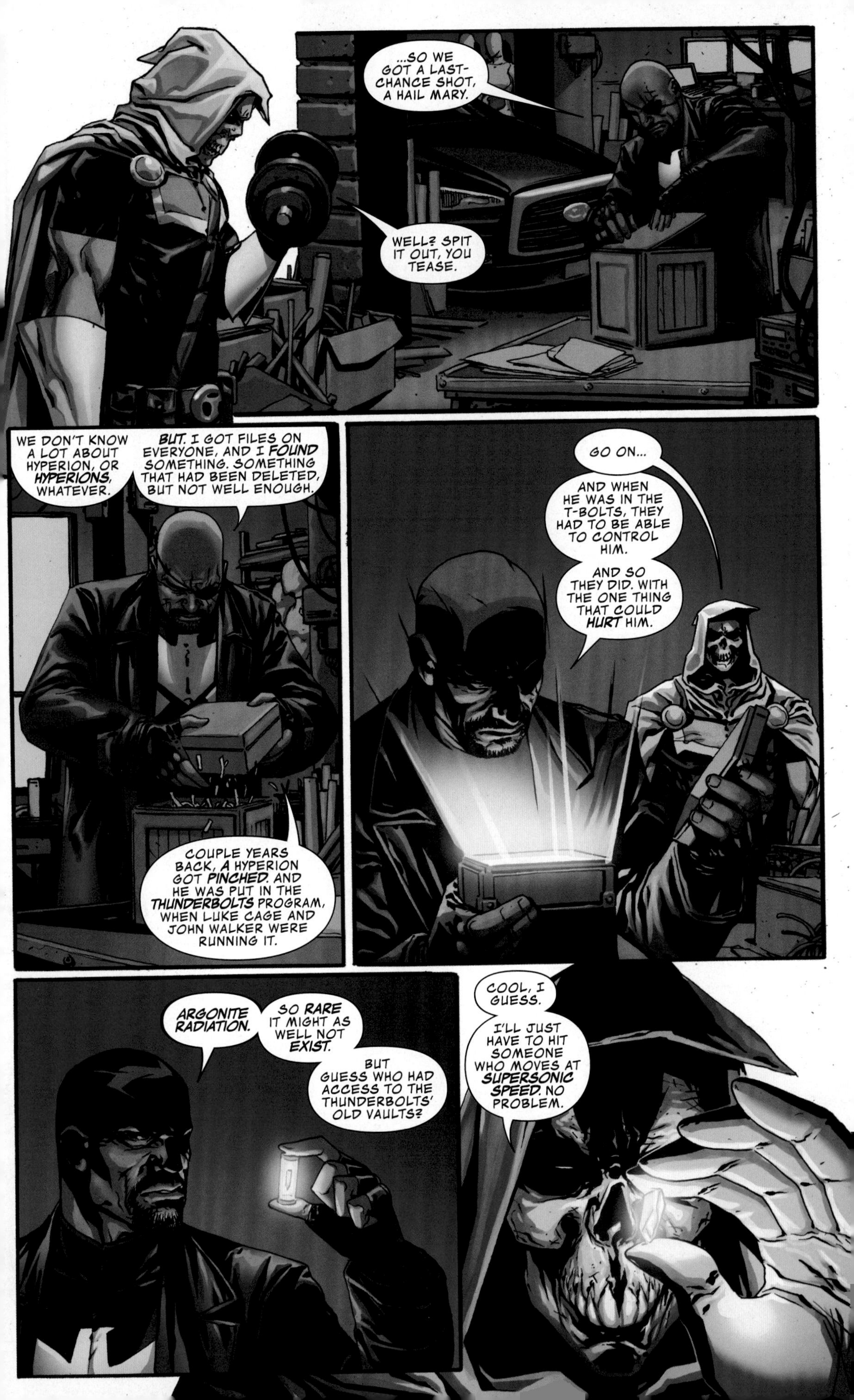
...SO WE GOT A LAST-CHANCE SHOT, A HAIL MARY.
WELL? SPIT IT OUT, YOU TEASE.
WE DON'T KNOW A LOT ABOUT HYPERION, OR HYPERIONS, WHATEVER.
BUT. I GOT FILES ON EVERYONE, AND I FOUND SOMETHING. SOMETHING THAT HAD BEEN DELETED, BUT NOT WELL ENOUGH.
COUPLE YEARS BACK, A HYPERION GOT PINCHED. AND HE WAS PUT IN THE THUNDERBOLTS PROGRAM, WHEN LUKE CAGE AND JOHN WALKER WERE RUNNING IT.
GO ON...
AND WHEN HE WAS IN THE T-BOLTS, THEY HAD TO BE ABLE TO CONTROL HIM.
AND SO THEY DID. WITH THE ONE THING THAT COULD HURT HIM.
ARGONITE RADIATION.
SO RARE IT MIGHT AS WELL NOT EXIST.
BUT GUESS WHO HAD ACCESS TO THE THUNDERBOLTS' OLD VAULTS?
COOL, I GUESS.
I'LL JUST HAVE TO HIT SOMEONE WHO MOVES AT SUPERSONIC SPEED. NO PROBLEM.

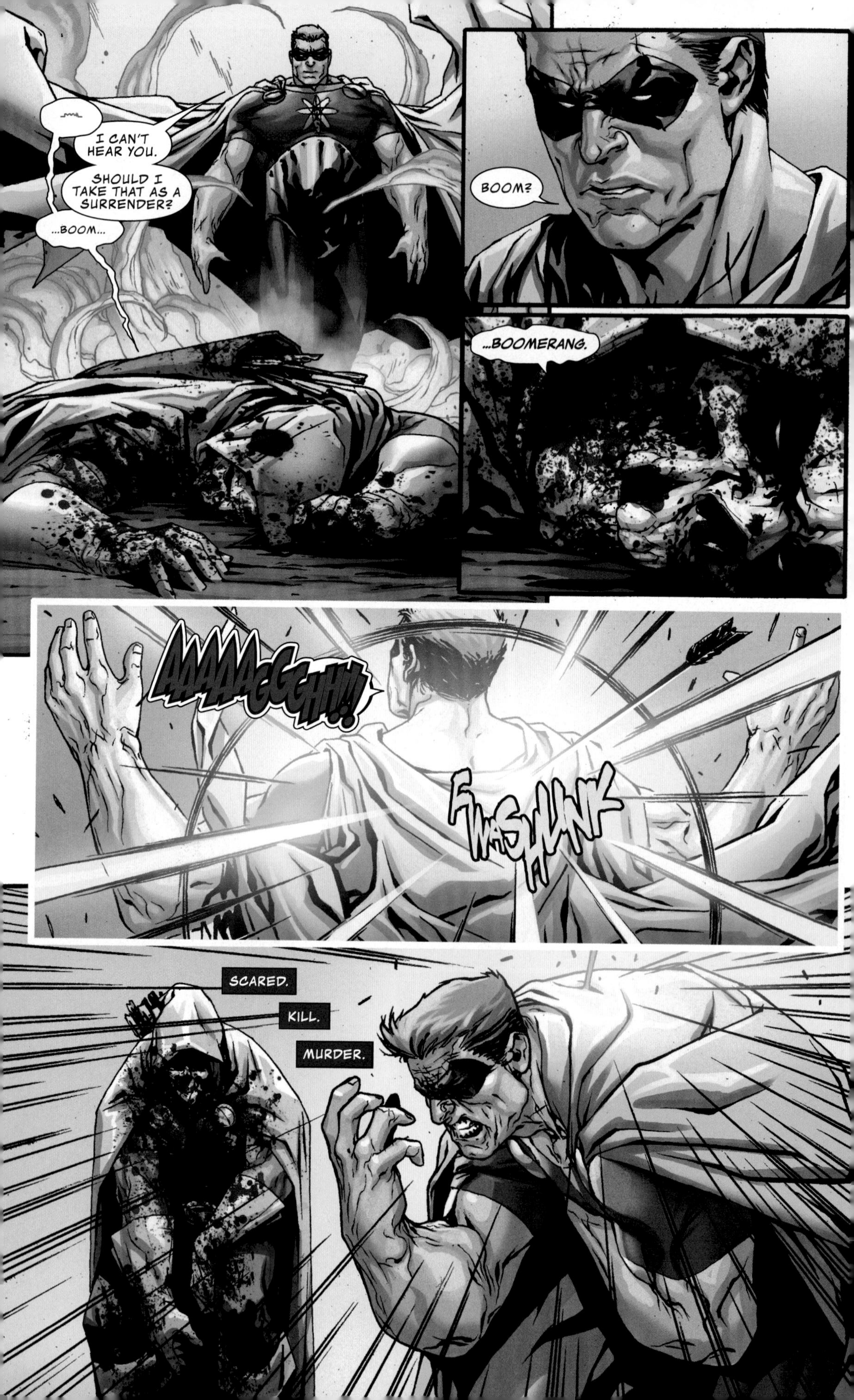

I CAN'T HEAR YOU.
SHOULD I TAKE THAT AS A SURRENDER?
...BOOM...
BOOM?
...BOOMERANG.
AAAAAGGGHH!!
FWASHUNK
SCARED.
KILL.
MURDER.

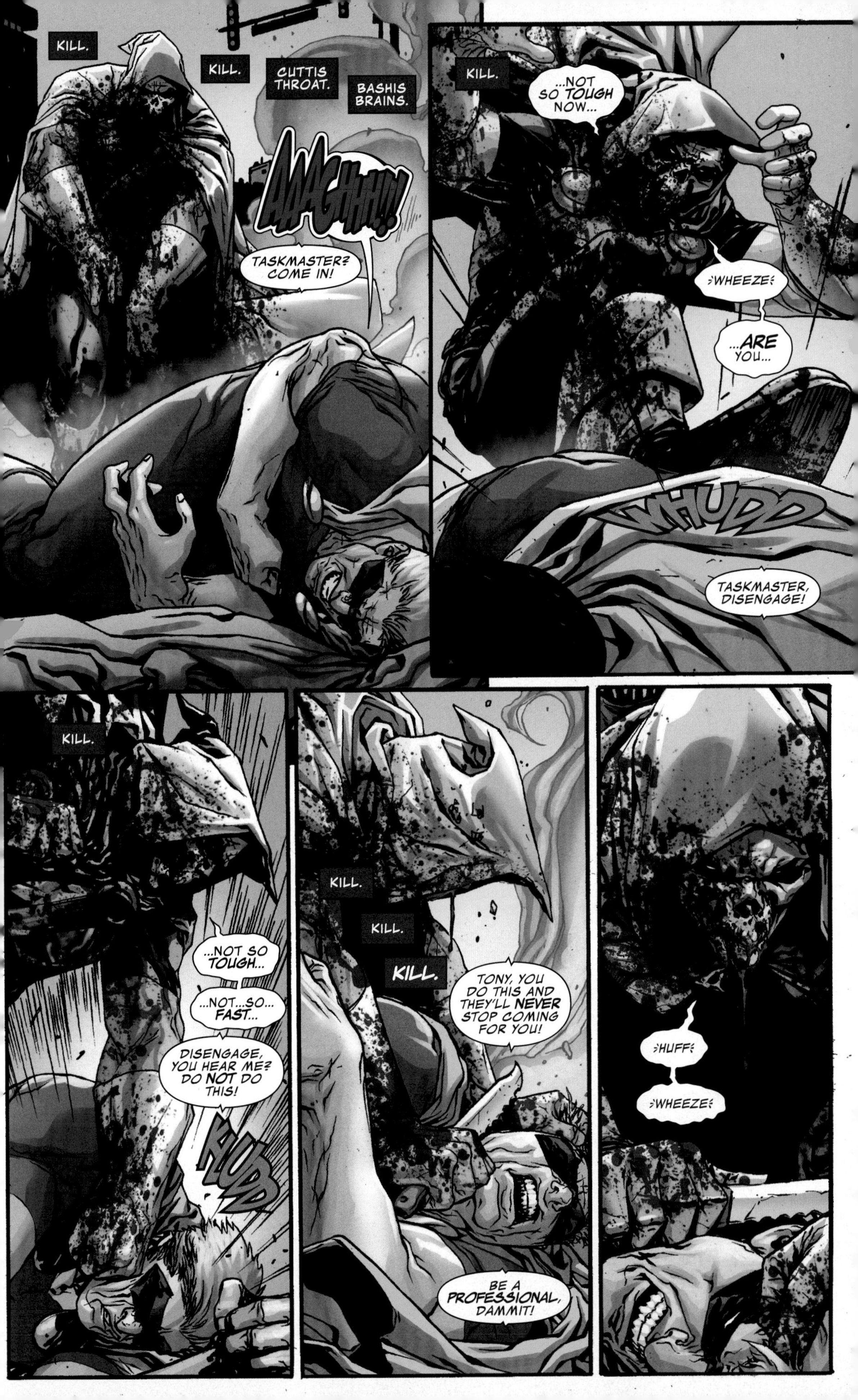
KILL.
KILL.
CUTTIS THROAT.
BASHIS BRAINS.
AAAGHHH!!
TASKMASTER? COME IN!
KILL.
...NOT SO TOUGH NOW...
WHEEZE
...ARE YOU...
WHUDD
TASKMASTER, DISENGAGE!
KILL.
...NOT SO TOUGH...
...NOT...SO... FAST...
DISENGAGE, YOU HEAR ME? DO NOT DO THIS!
THUDD
KILL.
KILL.
KILL.
TONY, YOU DO THIS AND THEY'LL NEVER STOP COMING FOR YOU!
BE A PROFESSIONAL, DAMMIT!
HUFF
WHEEZE

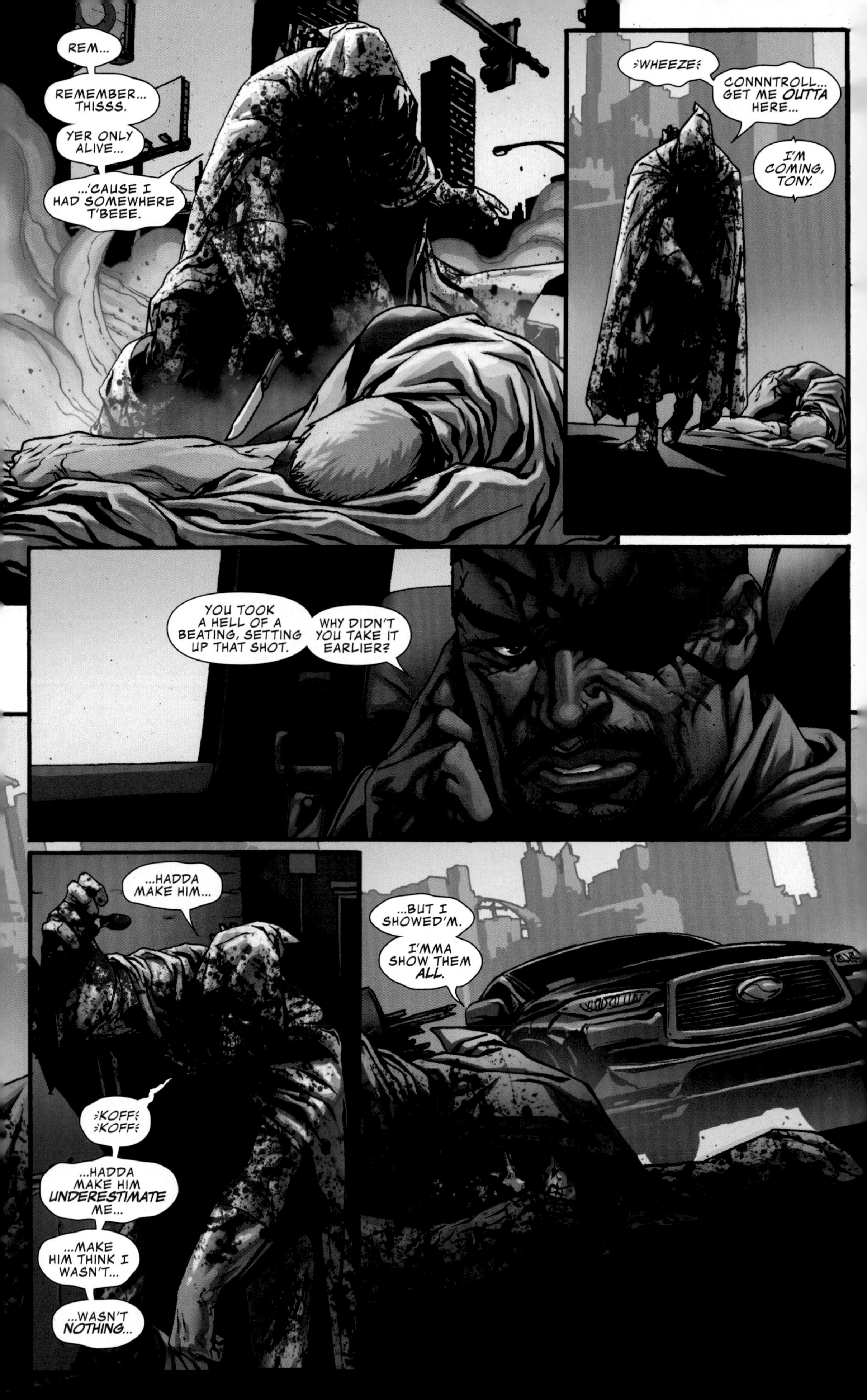
REM...
REMEMBER... THISSS.
YER ONLY ALIVE...
...'CAUSE I HAD SOMEWHERE T'BEEE.
*WHEEZE*
CONNNTROLL... GET ME OUTTA HERE...
I'M COMING, TONY.
YOU TOOK A HELL OF A BEATING, SETTING UP THAT SHOT.
WHY DIDN'T YOU TAKE IT EARLIER?
...HADDA MAKE HIM...
...BUT I SHOWED'M.
I'MMA SHOW THEM ALL.
*KOFF* *KOFF*
...HADDA MAKE HIM UNDERESTIMATE ME...
...MAKE HIM THINK I WASN'T...
...WASN'T NOTHING...

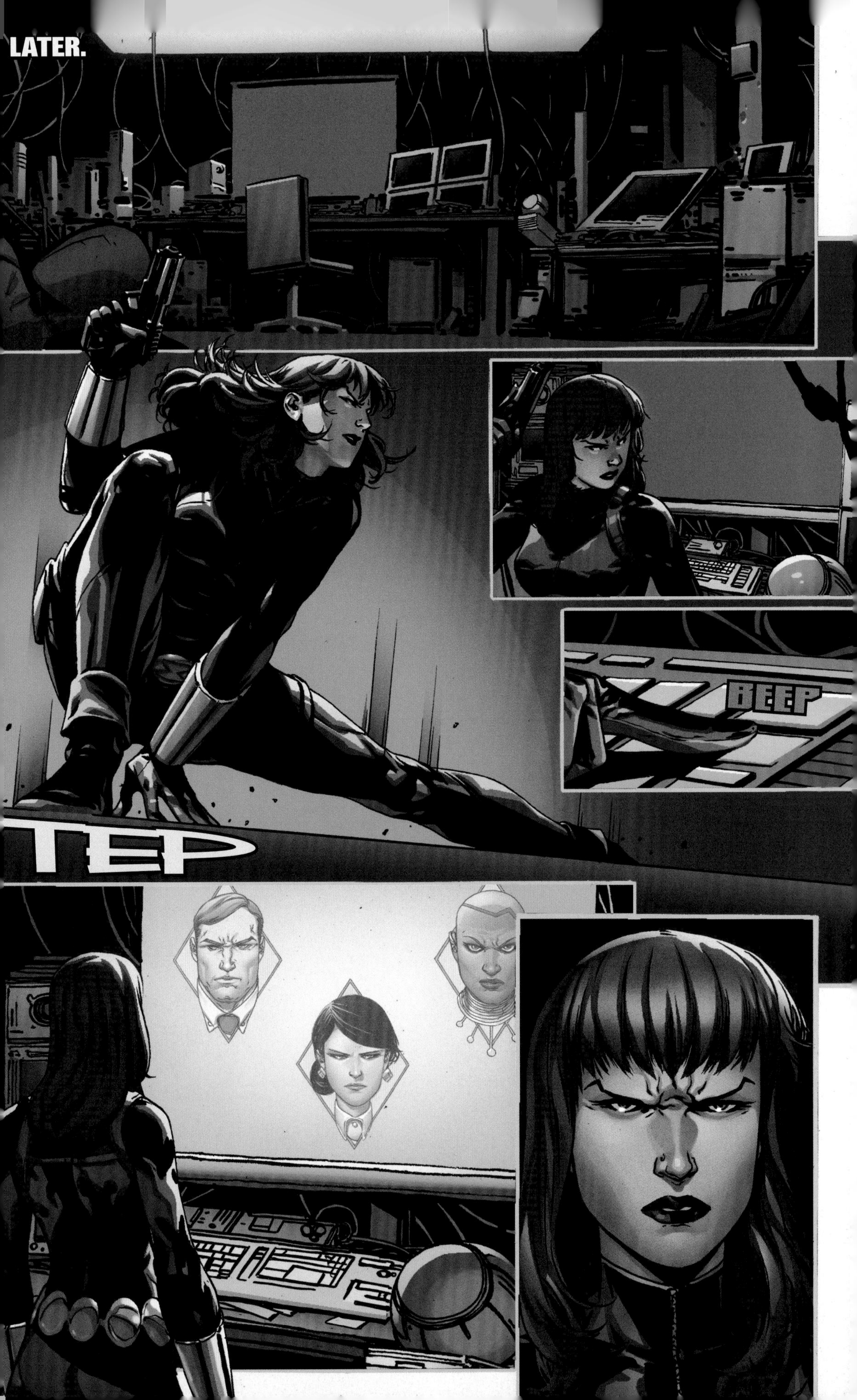
LATER.
TEP
BEEP

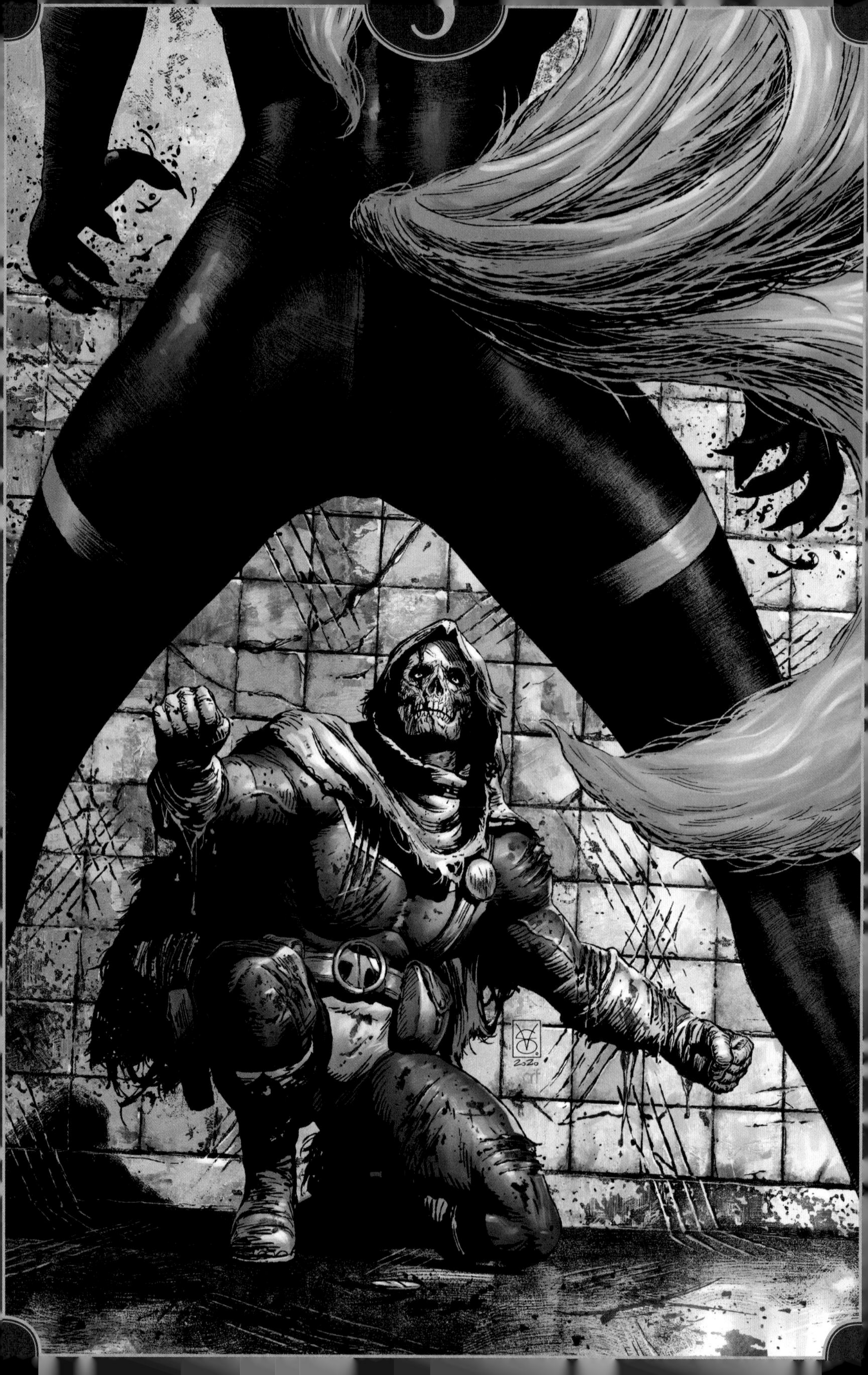

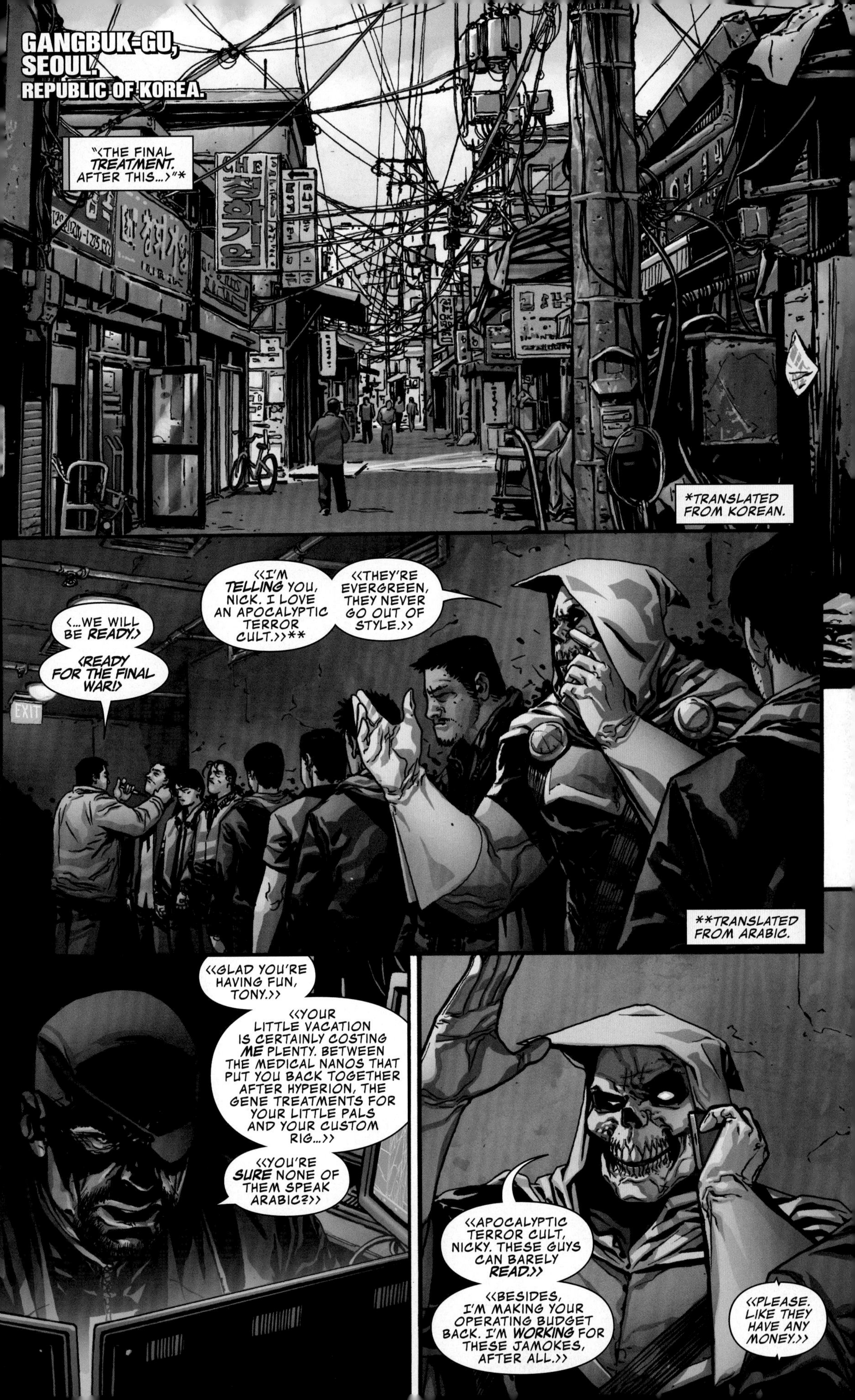
GANGBUK-GU, SEOUL. REPUBLIC OF KOREA.
"<THE FINAL TREATMENT. AFTER THIS...>"*
*TRANSLATED FROM KOREAN.
<...WE WILL BE READY.>
<READY FOR THE FINAL WAR!>
<<I'M TELLING YOU, NICK. I LOVE AN APOCALYPTIC TERROR CULT.>>**
<<THEY'RE EVERGREEN, THEY NEVER GO OUT OF STYLE.>>
**TRANSLATED FROM ARABIC.
<<GLAD YOU'RE HAVING FUN, TONY.>>
<<YOUR LITTLE VACATION IS CERTAINLY COSTING ME PLENTY. BETWEEN THE MEDICAL NANOS THAT PUT YOU BACK TOGETHER AFTER HYPERION, THE GENE TREATMENTS FOR YOUR LITTLE PALS AND YOUR CUSTOM RIG...>>
<<YOU'RE SURE NONE OF THEM SPEAK ARABIC?>>
<<APOCALYPTIC TERROR CULT, NICKY. THESE GUYS CAN BARELY READ.>>
<<BESIDES, I'M MAKING YOUR OPERATING BUDGET BACK. I'M WORKING FOR THESE JAMOKES, AFTER ALL.>>
<<PLEASE. LIKE THEY HAVE ANY MONEY.>>

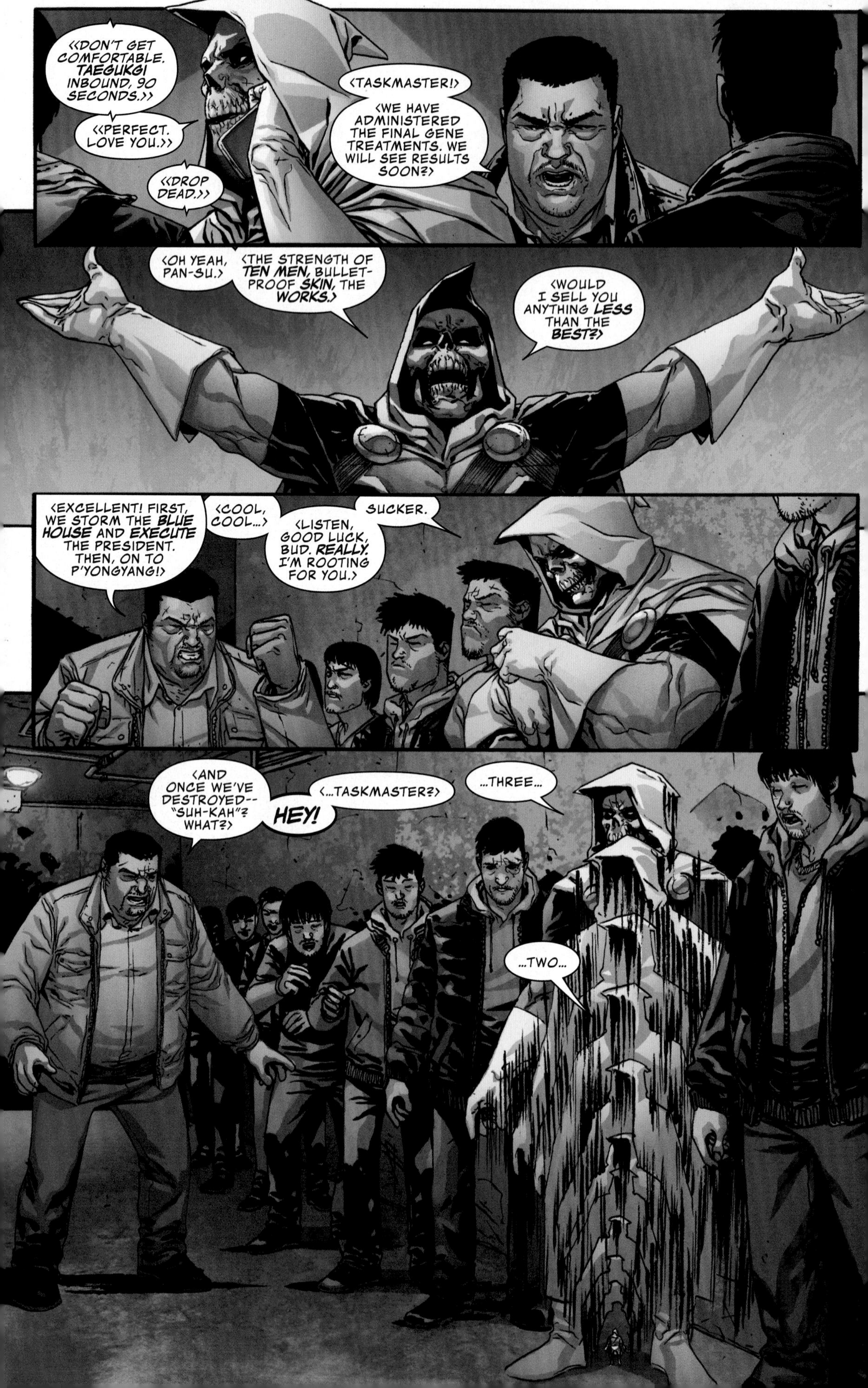

<<DON'T GET COMFORTABLE. TAEGUKGI INBOUND, 90 SECONDS.>>
<<PERFECT. LOVE YOU.>>
<<DROP DEAD.>>
<TASKMASTER!>
<WE HAVE ADMINISTERED THE FINAL GENE TREATMENTS. WE WILL SEE RESULTS SOON?>
<OH YEAH, PAN-SU.>
<THE STRENGTH OF TEN MEN, BULLET-PROOF SKIN, THE WORKS.>
<WOULD I SELL YOU ANYTHING LESS THAN THE BEST?>
<EXCELLENT! FIRST, WE STORM THE BLUE HOUSE AND EXECUTE THE PRESIDENT. THEN, ON TO P'YONGYANG!>
<COOL, COOL...>
<LISTEN, GOOD LUCK, BUD. REALLY. I'M ROOTING FOR YOU.>
SUCKER.
<AND ONCE WE'VE DESTROYED-- "SUH-KAH"? WHAT?>
HEY!
<...TASKMASTER?>
...THREE...
...TWO...

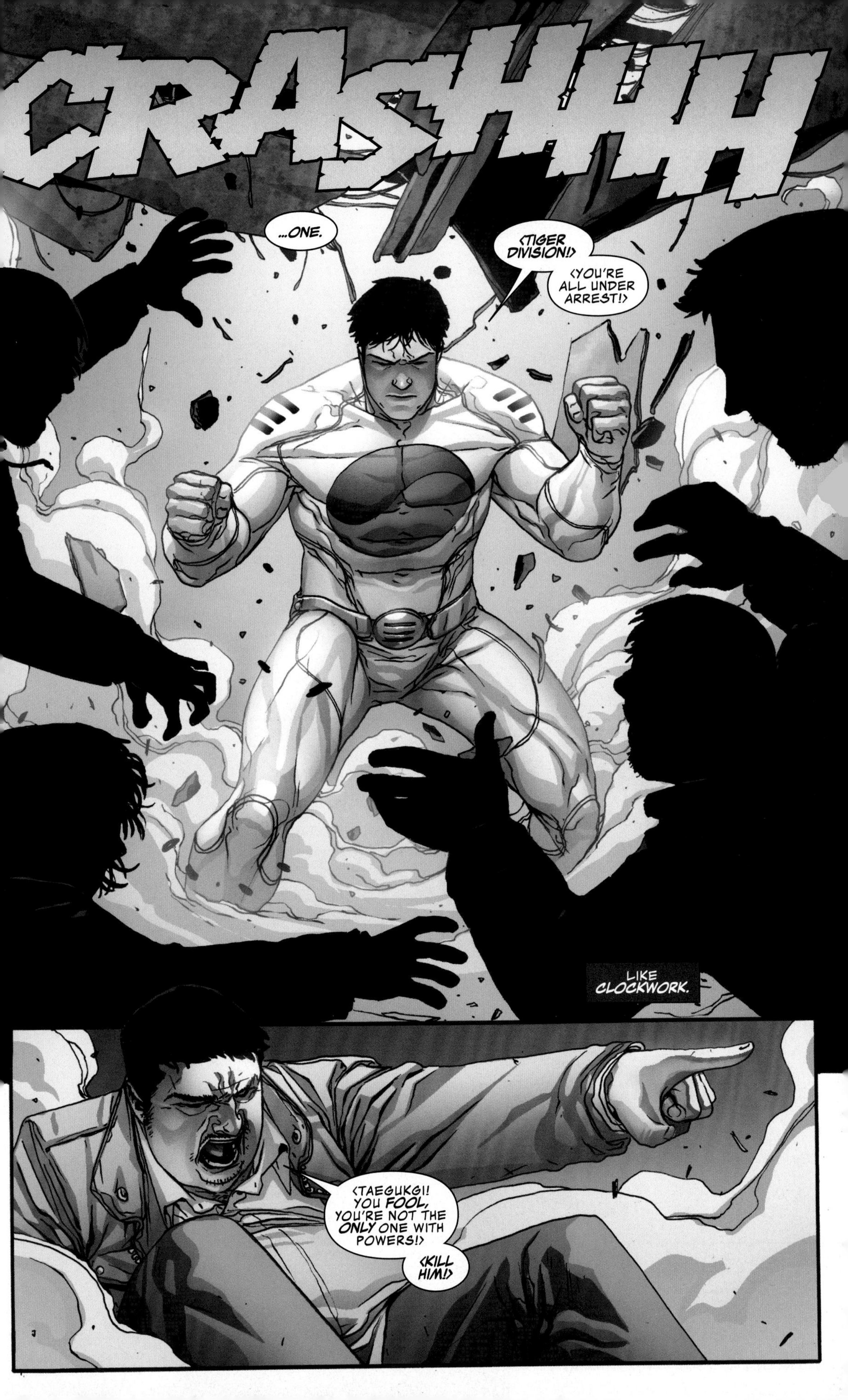
CRASHHH
...ONE.
‹TIGER DIVISION!›
‹YOU'RE ALL UNDER ARREST!›
LIKE CLOCKWORK.
‹TAEGUKGI! YOU FOOL, YOU'RE NOT THE ONLY ONE WITH POWERS!›
‹KILL HIM!›

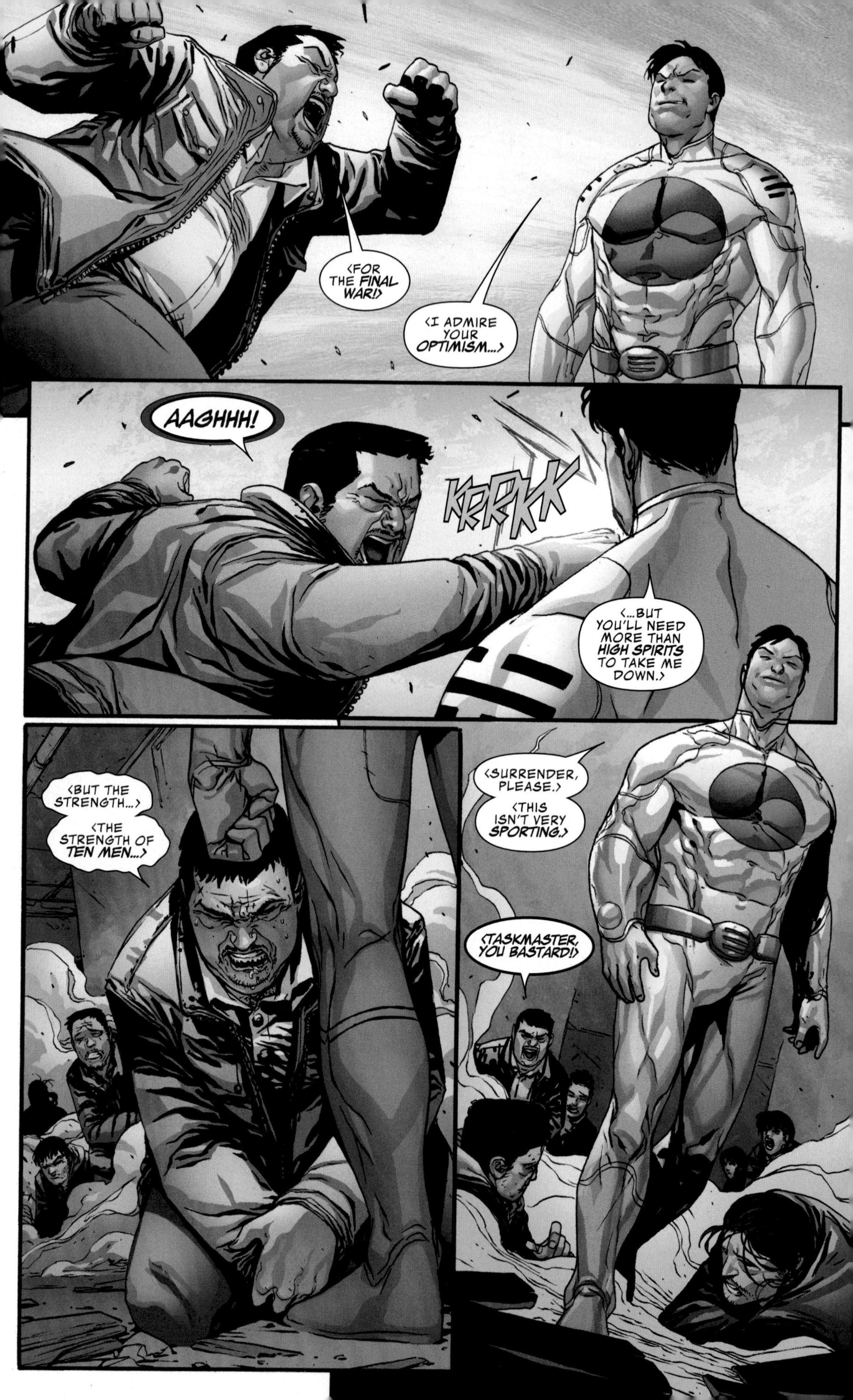
‹FOR THE FINAL WAR!›
‹I ADMIRE YOUR OPTIMISM...›
AAGHHH!
KRRKK
‹...BUT YOU'LL NEED MORE THAN HIGH SPIRITS TO TAKE ME DOWN.›
‹BUT THE STRENGTH...›
‹THE STRENGTH OF TEN MEN...›
‹SURRENDER, PLEASE.›
‹THIS ISN'T VERY SPORTING.›
‹TASKMASTER, YOU BASTARD!›

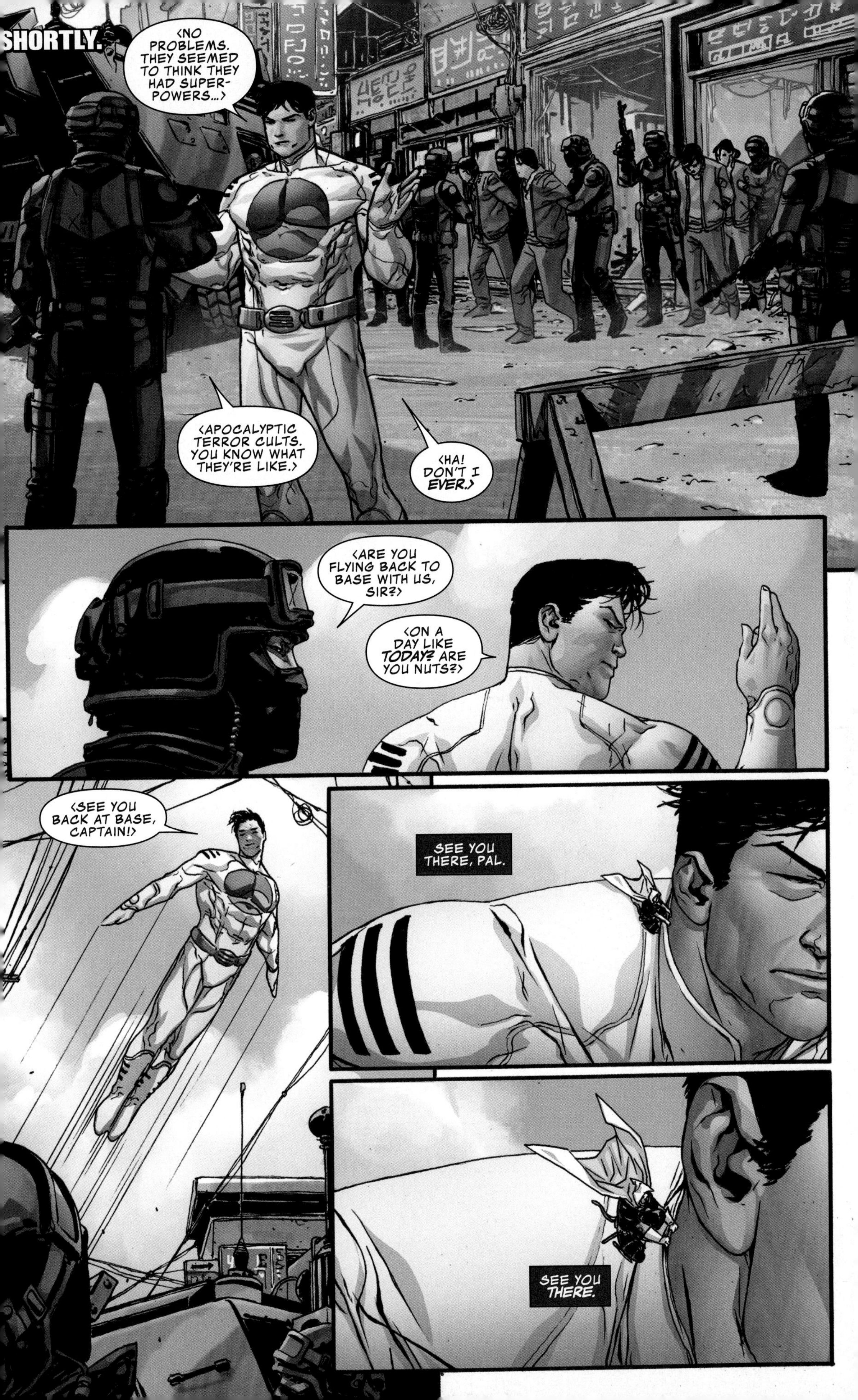
SHORTLY.
<NO PROBLEMS. THEY SEEMED TO THINK THEY HAD SUPER-POWERS...>
<APOCALYPTIC TERROR CULTS. YOU KNOW WHAT THEY'RE LIKE.>
<HA! DON'T I EVER.>
<ARE YOU FLYING BACK TO BASE WITH US, SIR?>
<ON A DAY LIKE TODAY? ARE YOU NUTS?>
<SEE YOU BACK AT BASE, CAPTAIN!>
SEE YOU THERE, PAL.
SEE YOU THERE.

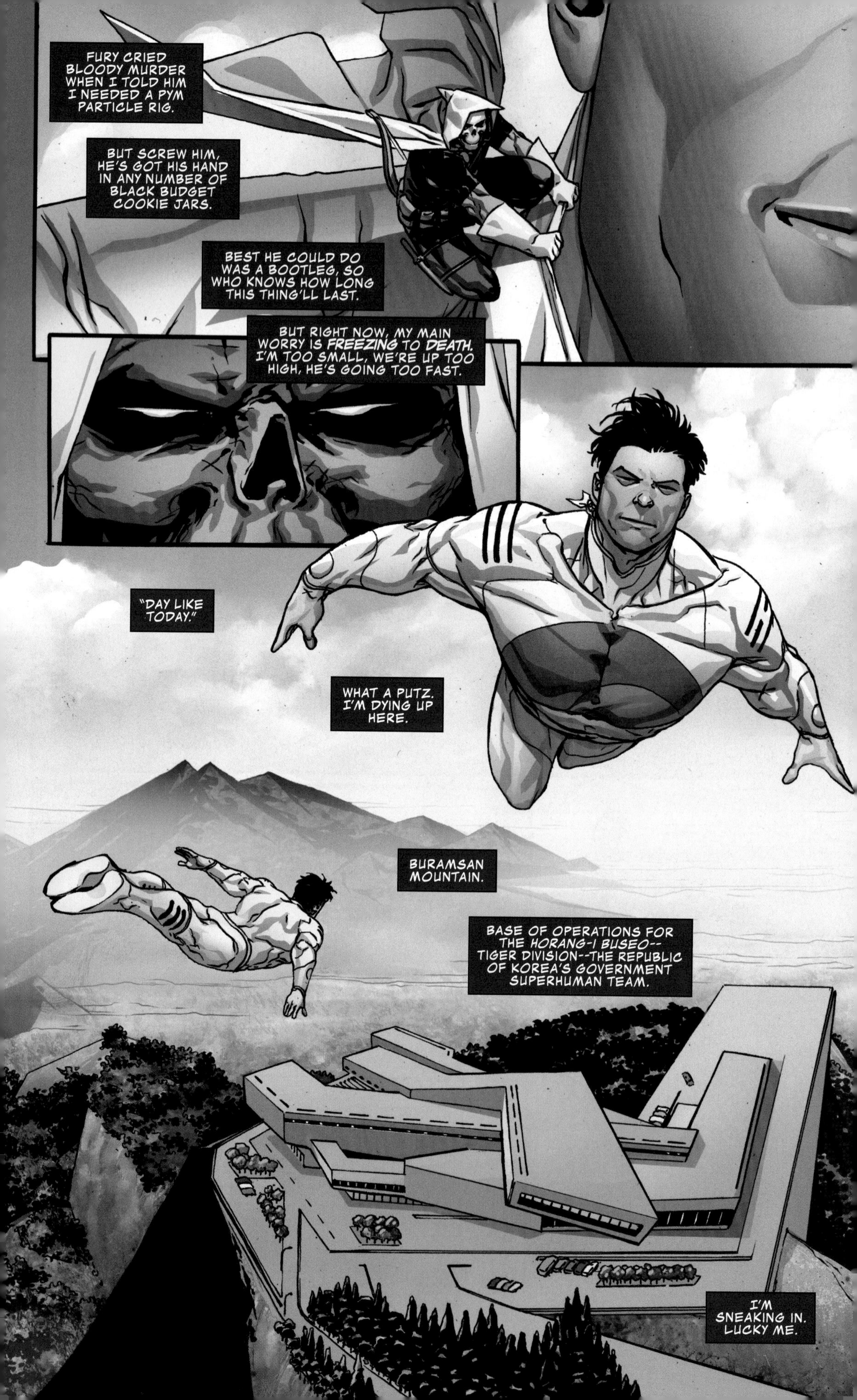
FURY CRIED BLOODY MURDER WHEN I TOLD HIM I NEEDED A PYM PARTICLE RIG.
BUT SCREW HIM, HE'S GOT HIS HAND IN ANY NUMBER OF BLACK BUDGET COOKIE JARS.
BEST HE COULD DO WAS A BOOTLEG, SO WHO KNOWS HOW LONG THIS THING'LL LAST.
BUT RIGHT NOW, MY MAIN WORRY IS *FREEZING* TO *DEATH*. I'M TOO SMALL, WE'RE UP TOO HIGH, HE'S GOING TOO FAST.
"DAY LIKE TODAY."
WHAT A PUTZ. I'M DYING UP HERE.
BURAMSAN MOUNTAIN.
BASE OF OPERATIONS FOR THE *HORANG-I BUSEO*--TIGER DIVISION--THE REPUBLIC OF KOREA'S GOVERNMENT SUPERHUMAN TEAM.
I'M SNEAKING IN. LUCKY ME.

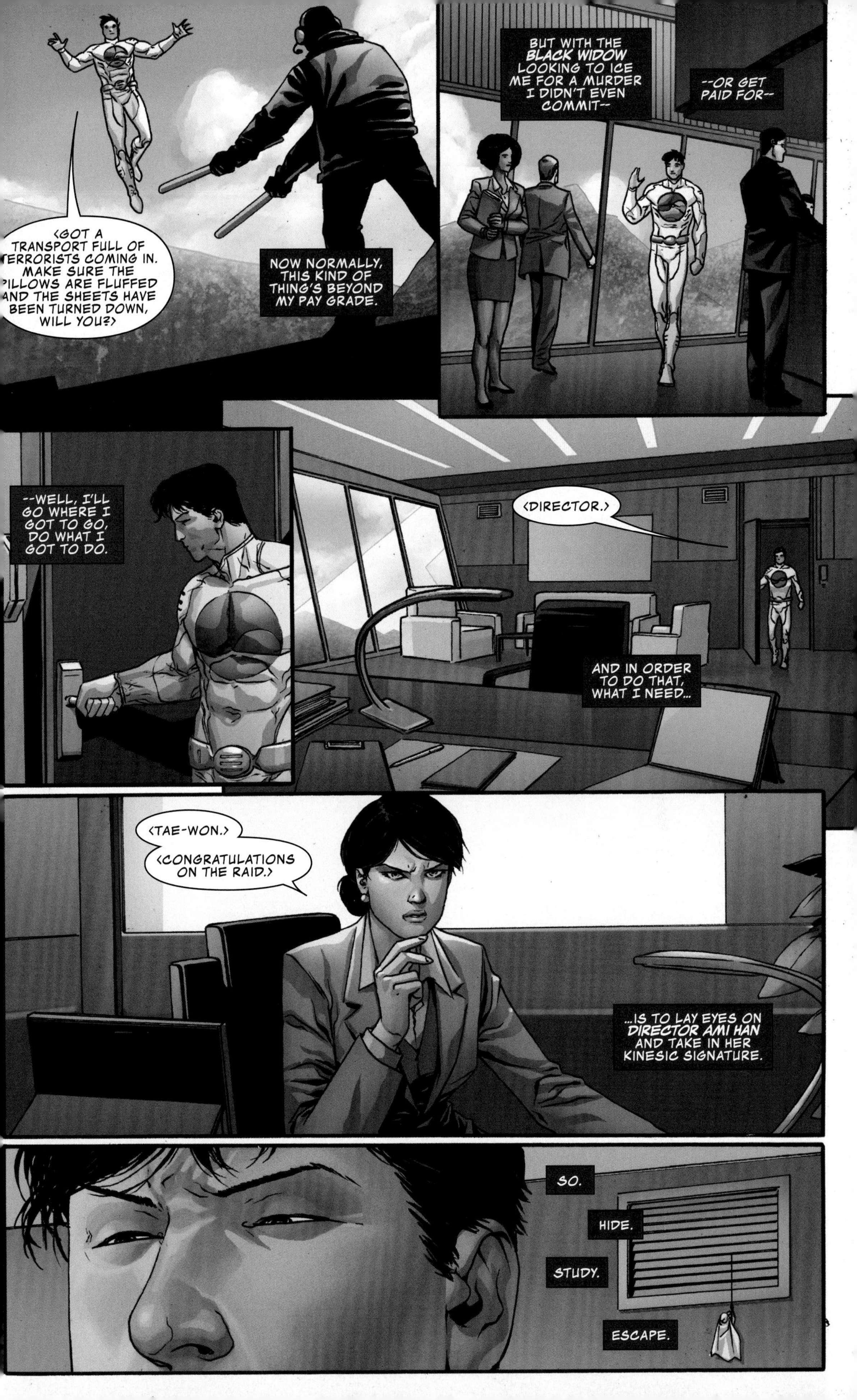

<GOT A TRANSPORT FULL OF TERRORISTS COMING IN. MAKE SURE THE PILLOWS ARE FLUFFED AND THE SHEETS HAVE BEEN TURNED DOWN, WILL YOU?>
NOW NORMALLY, THIS KIND OF THING'S BEYOND MY PAY GRADE.
BUT WITH THE BLACK WIDOW LOOKING TO ICE ME FOR A MURDER I DIDN'T EVEN COMMIT--
--OR GET PAID FOR--
--WELL, I'LL GO WHERE I GOT TO GO, DO WHAT I GOT TO DO.
<DIRECTOR.>
AND IN ORDER TO DO THAT, WHAT I NEED...
<TAE-WON.>
<CONGRATULATIONS ON THE RAID.>
...IS TO LAY EYES ON DIRECTOR AMI HAN AND TAKE IN HER KINESIC SIGNATURE.
SO.
HIDE.
STUDY.
ESCAPE.

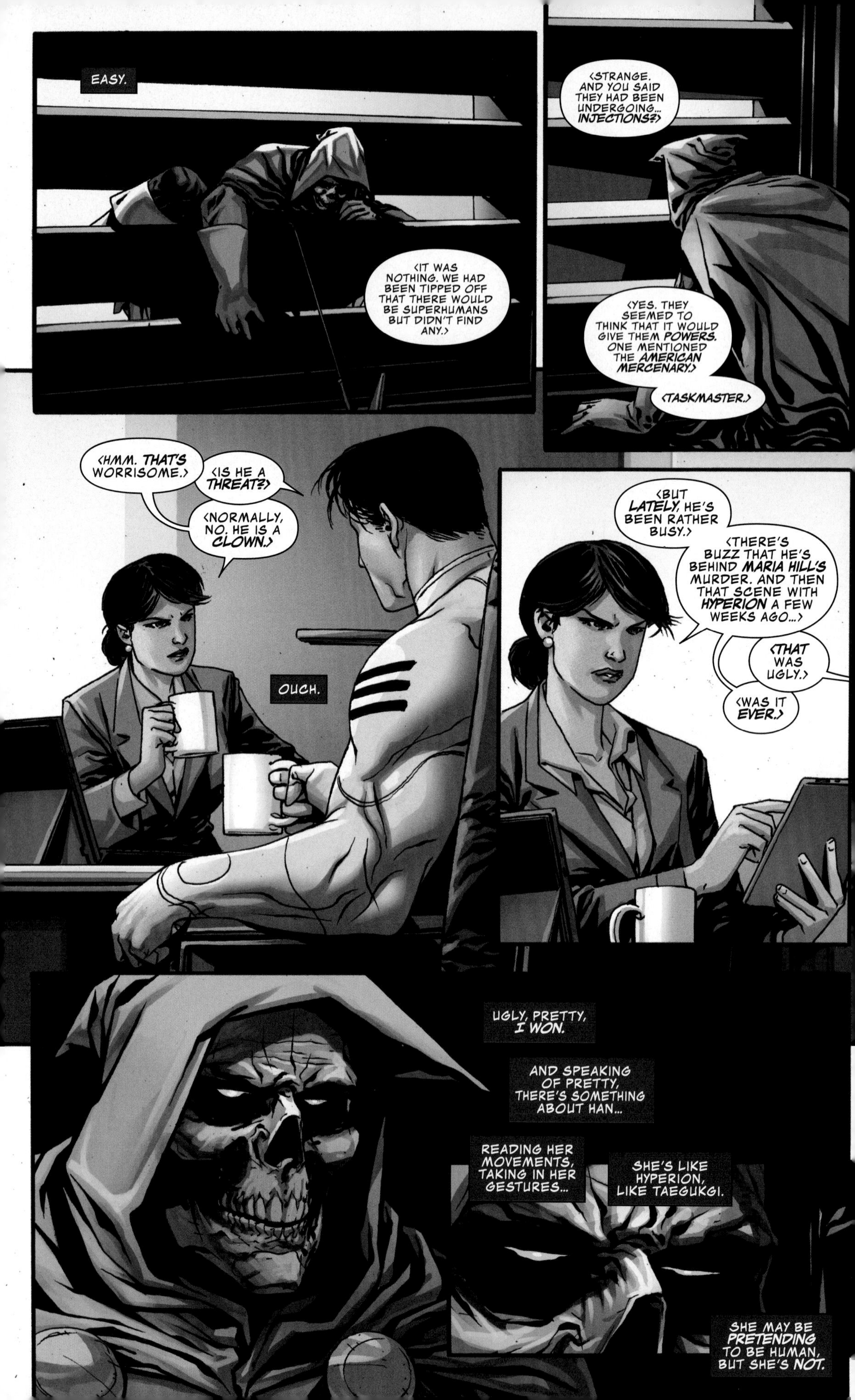
EASY.
<IT WAS NOTHING. WE HAD BEEN TIPPED OFF THAT THERE WOULD BE SUPERHUMANS BUT DIDN'T FIND ANY.>
<STRANGE. AND YOU SAID THEY HAD BEEN UNDERGOING... INJECTIONS?>
<YES. THEY SEEMED TO THINK THAT IT WOULD GIVE THEM POWERS. ONE MENTIONED THE AMERICAN MERCENARY.>
<TASKMASTER.>
<HMM. THAT'S WORRISOME.>
<IS HE A THREAT?>
<NORMALLY, NO. HE IS A CLOWN.>
OUCH.
<BUT LATELY, HE'S BEEN RATHER BUSY.>
<THERE'S BUZZ THAT HE'S BEHIND MARIA HILL'S MURDER. AND THEN THAT SCENE WITH HYPERION A FEW WEEKS AGO...>
<THAT WAS UGLY.>
<WAS IT EVER.>
UGLY, PRETTY, I WON.
AND SPEAKING OF PRETTY, THERE'S SOMETHING ABOUT HAN...
READING HER MOVEMENTS, TAKING IN HER GESTURES...
SHE'S LIKE HYPERION, LIKE TAEGUKGI.
SHE MAY BE PRETENDING TO BE HUMAN, BUT SHE'S NOT.

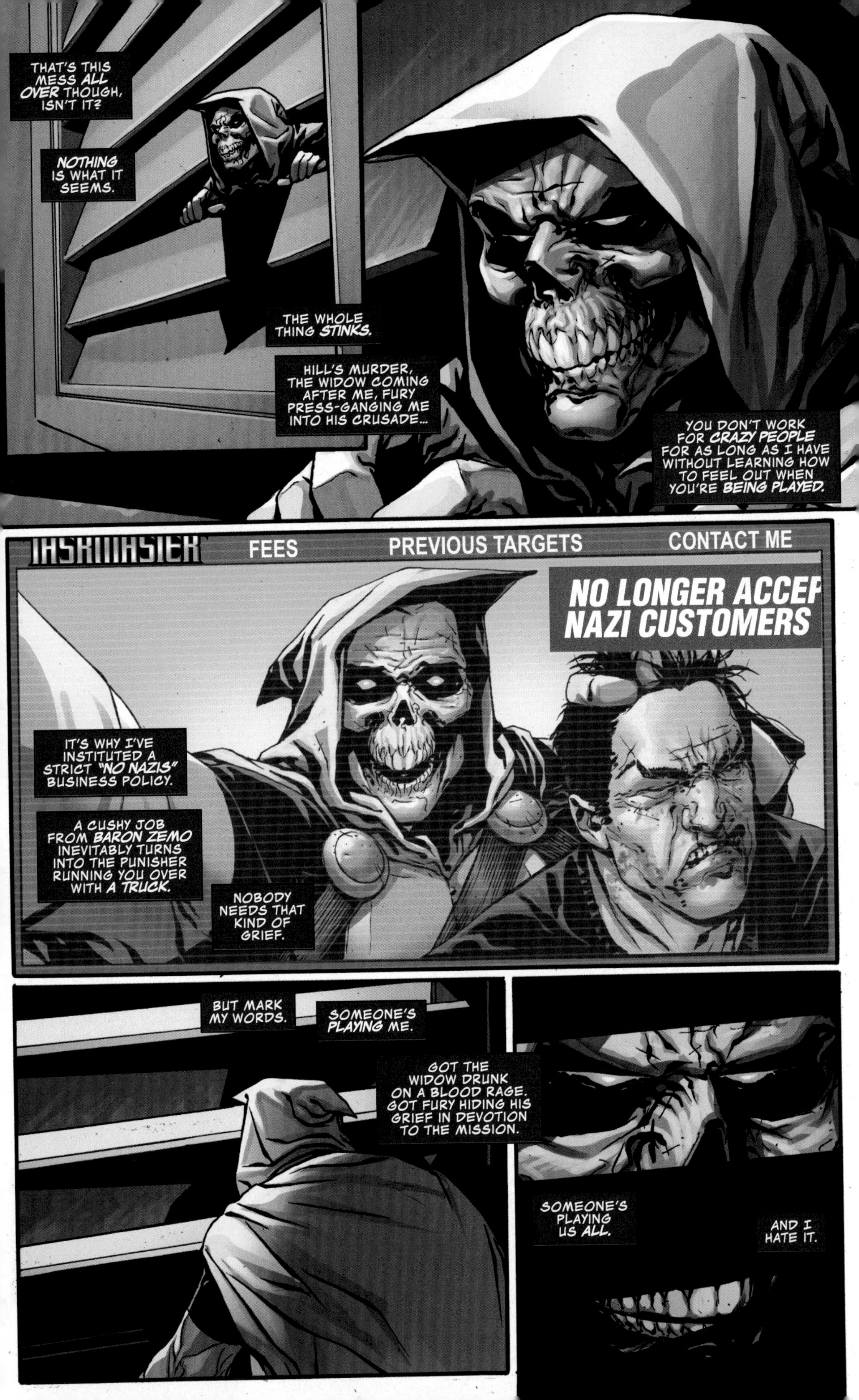

THAT'S THIS MESS ALL OVER THOUGH, ISN'T IT?
NOTHING IS WHAT IT SEEMS.
THE WHOLE THING STINKS.
HILL'S MURDER, THE WIDOW COMING AFTER ME, FURY PRESS-GANGING ME INTO HIS CRUSADE...
YOU DON'T WORK FOR CRAZY PEOPLE FOR AS LONG AS I HAVE WITHOUT LEARNING HOW TO FEEL OUT WHEN YOU'RE BEING PLAYED.
TASKMASTER
FEES
PREVIOUS TARGETS
CONTACT ME
NO LONGER ACCEP
NAZI CUSTOMERS
IT'S WHY I'VE INSTITUTED A STRICT "NO NAZIS" BUSINESS POLICY.
A CUSHY JOB FROM BARON ZEMO INEVITABLY TURNS INTO THE PUNISHER RUNNING YOU OVER WITH A TRUCK.
NOBODY NEEDS THAT KIND OF GRIEF.
BUT MARK MY WORDS.
SOMEONE'S PLAYING ME.
GOT THE WIDOW DRUNK ON A BLOOD RAGE. GOT FURY HIDING HIS GRIEF IN DEVOTION TO THE MISSION.
SOMEONE'S PLAYING US ALL.
AND I HATE IT.

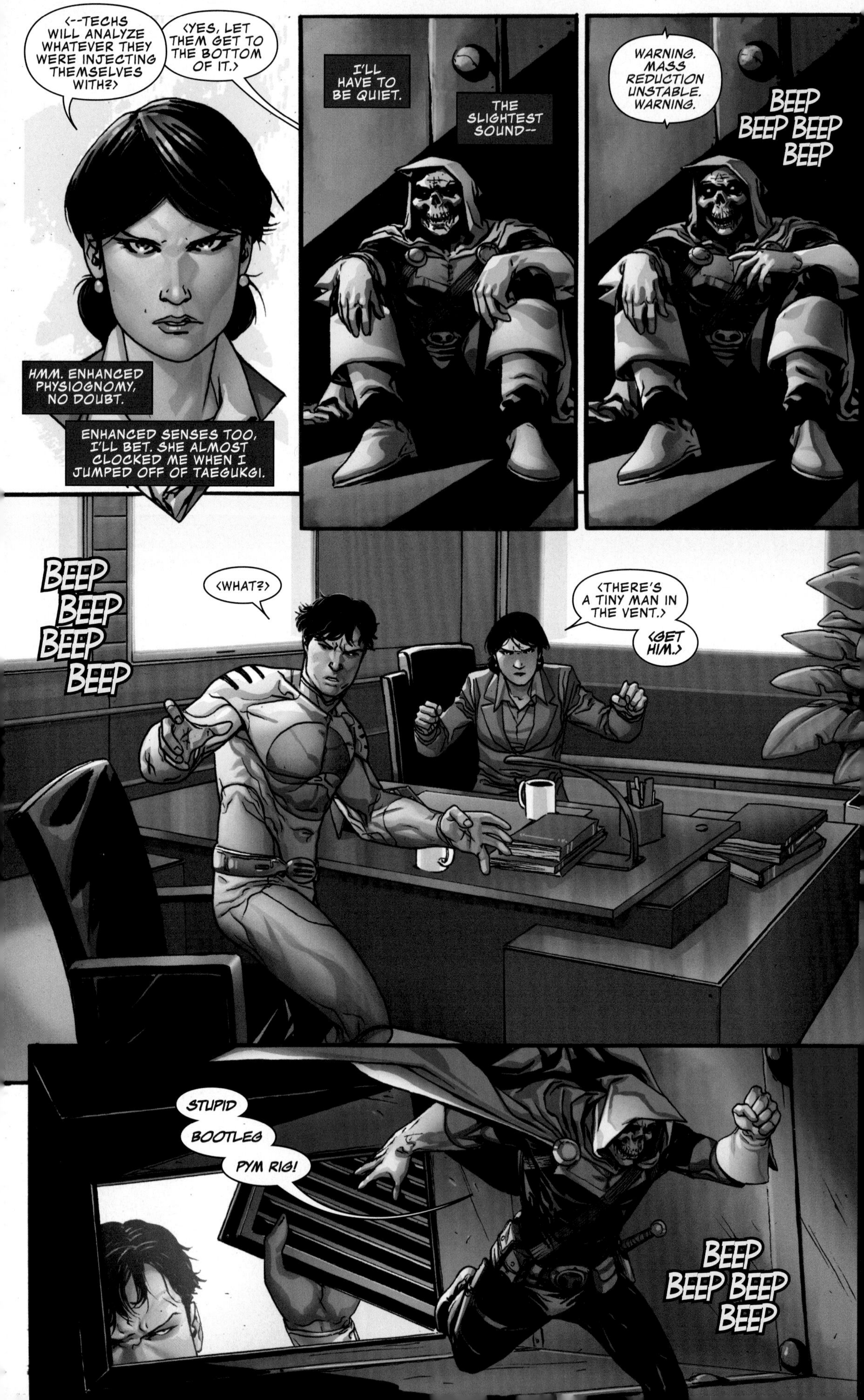
<--TECHS WILL ANALYZE WHATEVER THEY WERE INJECTING THEMSELVES WITH?>
<YES, LET THEM GET TO THE BOTTOM OF IT.>
HMM. ENHANCED PHYSIOGNOMY, NO DOUBT.
ENHANCED SENSES TOO, I'LL BET. SHE ALMOST CLOCKED ME WHEN I JUMPED OFF OF TAEGUKGI.
I'LL HAVE TO BE QUIET.
THE SLIGHTEST SOUND--
WARNING. MASS REDUCTION UNSTABLE. WARNING.
BEEP BEEP BEEP BEEP
BEEP BEEP BEEP BEEP
<WHAT?>
<THERE'S A TINY MAN IN THE VENT.>
<GET HIM.>
STUPID
BOOTLEG
PYM RIG!
BEEP BEEP BEEP BEEP

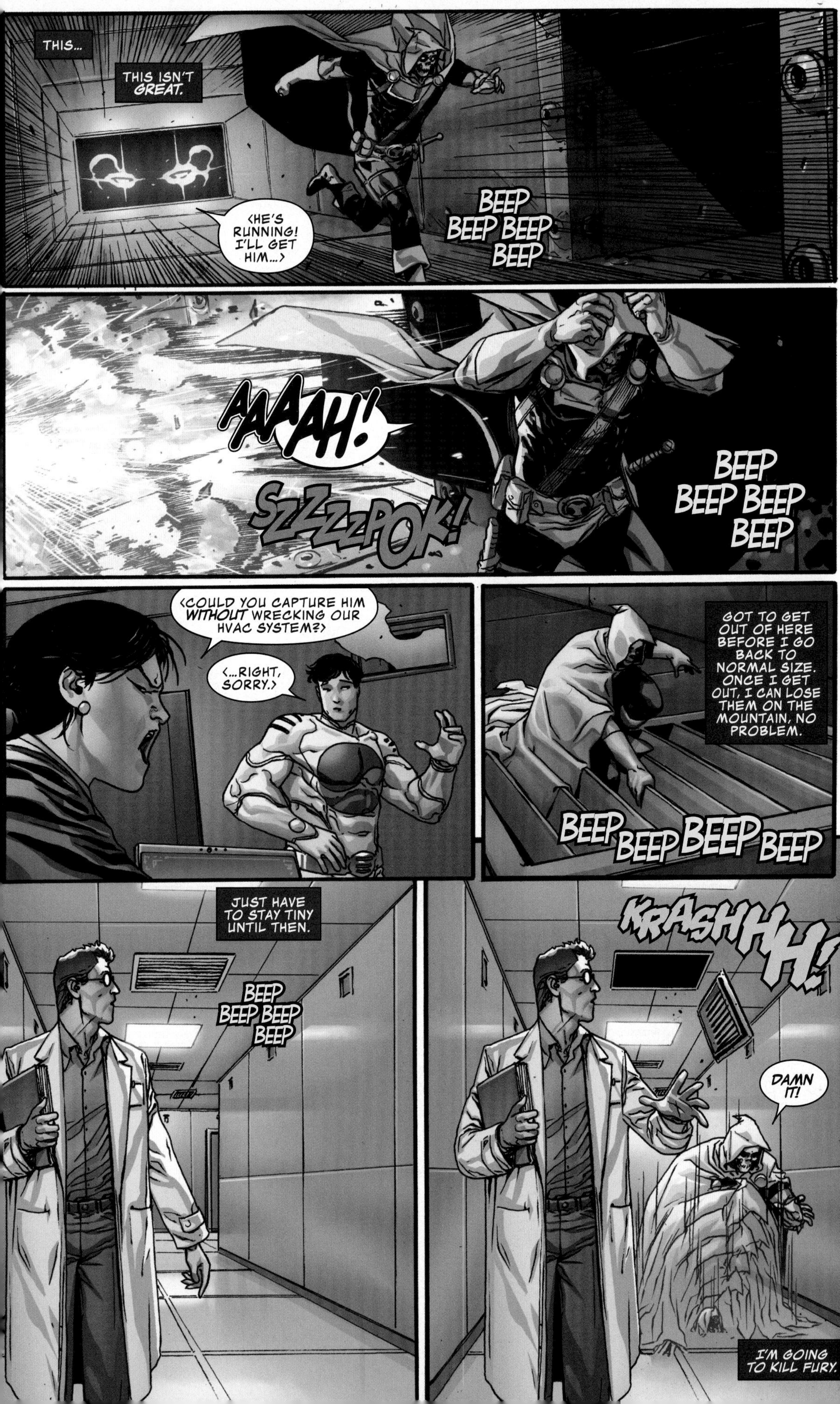
THIS...
THIS ISN'T GREAT.
<HE'S RUNNING! I'LL GET HIM...>
BEEP BEEP BEEP BEEP
AAAAH!
SZZZZPOK!
BEEP BEEP BEEP BEEP
<COULD YOU CAPTURE HIM WITHOUT WRECKING OUR HVAC SYSTEM?>
<...RIGHT, SORRY.>
GOT TO GET OUT OF HERE BEFORE I GO BACK TO NORMAL SIZE. ONCE I GET OUT, I CAN LOSE THEM ON THE MOUNTAIN, NO PROBLEM.
BEEP BEEP BEEP BEEP
JUST HAVE TO STAY TINY UNTIL THEN.
BEEP BEEP BEEP BEEP
KRASHHH!
DAMN IT!
I'M GOING TO KILL FURY.

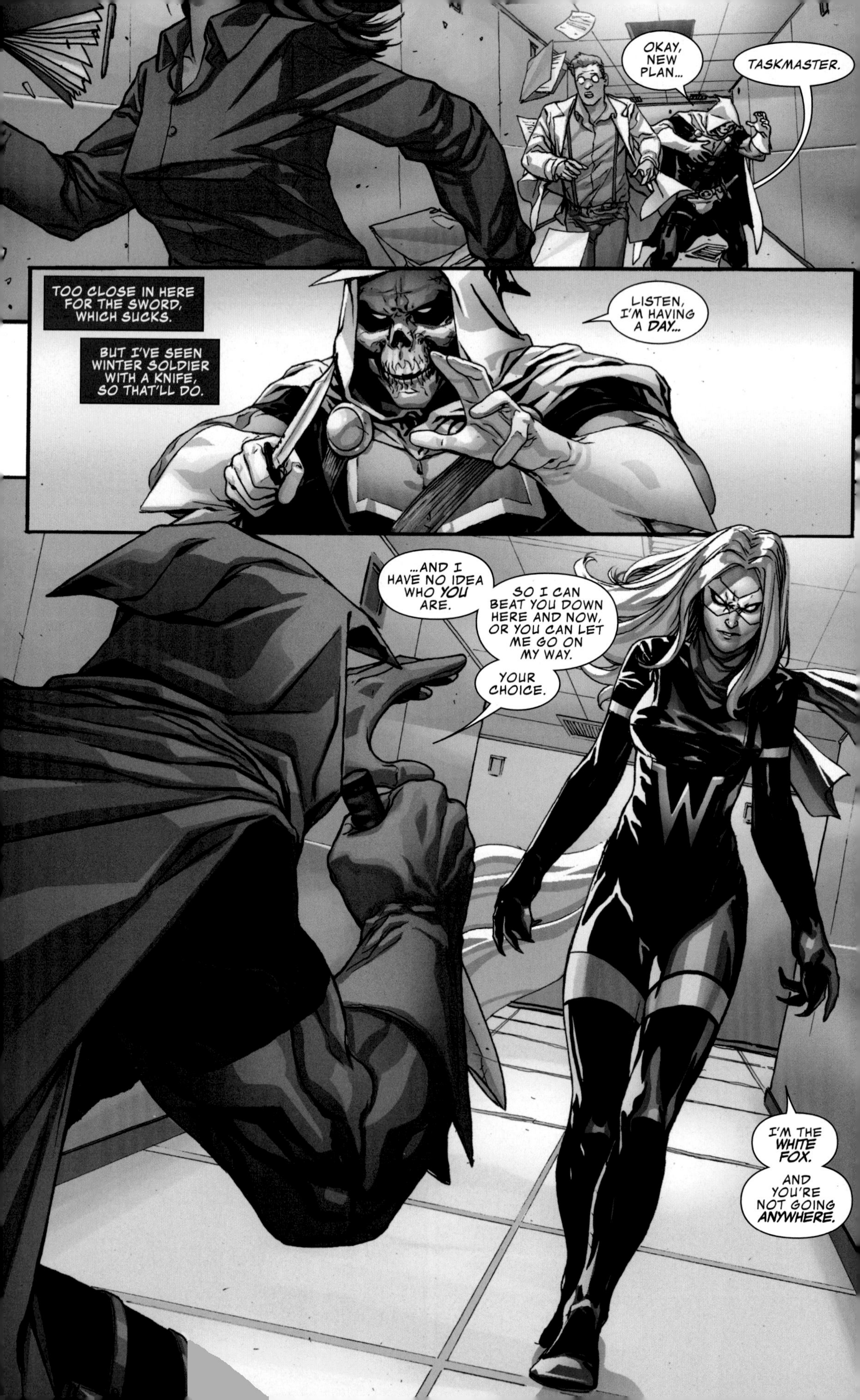
OKAY, NEW PLAN...
TASKMASTER.
TOO CLOSE IN HERE FOR THE SWORD, WHICH SUCKS.
BUT I'VE SEEN WINTER SOLDIER WITH A KNIFE, SO THAT'LL DO.
LISTEN, I'M HAVING A DAY...
...AND I HAVE NO IDEA WHO YOU ARE.
SO I CAN BEAT YOU DOWN HERE AND NOW, OR YOU CAN LET ME GO ON MY WAY.
YOUR CHOICE.
I'M THE WHITE FOX.
AND YOU'RE NOT GOING ANYWHERE.

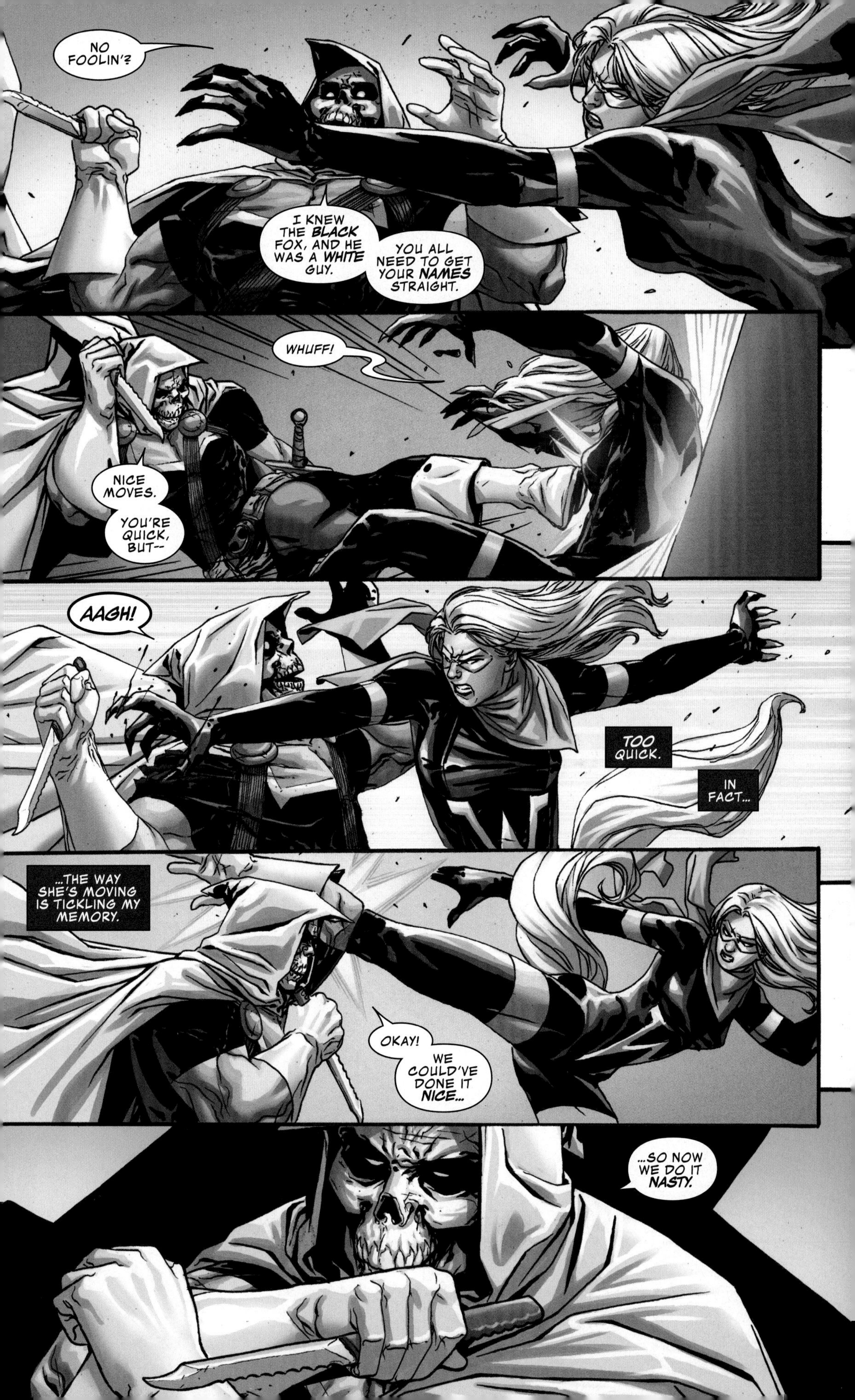

NO FOOLIN'?
I KNEW THE BLACK FOX, AND HE WAS A WHITE GUY.
YOU ALL NEED TO GET YOUR NAMES STRAIGHT.
WHUFF!
NICE MOVES.
YOU'RE QUICK, BUT--
AAGH!
TOO QUICK.
IN FACT...
...THE WAY SHE'S MOVING IS TICKLING MY MEMORY.
OKAY!
WE COULD'VE DONE IT NICE...
...SO NOW WE DO IT NASTY.

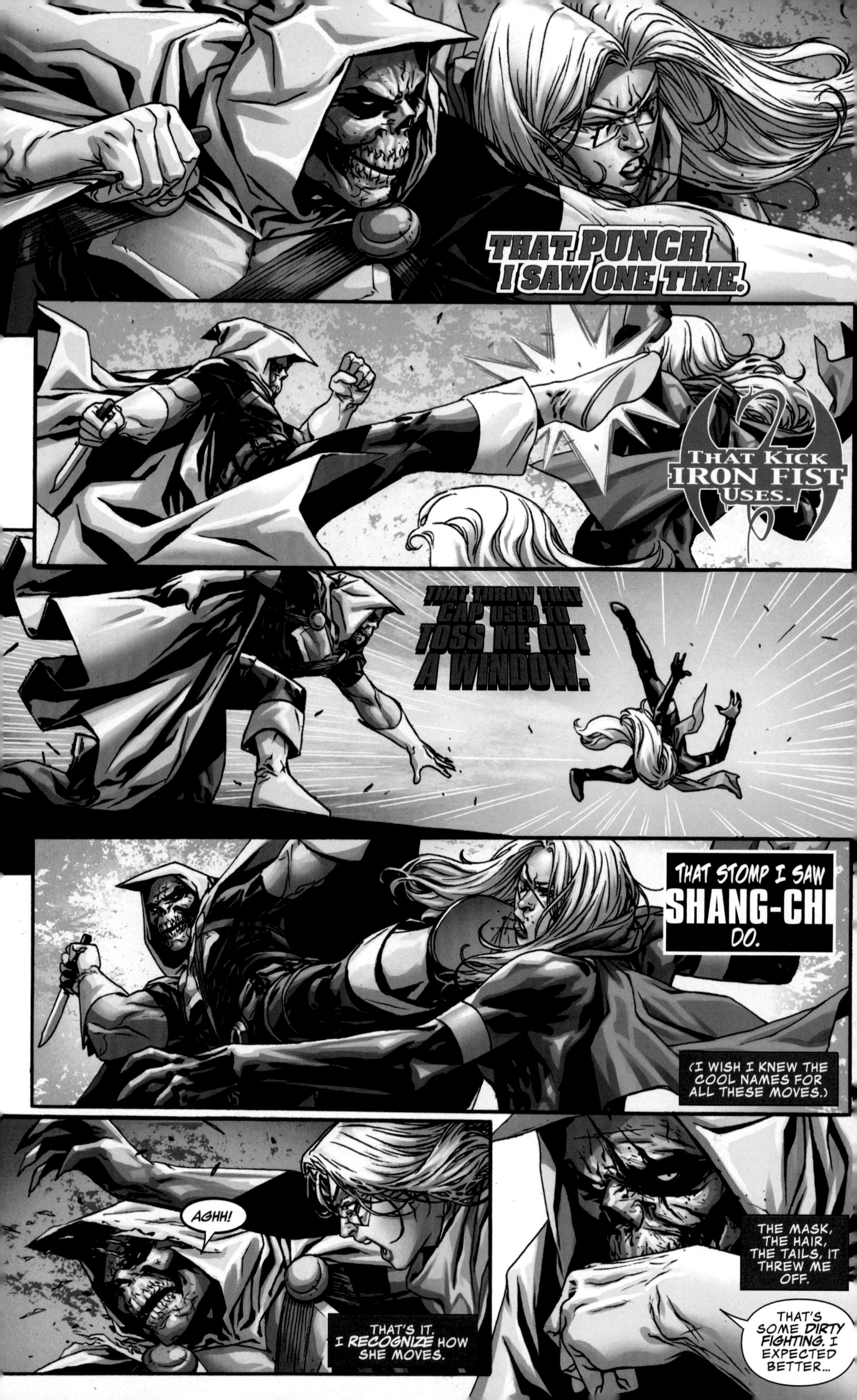

THAT PUNCH I SAW ONE TIME.
THAT KICK IRON FIST USES.
THAT THROW THAT CAP USED TO TOSS ME OUT A WINDOW.
THAT STOMP I SAW SHANG-CHI DO.
(I WISH I KNEW THE COOL NAMES FOR ALL THESE MOVES.)
AGHH!
THAT'S IT. I RECOGNIZE HOW SHE MOVES.
THE MASK, THE HAIR, THE TAILS, IT THREW ME OFF.
THAT'S SOME DIRTY FIGHTING. I EXPECTED BETTER...

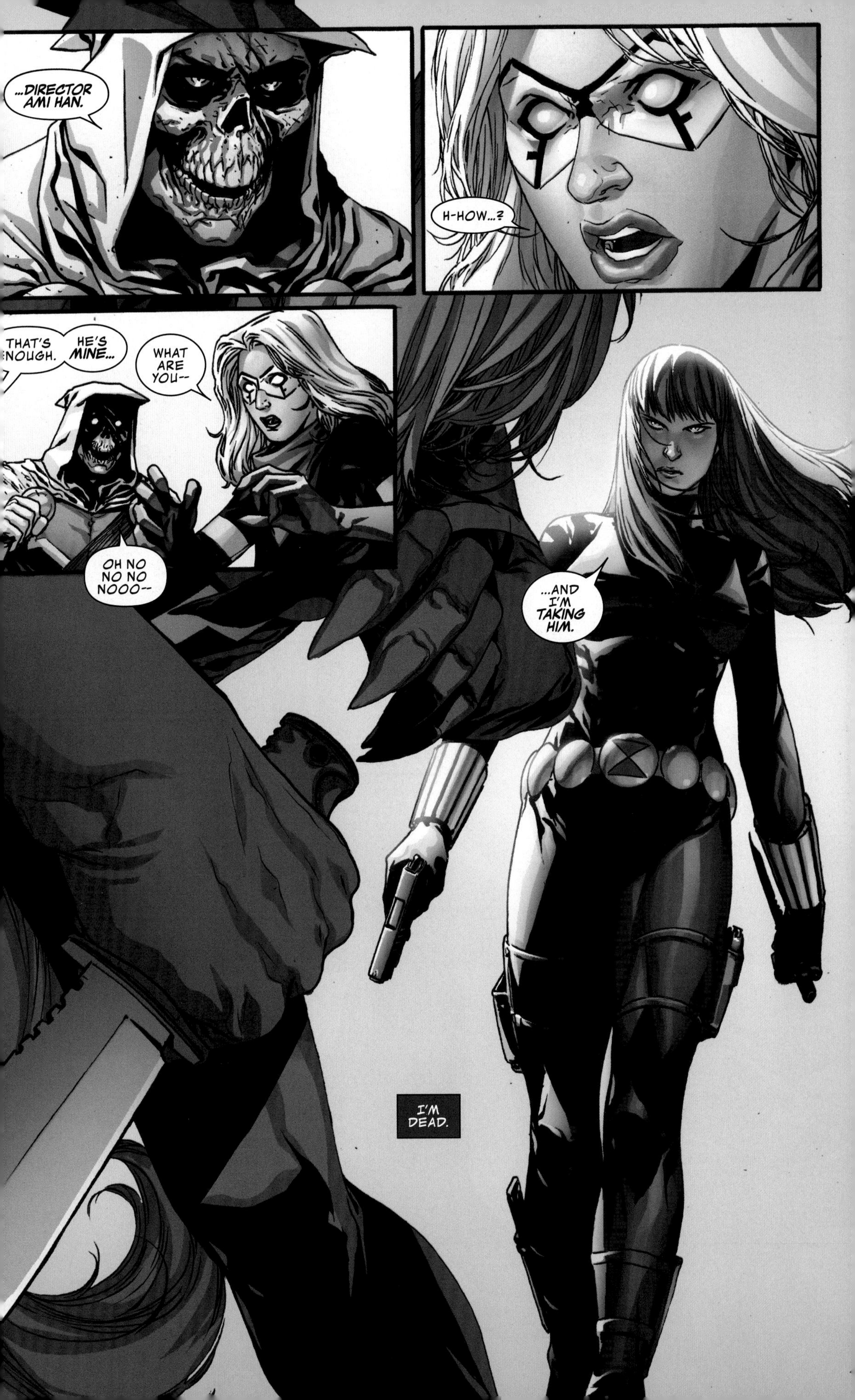
...DIRECTOR AMI HAN.
H-HOW...?
THAT'S ENOUGH.
HE'S MINE...
WHAT ARE YOU--
OH NO NO NO NOOO--
...AND I'M TAKING HIM.
I'M DEAD.

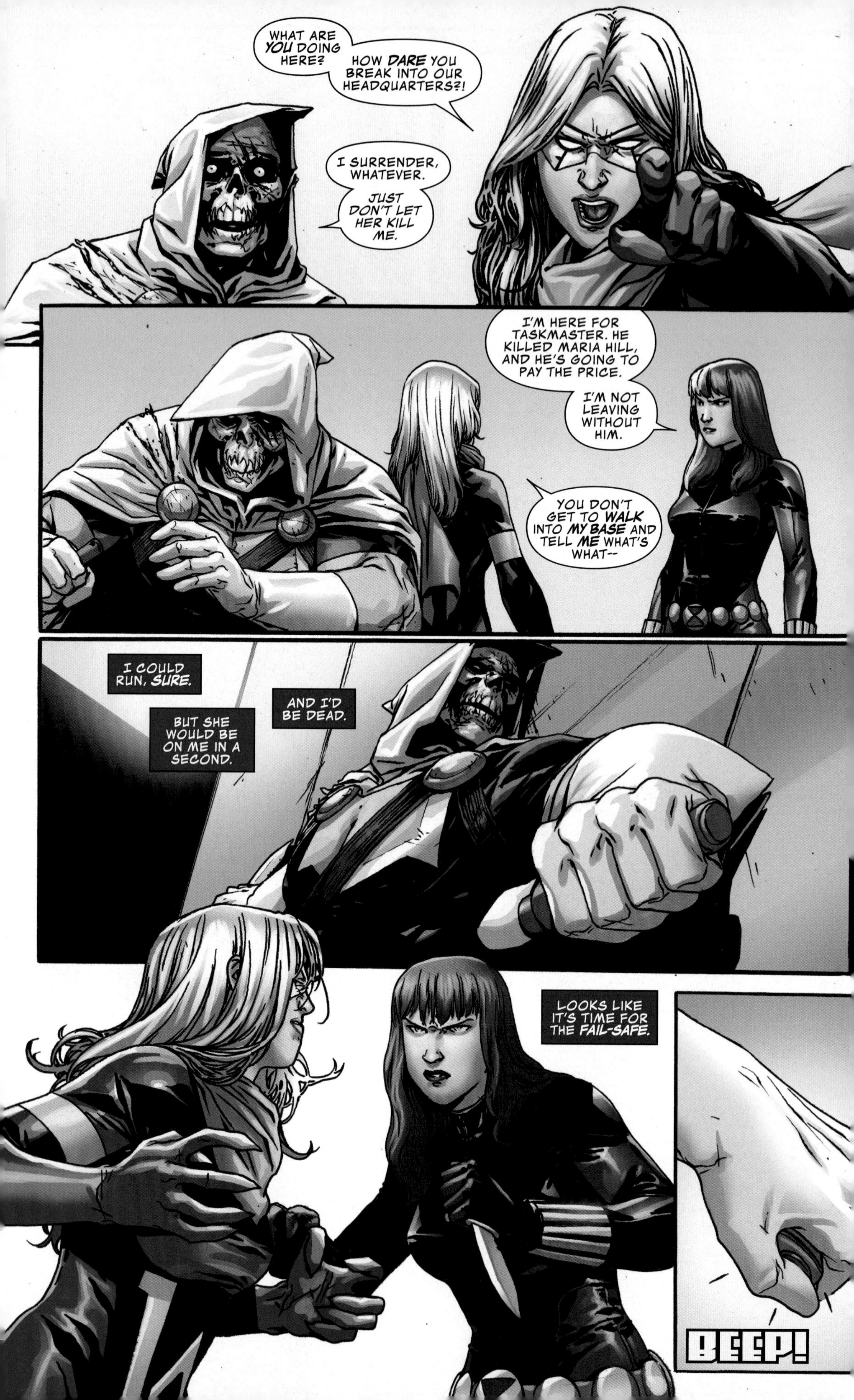
WHAT ARE YOU DOING HERE?
HOW DARE YOU BREAK INTO OUR HEADQUARTERS?!
I SURRENDER, WHATEVER.
JUST DON'T LET HER KILL ME.
I'M HERE FOR TASKMASTER. HE KILLED MARIA HILL, AND HE'S GOING TO PAY THE PRICE.
I'M NOT LEAVING WITHOUT HIM.
YOU DON'T GET TO WALK INTO MY BASE AND TELL ME WHAT'S WHAT--
I COULD RUN, SURE.
BUT SHE WOULD BE ON ME IN A SECOND.
AND I'D BE DEAD.
LOOKS LIKE IT'S TIME FOR THE FAIL-SAFE.
BEEP!

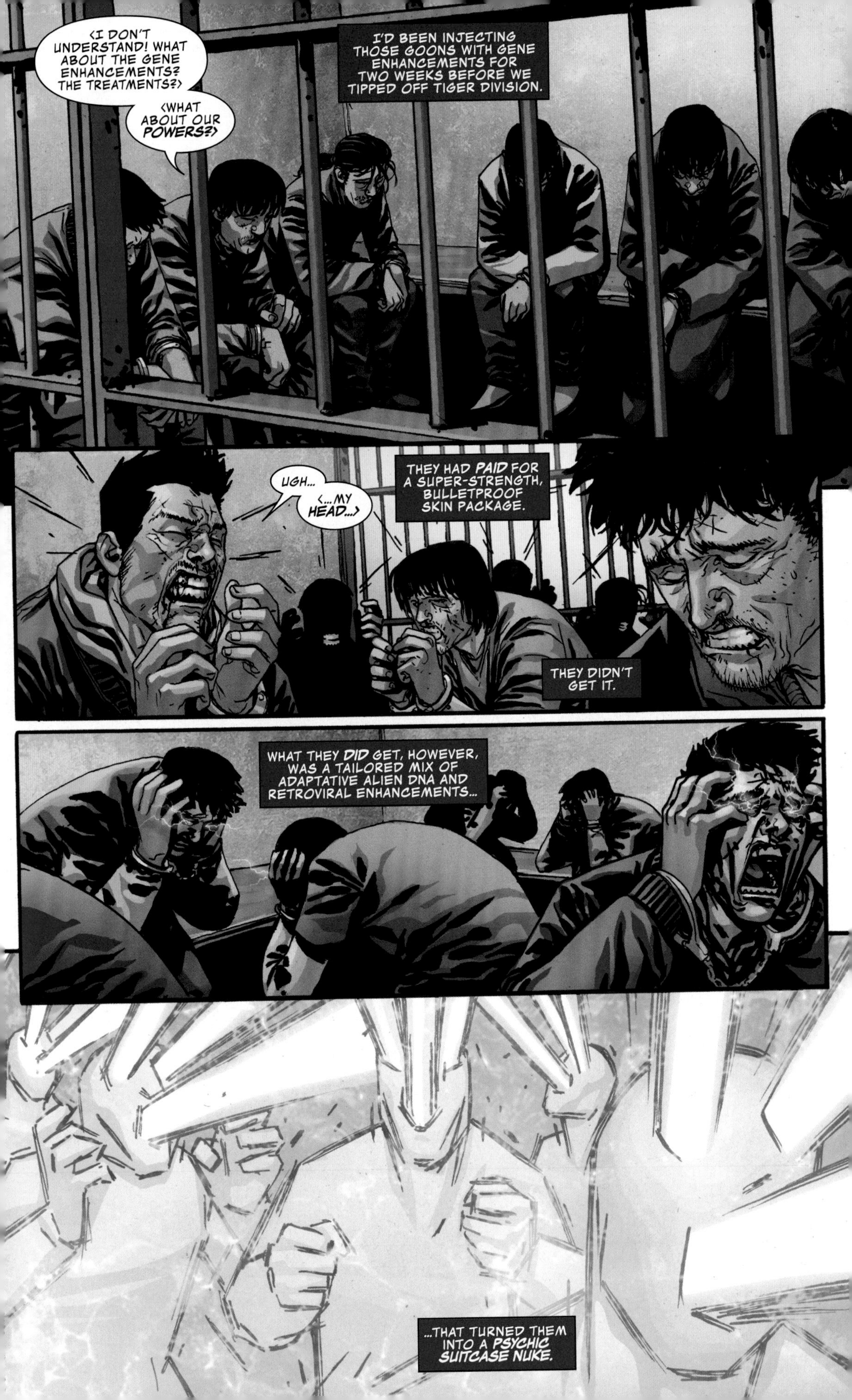

<I DON'T UNDERSTAND! WHAT ABOUT THE GENE ENHANCEMENTS? THE TREATMENTS?>
<WHAT ABOUT OUR POWERS?>
I'D BEEN INJECTING THOSE GOONS WITH GENE ENHANCEMENTS FOR TWO WEEKS BEFORE WE TIPPED OFF TIGER DIVISION.
UGH...
<...MY HEAD...>
THEY HAD PAID FOR A SUPER-STRENGTH, BULLETPROOF SKIN PACKAGE.
THEY DIDN'T GET IT.
WHAT THEY DID GET, HOWEVER, WAS A TAILORED MIX OF ADAPTATIVE ALIEN DNA AND RETROVIRAL ENHANCEMENTS...
...THAT TURNED THEM INTO A PSYCHIC SUITCASE NUKE.

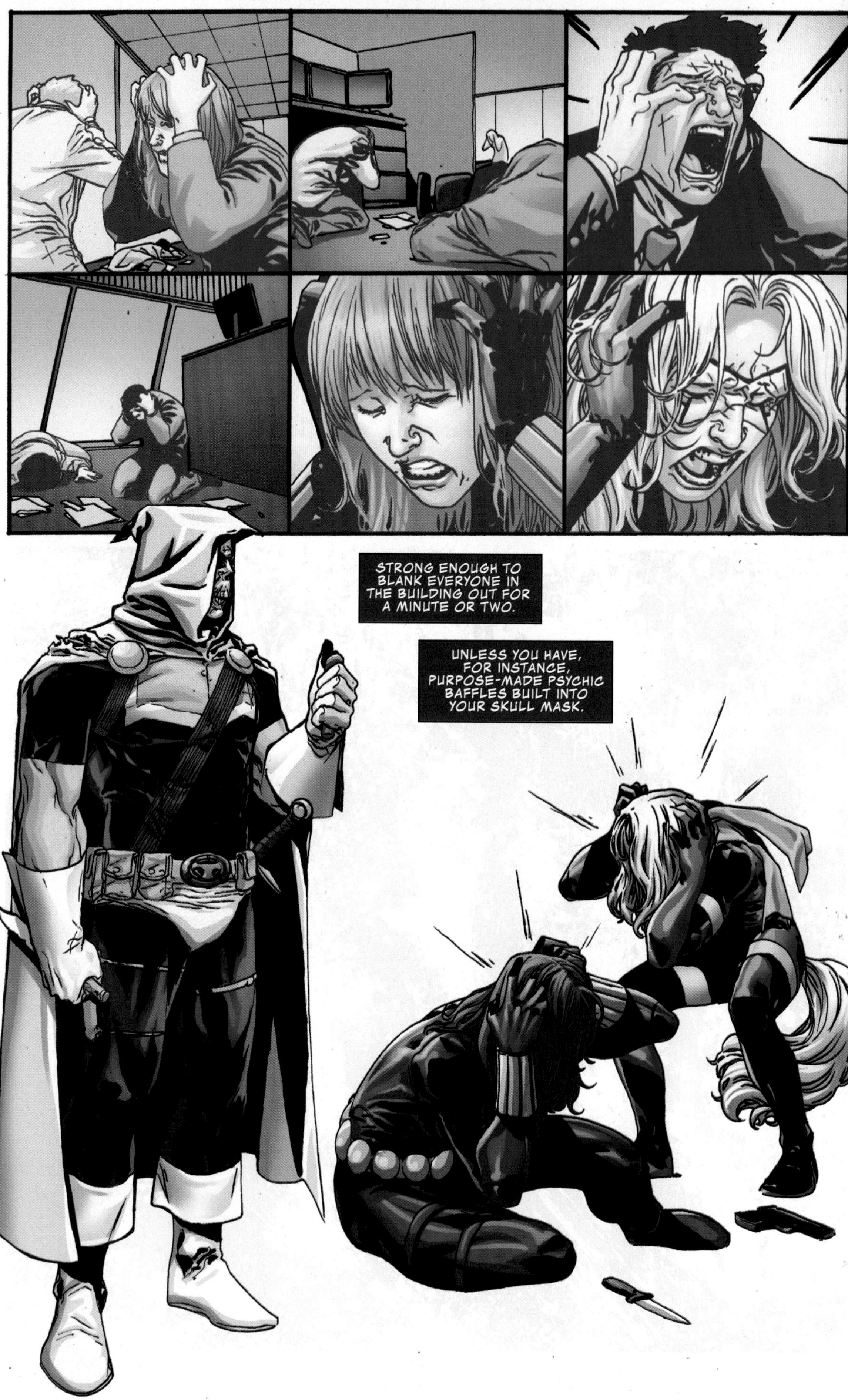
STRONG ENOUGH TO BLANK EVERYONE IN THE BUILDING OUT FOR A MINUTE OR TWO.
UNLESS YOU HAVE, FOR INSTANCE, PURPOSE-MADE PSYCHIC BAFFLES BUILT INTO YOUR SKULL MASK.

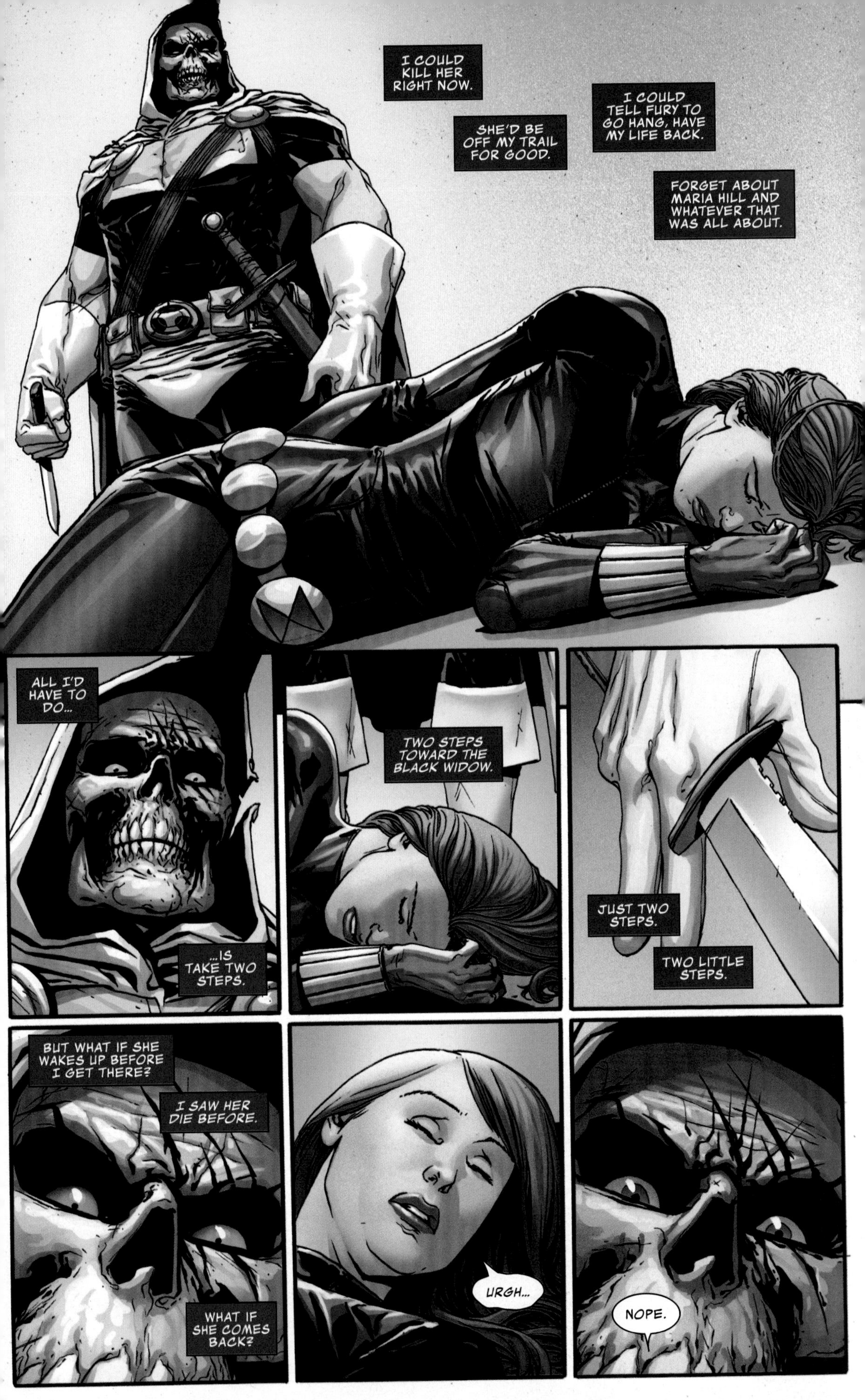
I COULD KILL HER RIGHT NOW.
SHE'D BE OFF MY TRAIL FOR GOOD.
I COULD TELL FURY TO GO HANG, HAVE MY LIFE BACK.
FORGET ABOUT MARIA HILL AND WHATEVER THAT WAS ALL ABOUT.
ALL I'D HAVE TO DO...
...IS TAKE TWO STEPS.
TWO STEPS TOWARD THE BLACK WIDOW.
JUST TWO STEPS.
TWO LITTLE STEPS.
BUT WHAT IF SHE WAKES UP BEFORE I GET THERE?
I SAW HER DIE BEFORE.
WHAT IF SHE COMES BACK?
URGH...
NOPE.

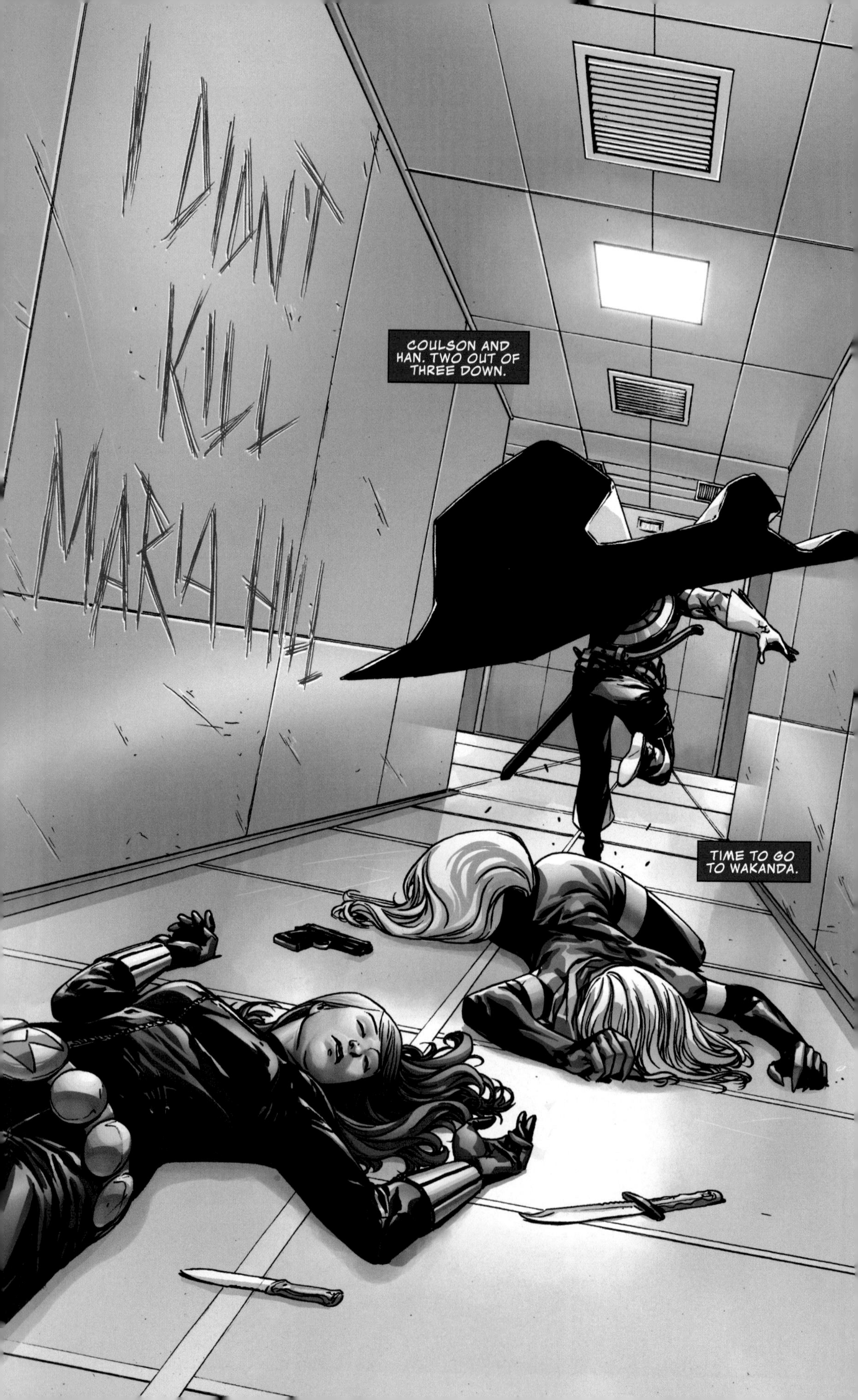

I DIDN'T KILL MARIA HILL
COULSON AND HAN. TWO OUT OF THREE DOWN.
TIME TO GO TO WAKANDA.

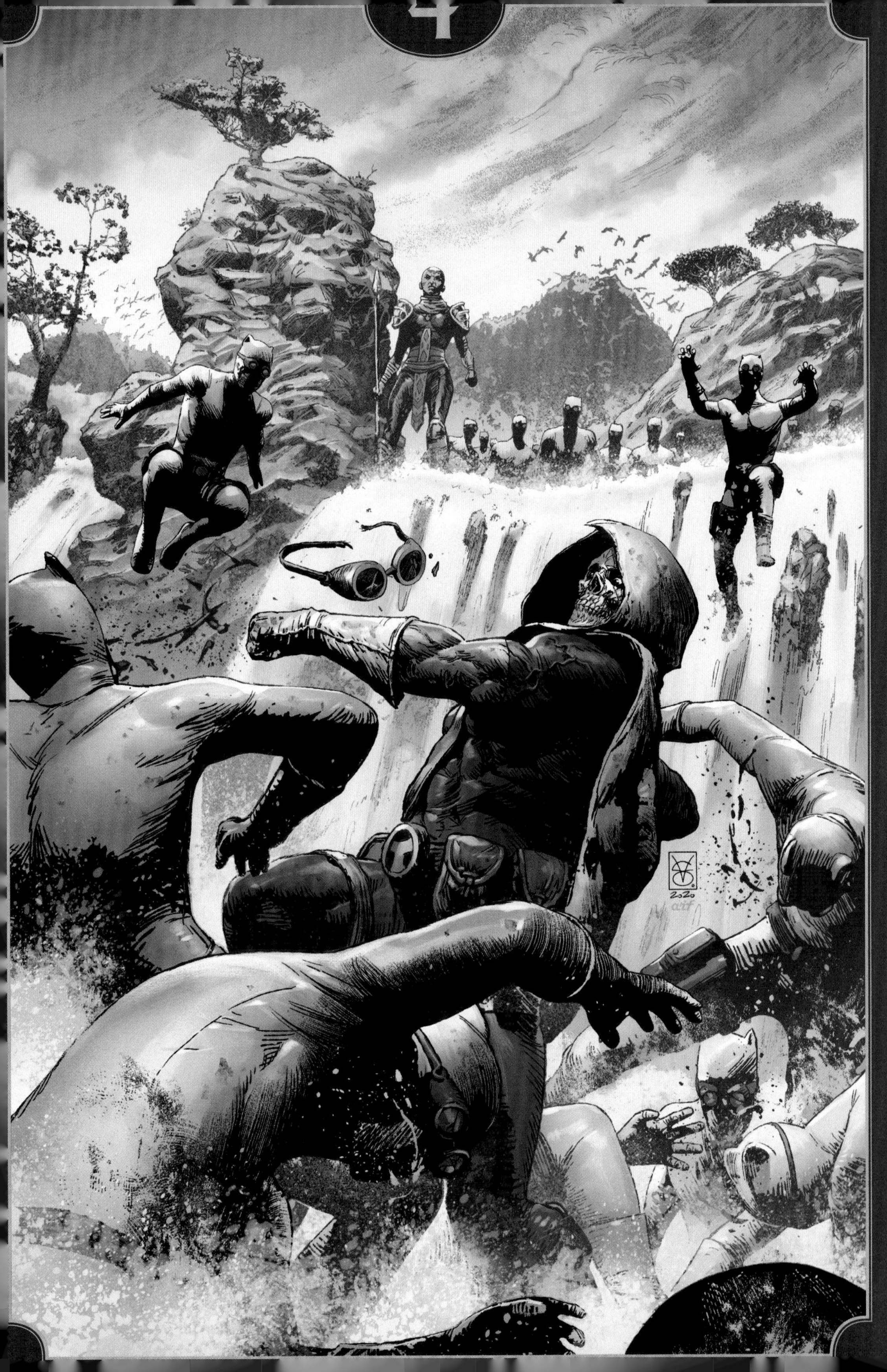
4

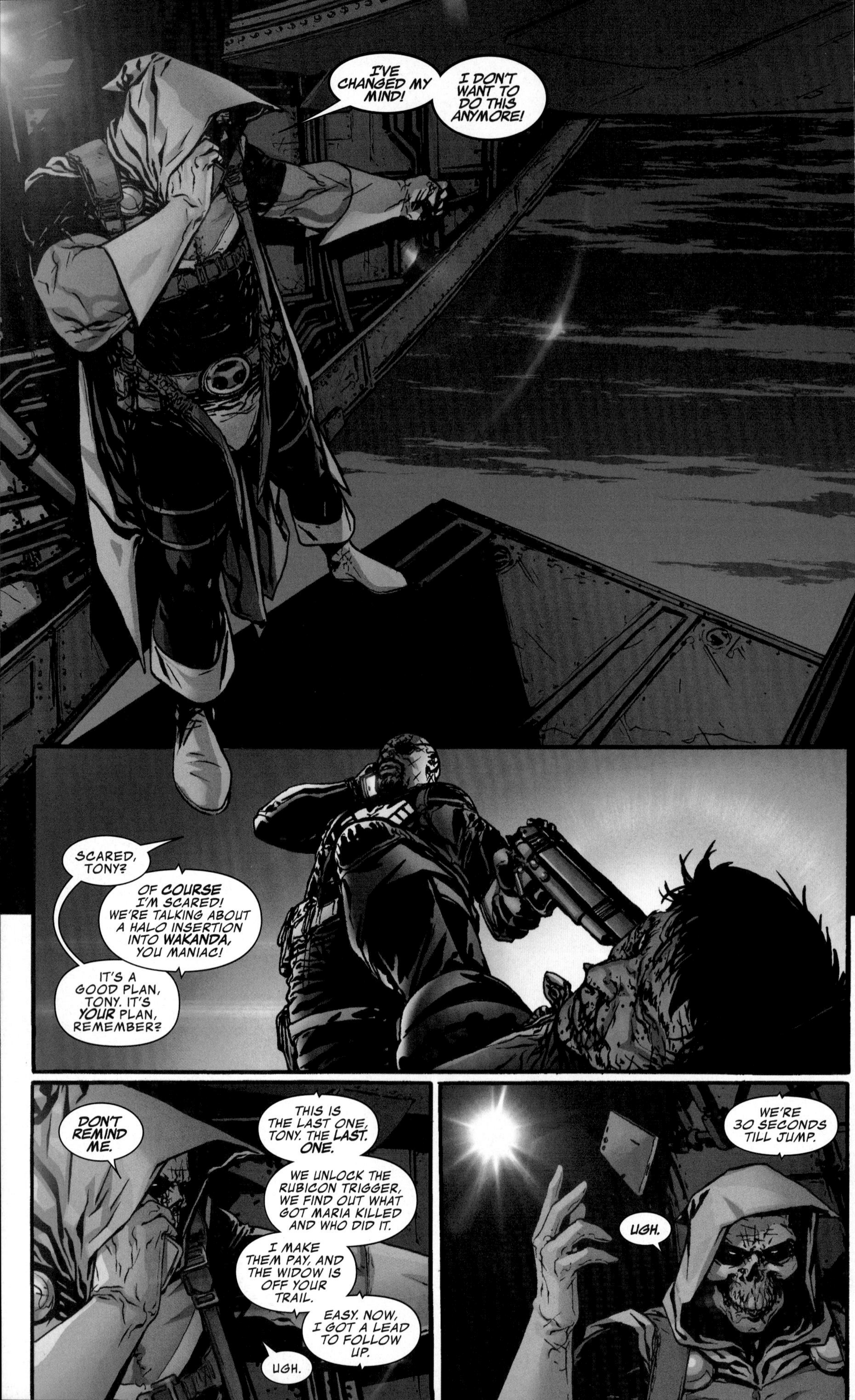
I'VE CHANGED MY MIND!
I DON'T WANT TO DO THIS ANYMORE!
SCARED, TONY?
OF COURSE I'M SCARED! WE'RE TALKING ABOUT A HALO INSERTION INTO WAKANDA, YOU MANIAC!
IT'S A GOOD PLAN, TONY. IT'S YOUR PLAN, REMEMBER?
DON'T REMIND ME.
THIS IS THE LAST ONE, TONY. THE LAST. ONE.
WE UNLOCK THE RUBICON TRIGGER, WE FIND OUT WHAT GOT MARIA KILLED AND WHO DID IT.
I MAKE THEM PAY, AND THE WIDOW IS OFF YOUR TRAIL.
EASY. NOW, I GOT A LEAD TO FOLLOW UP.
UGH.
WE'RE 30 SECONDS TILL JUMP.
UGH.

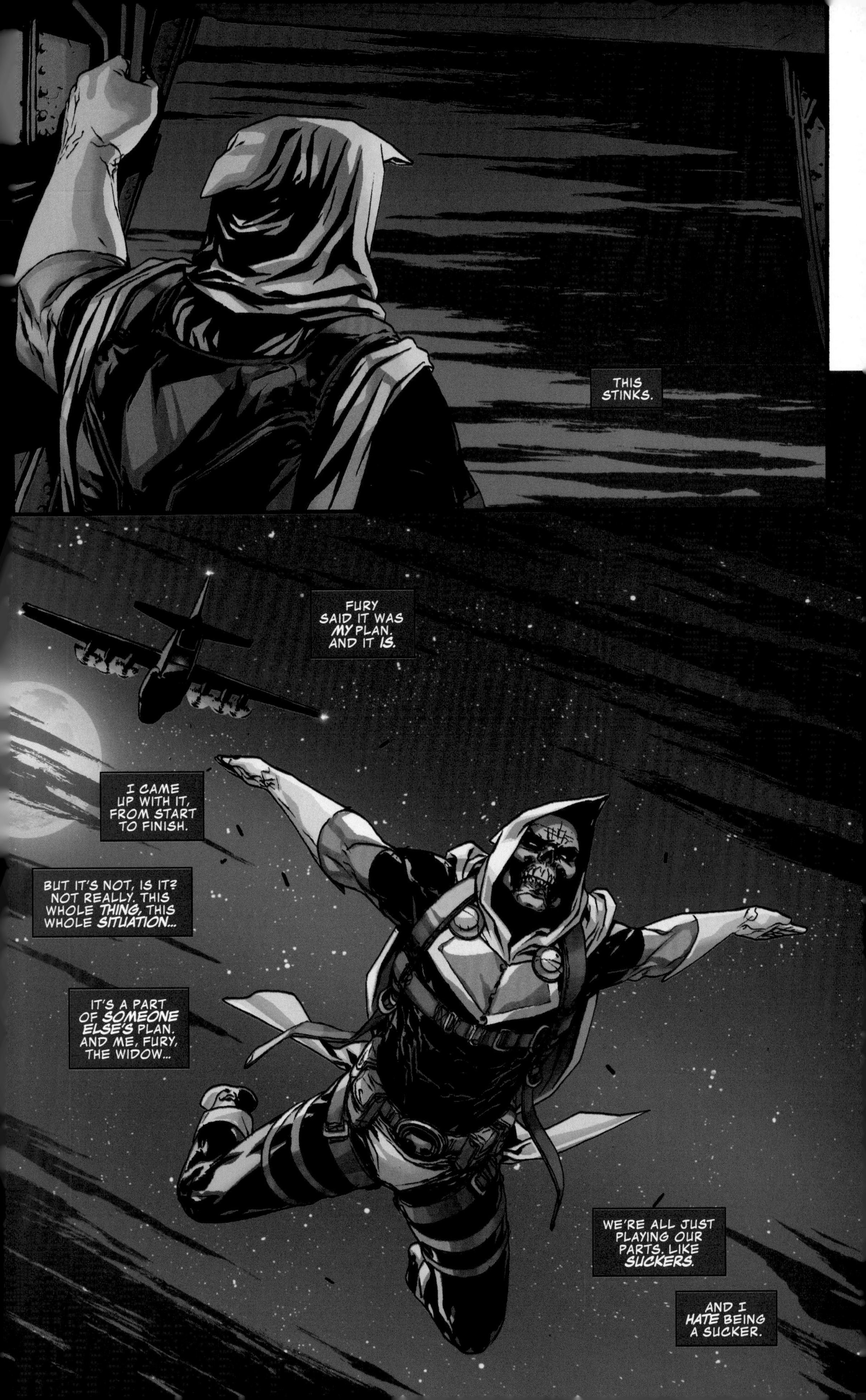
THIS STINKS.
FURY SAID IT WAS MY PLAN. AND IT IS.
I CAME UP WITH IT, FROM START TO FINISH.
BUT IT'S NOT, IS IT? NOT REALLY. THIS WHOLE THING, THIS WHOLE SITUATION...
IT'S A PART OF SOMEONE ELSE'S PLAN. AND ME, FURY, THE WIDOW...
WE'RE ALL JUST PLAYING OUR PARTS. LIKE SUCKERS.
AND I HATE BEING A SUCKER.

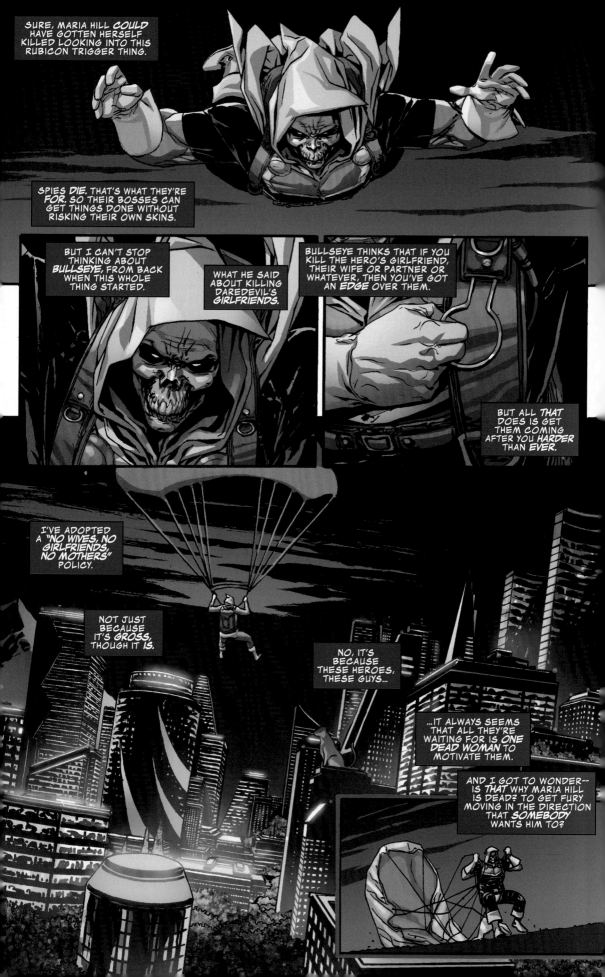

SURE, MARIA HILL *COULD* HAVE GOTTEN HERSELF KILLED LOOKING INTO THIS RUBICON TRIGGER THING.

SPIES *DIE.* THAT'S WHAT THEY'RE *FOR.* SO THEIR BOSSES CAN GET THINGS DONE WITHOUT RISKING THEIR OWN SKINS.

BUT I CAN'T STOP THINKING ABOUT *BULLSEYE,* FROM BACK WHEN THIS WHOLE THING STARTED.

WHAT HE SAID ABOUT KILLING DAREDEVIL'S *GIRLFRIENDS.*

BULLSEYE THINKS THAT IF YOU KILL THE HERO'S GIRLFRIEND, THEIR WIFE OR PARTNER OR WHATEVER, THEN YOU'VE GOT AN *EDGE* OVER THEM.

BUT ALL *THAT* DOES IS GET THEM COMING AFTER YOU *HARDER* THAN *EVER.*

I'VE ADOPTED A *"NO WIVES, NO GIRLFRIENDS, NO MOTHERS"* POLICY.

NOT JUST BECAUSE IT'S *GROSS,* THOUGH IT *IS.*

NO, IT'S BECAUSE THESE HEROES, THESE GUYS...

...IT ALWAYS SEEMS THAT ALL THEY'RE WAITING FOR IS *ONE DEAD WOMAN* TO MOTIVATE THEM.

AND I GOT TO WONDER-- IS *THAT* WHY MARIA HILL IS DEAD? TO GET FURY MOVING IN THE DIRECTION THAT *SOMEBODY* WANTS HIM TO?

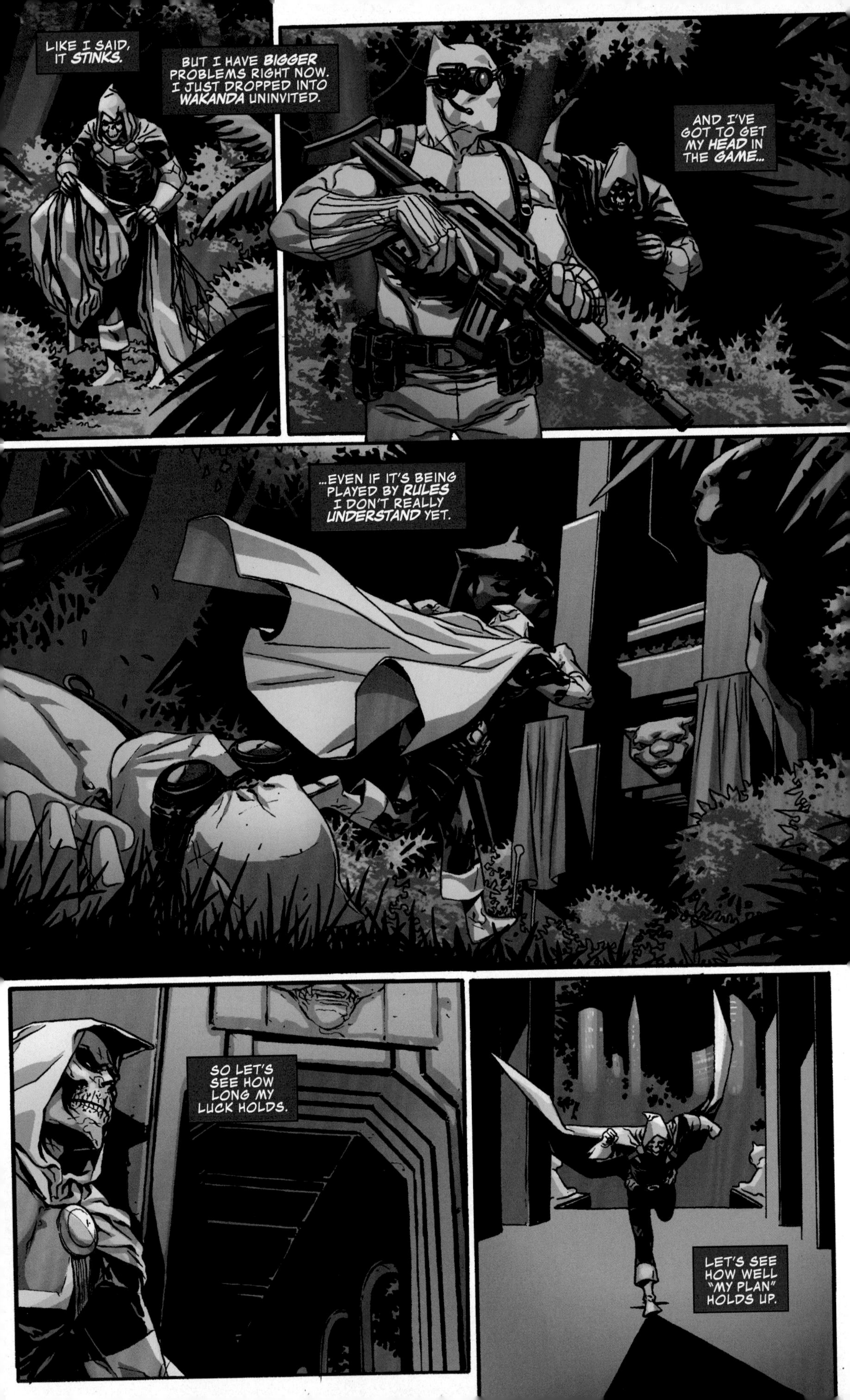

LIKE I SAID, IT STINKS.
BUT I HAVE BIGGER PROBLEMS RIGHT NOW. I JUST DROPPED INTO WAKANDA UNINVITED.
AND I'VE GOT TO GET MY HEAD IN THE GAME...
...EVEN IF IT'S BEING PLAYED BY RULES I DON'T REALLY UNDERSTAND YET.
SO LET'S SEE HOW LONG MY LUCK HOLDS.
LET'S SEE HOW WELL "MY PLAN" HOLDS UP.

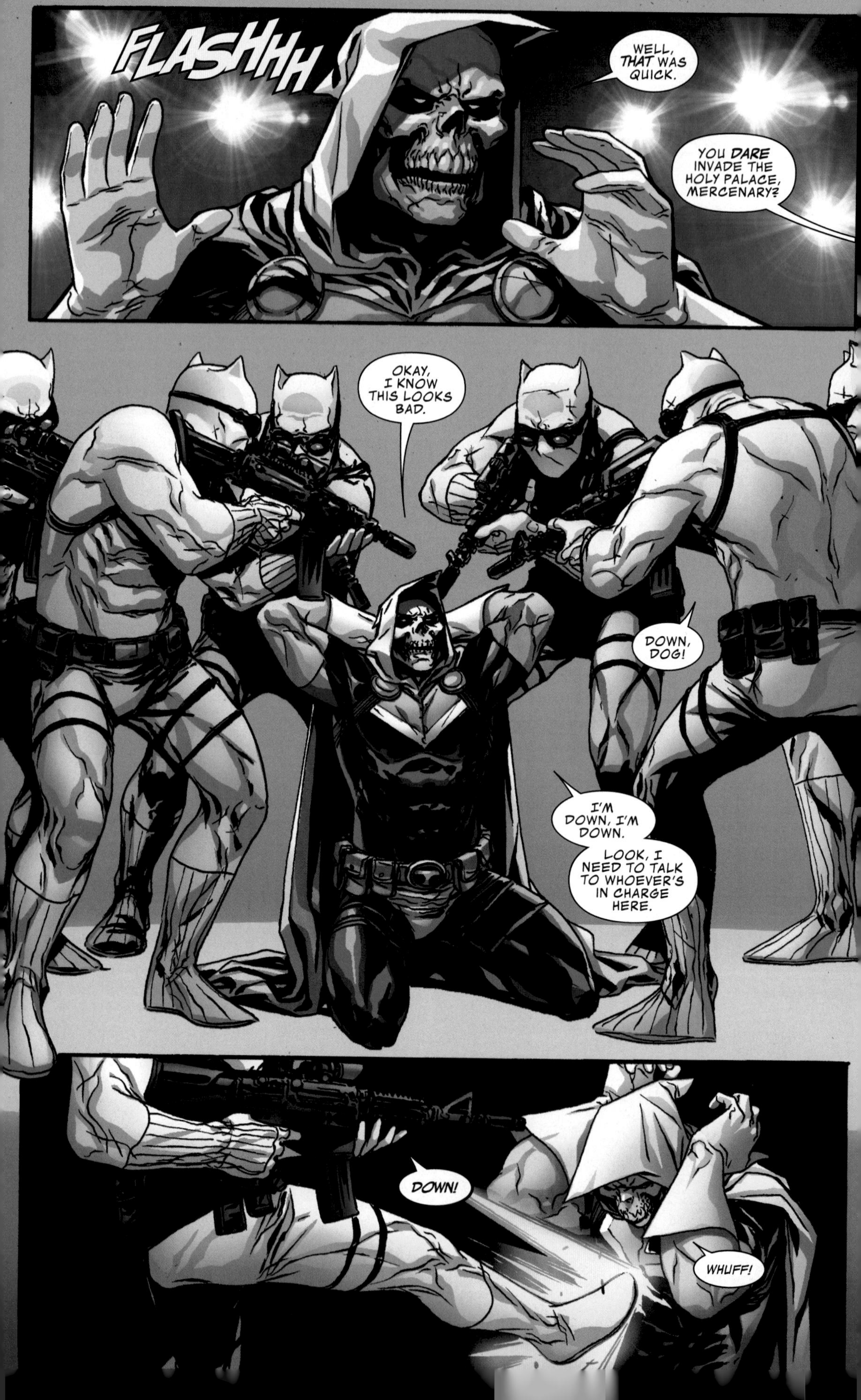
FLASHHH
WELL, THAT WAS QUICK.
YOU DARE INVADE THE HOLY PALACE, MERCENARY?
OKAY, I KNOW THIS LOOKS BAD.
DOWN, DOG!
I'M DOWN, I'M DOWN.
LOOK, I NEED TO TALK TO WHOEVER'S IN CHARGE HERE.
DOWN!
WHUFF!

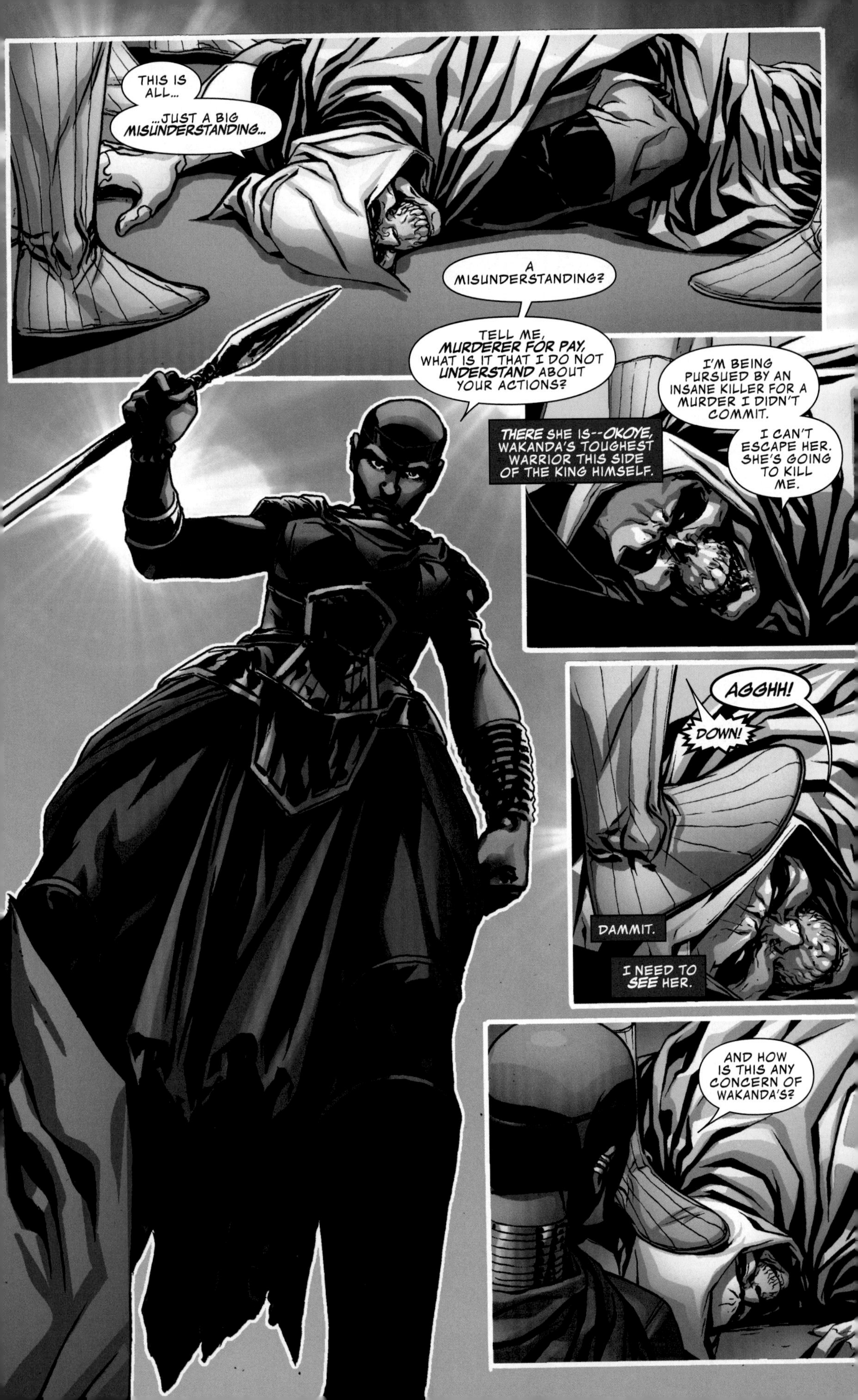

THIS IS ALL...
...JUST A BIG MISUNDERSTANDING...
A MISUNDERSTANDING?
TELL ME, MURDERER FOR PAY, WHAT IS IT THAT I DO NOT UNDERSTAND ABOUT YOUR ACTIONS?
THERE SHE IS--OKOYE, WAKANDA'S TOUGHEST WARRIOR THIS SIDE OF THE KING HIMSELF.
I'M BEING PURSUED BY AN INSANE KILLER FOR A MURDER I DIDN'T COMMIT.
I CAN'T ESCAPE HER. SHE'S GOING TO KILL ME.
AGGHH!
DOWN!
DAMMIT.
I NEED TO SEE HER.
AND HOW IS THIS ANY CONCERN OF WAKANDA'S?

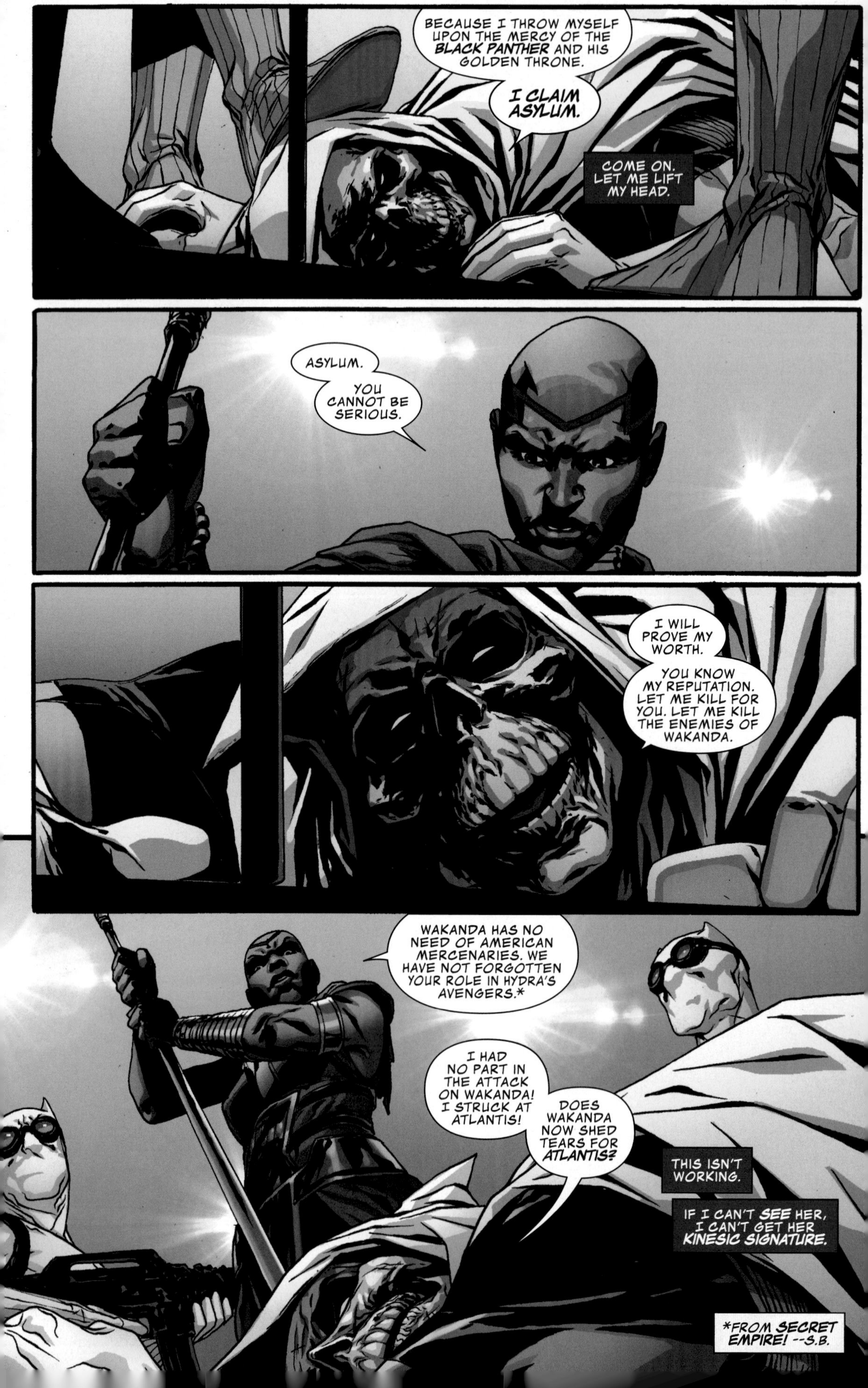
BECAUSE I THROW MYSELF UPON THE MERCY OF THE BLACK PANTHER AND HIS GOLDEN THRONE.
I CLAIM ASYLUM.
COME ON. LET ME LIFT MY HEAD.
ASYLUM.
YOU CANNOT BE SERIOUS.
I WILL PROVE MY WORTH.
YOU KNOW MY REPUTATION. LET ME KILL FOR YOU. LET ME KILL THE ENEMIES OF WAKANDA.
WAKANDA HAS NO NEED OF AMERICAN MERCENARIES. WE HAVE NOT FORGOTTEN YOUR ROLE IN HYDRA'S AVENGERS.*
I HAD NO PART IN THE ATTACK ON WAKANDA! I STRUCK AT ATLANTIS!
DOES WAKANDA NOW SHED TEARS FOR ATLANTIS?
THIS ISN'T WORKING.
IF I CAN'T SEE HER, I CAN'T GET HER KINESIC SIGNATURE.
*FROM SECRET EMPIRE! --S.B.

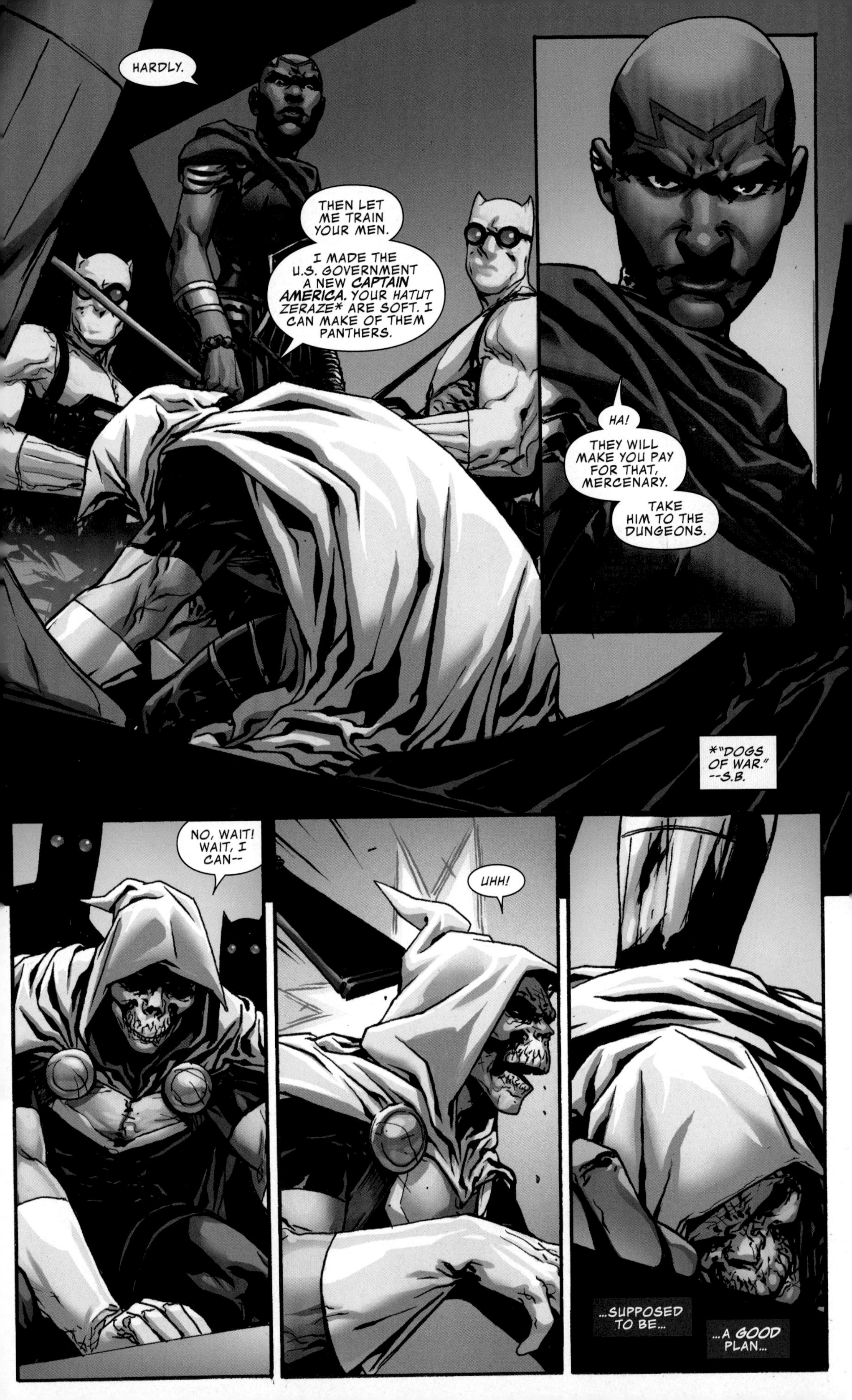
HARDLY.
THEN LET ME TRAIN YOUR MEN.
I MADE THE U.S. GOVERNMENT A NEW CAPTAIN AMERICA. YOUR HATUT ZERAZE* ARE SOFT. I CAN MAKE OF THEM PANTHERS.
HA!
THEY WILL MAKE YOU PAY FOR THAT, MERCENARY.
TAKE HIM TO THE DUNGEONS.
*"DOGS OF WAR." --S.B.
NO, WAIT! WAIT, I CAN--
UHH!
...SUPPOSED TO BE...
...A GOOD PLAN...

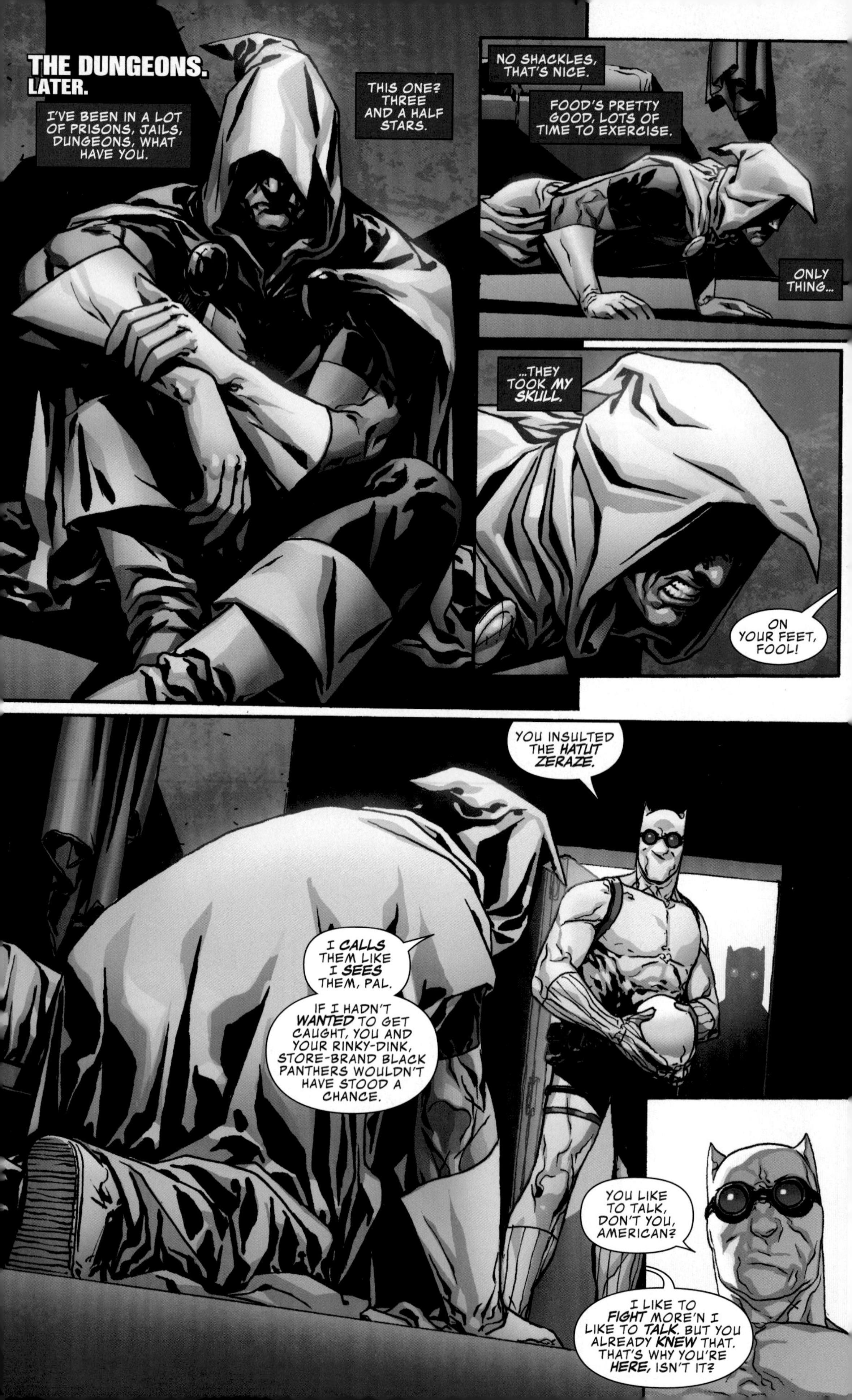
THE DUNGEONS. LATER.
I'VE BEEN IN A LOT OF PRISONS, JAILS, DUNGEONS, WHAT HAVE YOU.
THIS ONE? THREE AND A HALF STARS.
NO SHACKLES, THAT'S NICE.
FOOD'S PRETTY GOOD, LOTS OF TIME TO EXERCISE.
ONLY THING...
...THEY TOOK MY SKULL.
ON YOUR FEET, FOOL!
YOU INSULTED THE HATUT ZERAZE.
I CALLS THEM LIKE I SEES THEM, PAL.
IF I HADN'T WANTED TO GET CAUGHT, YOU AND YOUR RINKY-DINK, STORE-BRAND BLACK PANTHERS WOULDN'T HAVE STOOD A CHANCE.
YOU LIKE TO TALK, DON'T YOU, AMERICAN?
I LIKE TO FIGHT MORE'N I LIKE TO TALK. BUT YOU ALREADY KNEW THAT. THAT'S WHY YOU'RE HERE, ISN'T IT?

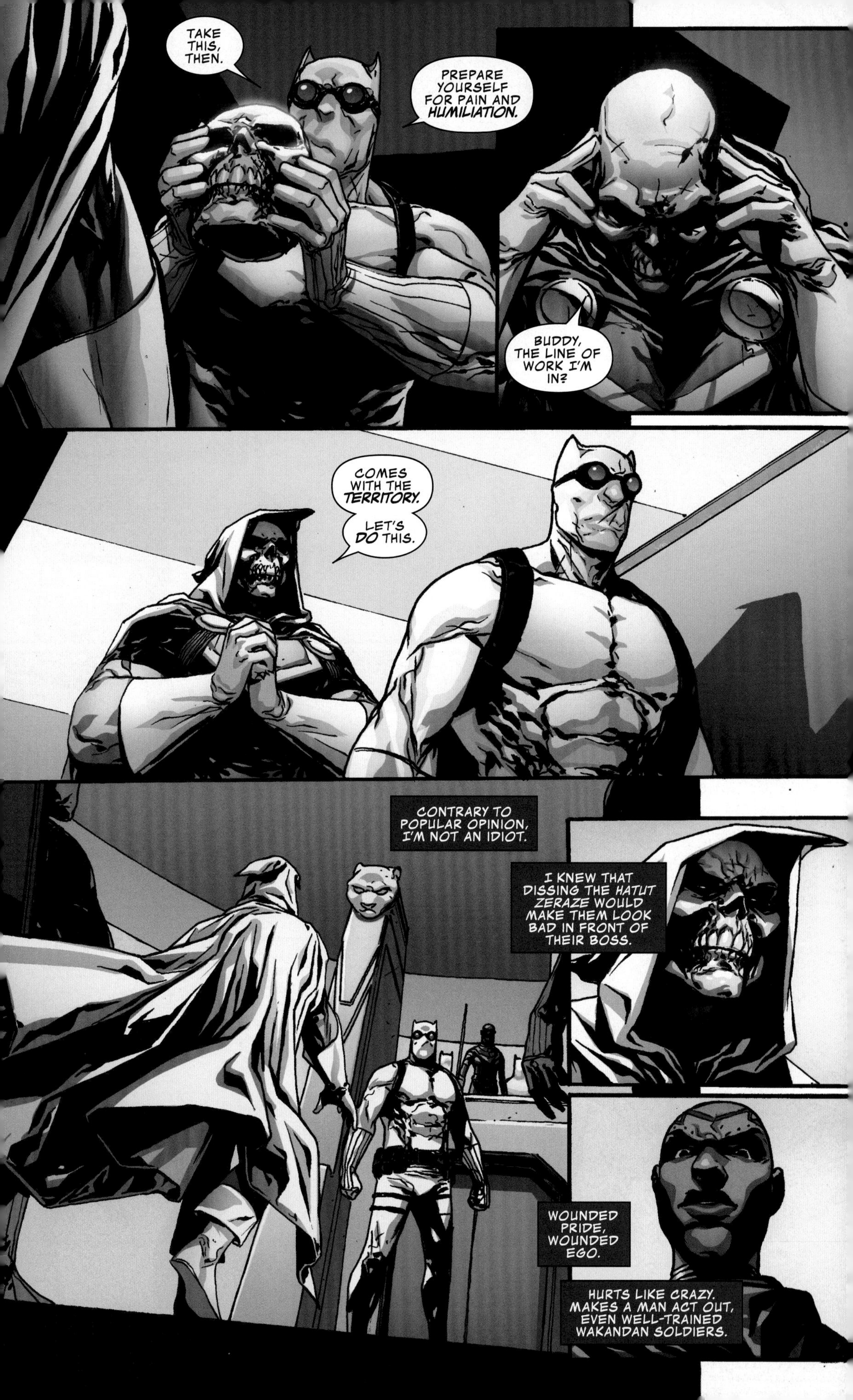
TAKE THIS, THEN.
PREPARE YOURSELF FOR PAIN AND HUMILIATION.
BUDDY, THE LINE OF WORK I'M IN?
COMES WITH THE TERRITORY.
LET'S DO THIS.
CONTRARY TO POPULAR OPINION, I'M NOT AN IDIOT.
I KNEW THAT DISSING THE HATUT ZERAZE WOULD MAKE THEM LOOK BAD IN FRONT OF THEIR BOSS.
WOUNDED PRIDE, WOUNDED EGO.
HURTS LIKE CRAZY. MAKES A MAN ACT OUT, EVEN WELL-TRAINED WAKANDAN SOLDIERS.

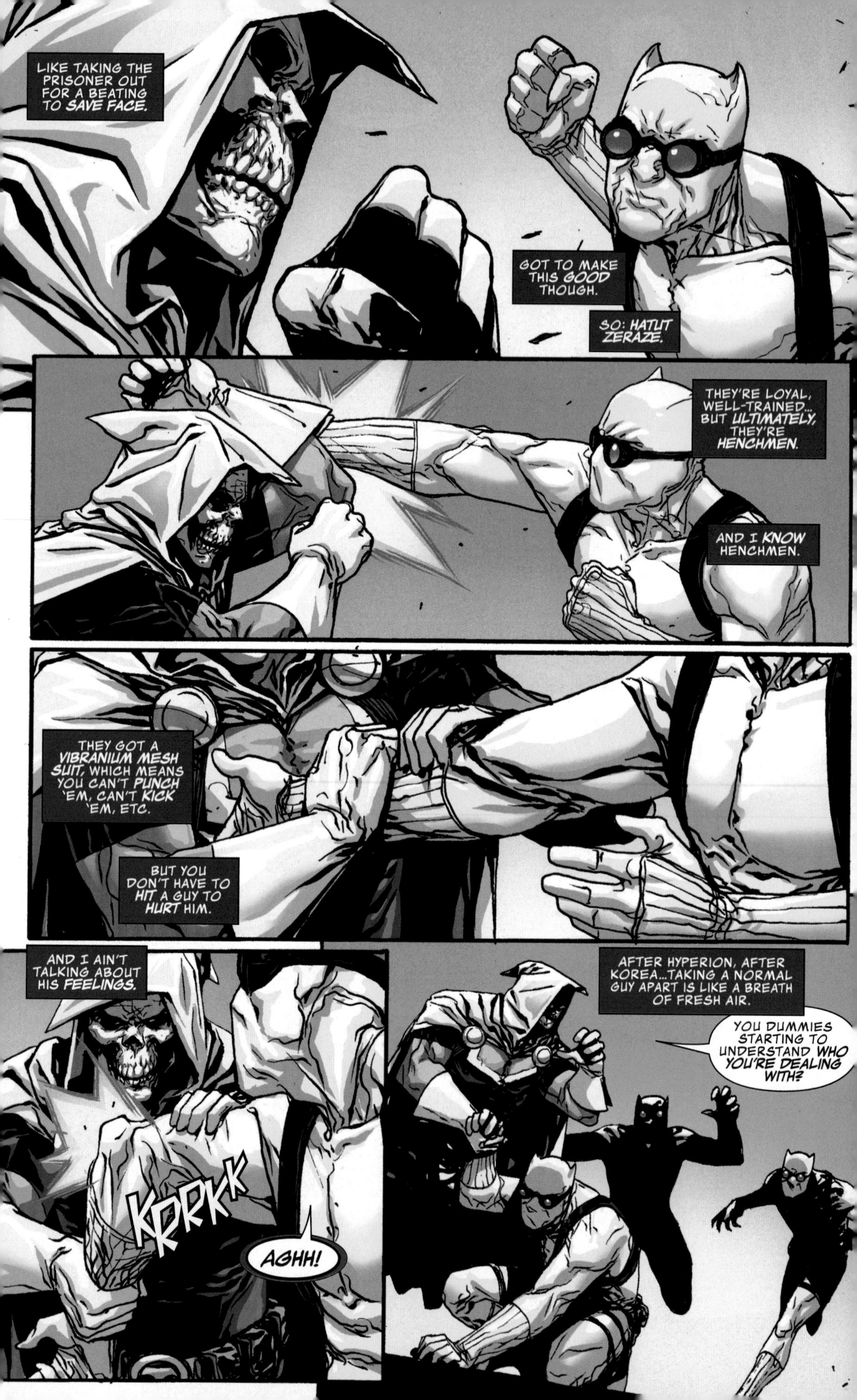
LIKE TAKING THE PRISONER OUT FOR A BEATING TO SAVE FACE.
GOT TO MAKE THIS GOOD THOUGH.
SO: HATUT ZERAZE.
THEY'RE LOYAL, WELL-TRAINED... BUT ULTIMATELY, THEY'RE HENCHMEN.
AND I KNOW HENCHMEN.
THEY GOT A VIBRANIUM MESH SUIT, WHICH MEANS YOU CAN'T PUNCH 'EM, CAN'T KICK 'EM, ETC.
BUT YOU DON'T HAVE TO HIT A GUY TO HURT HIM.
AND I AIN'T TALKING ABOUT HIS FEELINGS.
KRRKK
AGHH!
AFTER HYPERION, AFTER KOREA...TAKING A NORMAL GUY APART IS LIKE A BREATH OF FRESH AIR.
YOU DUMMIES STARTING TO UNDERSTAND WHO YOU'RE DEALING WITH?

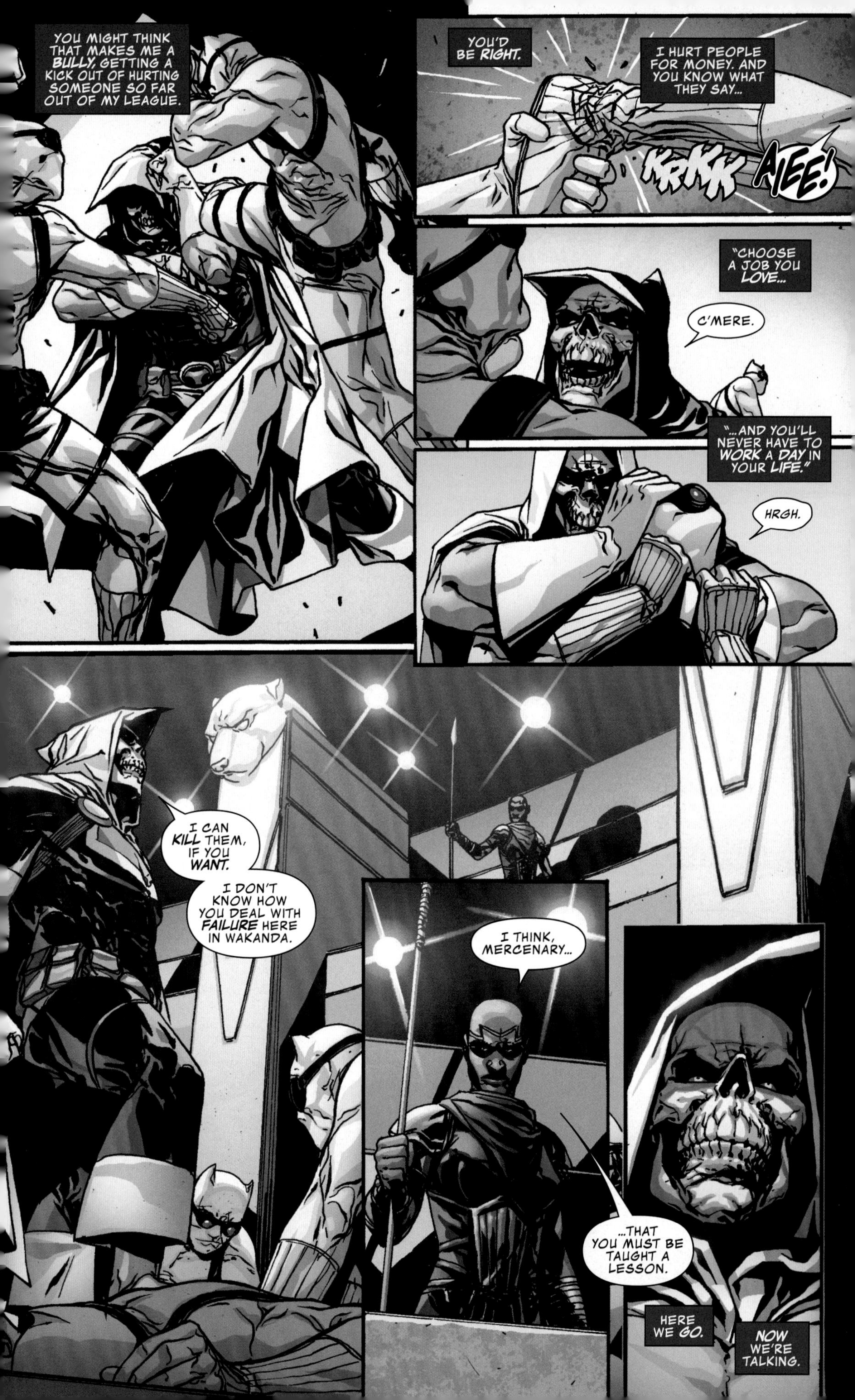
YOU MIGHT THINK THAT MAKES ME A BULLY, GETTING A KICK OUT OF HURTING SOMEONE SO FAR OUT OF MY LEAGUE.
YOU'D BE RIGHT.
I HURT PEOPLE FOR MONEY. AND YOU KNOW WHAT THEY SAY...
KRKK
AIEE!
"CHOOSE A JOB YOU LOVE...
C'MERE.
"...AND YOU'LL NEVER HAVE TO WORK A DAY IN YOUR LIFE."
HRGH.
I CAN KILL THEM, IF YOU WANT.
I DON'T KNOW HOW YOU DEAL WITH FAILURE HERE IN WAKANDA.
I THINK, MERCENARY...
...THAT YOU MUST BE TAUGHT A LESSON.
HERE WE GO.
NOW WE'RE TALKING.

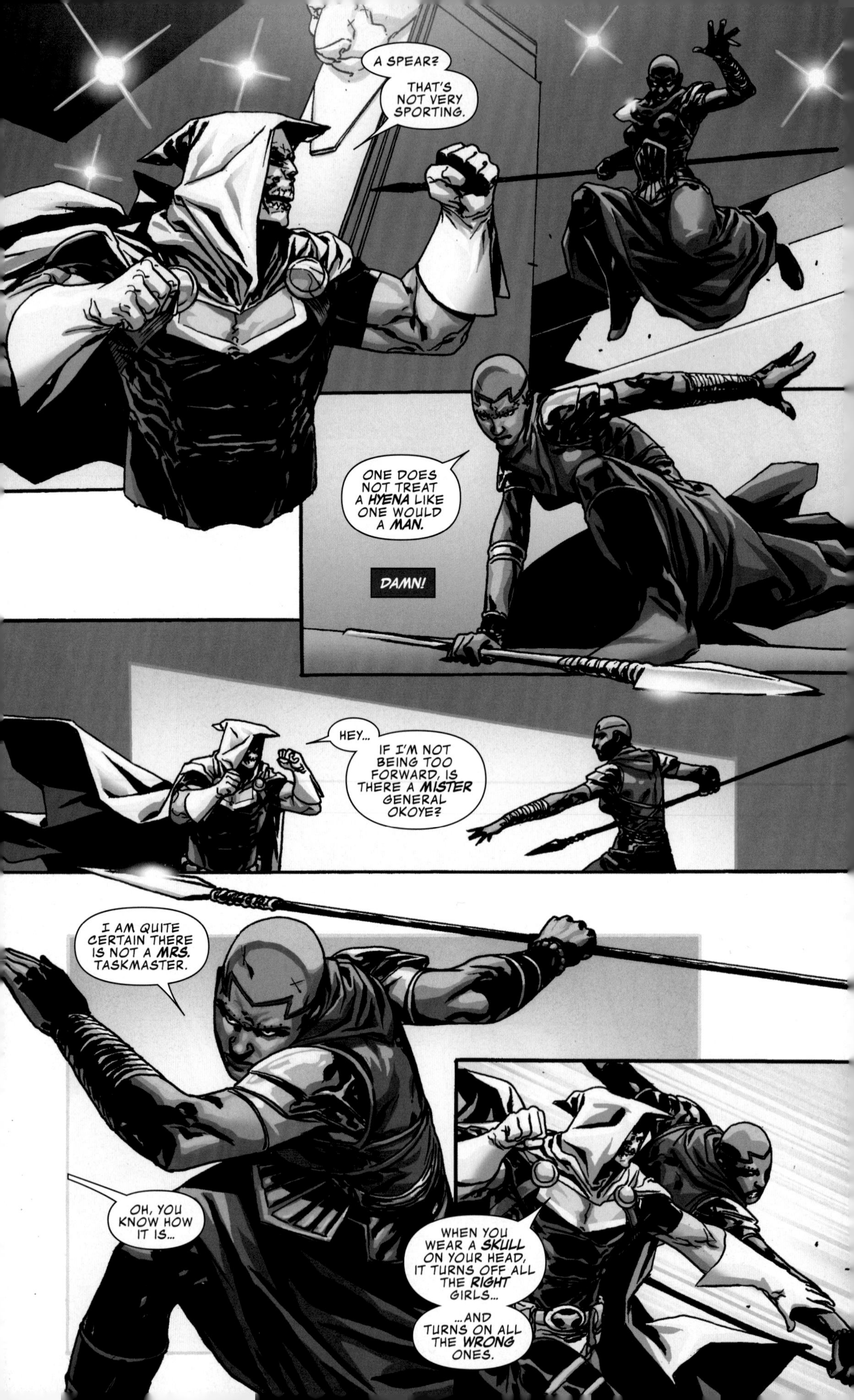
A SPEAR?
THAT'S NOT VERY SPORTING.
ONE DOES NOT TREAT A HYENA LIKE ONE WOULD A MAN.
DAMN!
HEY...
IF I'M NOT BEING TOO FORWARD, IS THERE A MISTER GENERAL OKOYE?
I AM QUITE CERTAIN THERE IS NOT A MRS. TASKMASTER.
OH, YOU KNOW HOW IT IS...
WHEN YOU WEAR A SKULL ON YOUR HEAD, IT TURNS OFF ALL THE RIGHT GIRLS...
...AND TURNS ON ALL THE WRONG ONES.

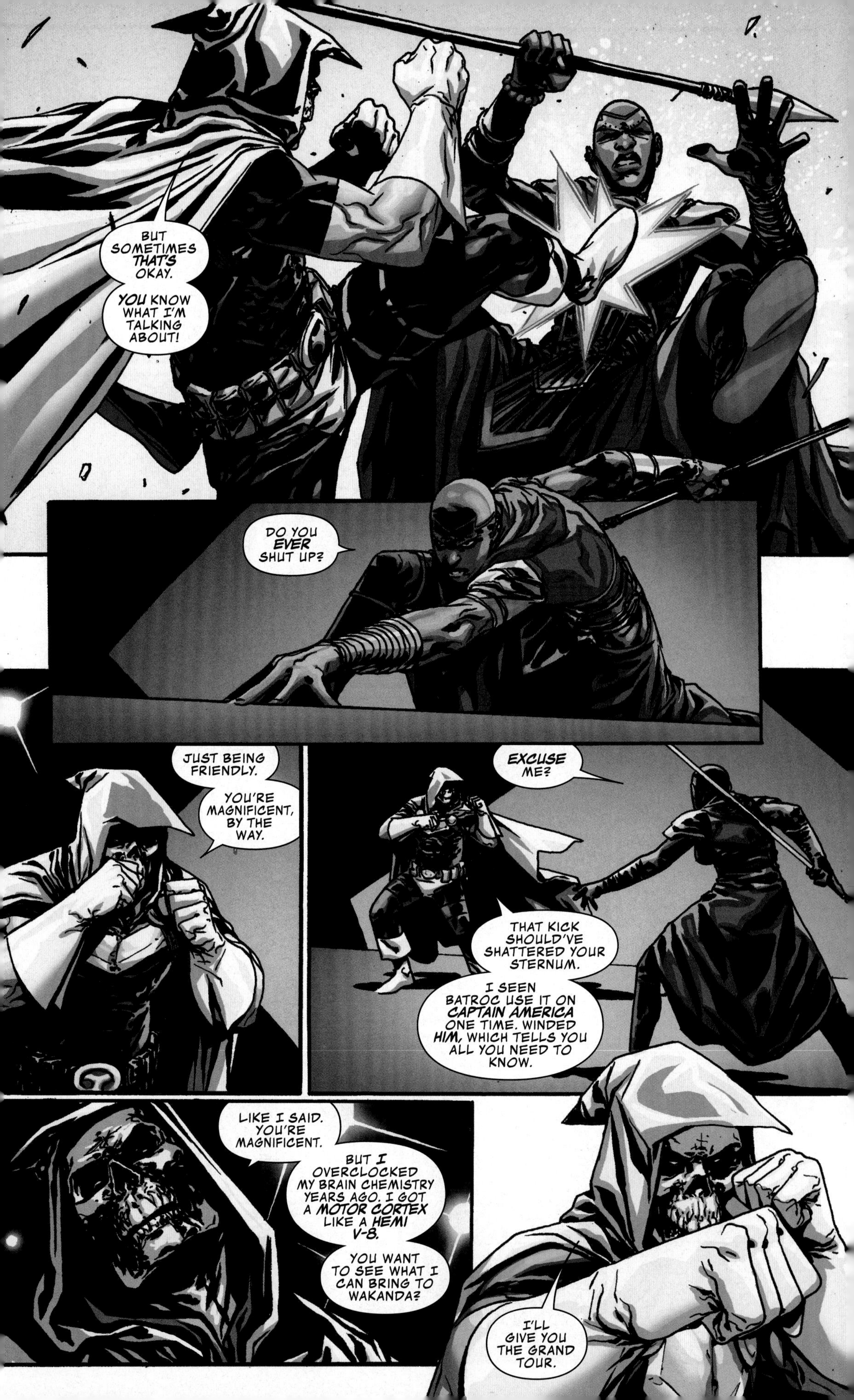
BUT SOMETIMES *THAT'S* OKAY.
*YOU* KNOW WHAT I'M TALKING ABOUT!
DO YOU *EVER* SHUT UP?
JUST BEING FRIENDLY.
YOU'RE MAGNIFICENT, BY THE WAY.
*EXCUSE* ME?
THAT KICK SHOULD'VE SHATTERED YOUR STERNUM.
I SEEN BATROC USE IT ON *CAPTAIN AMERICA* ONE TIME. WINDED *HIM,* WHICH TELLS YOU ALL YOU NEED TO KNOW.
LIKE I SAID. YOU'RE MAGNIFICENT.
BUT *I* OVERCLOCKED MY BRAIN CHEMISTRY YEARS AGO. I GOT A *MOTOR CORTEX* LIKE A *HEMI V-8.*
YOU WANT TO SEE WHAT I CAN BRING TO WAKANDA?
I'LL GIVE YOU THE GRAND TOUR.

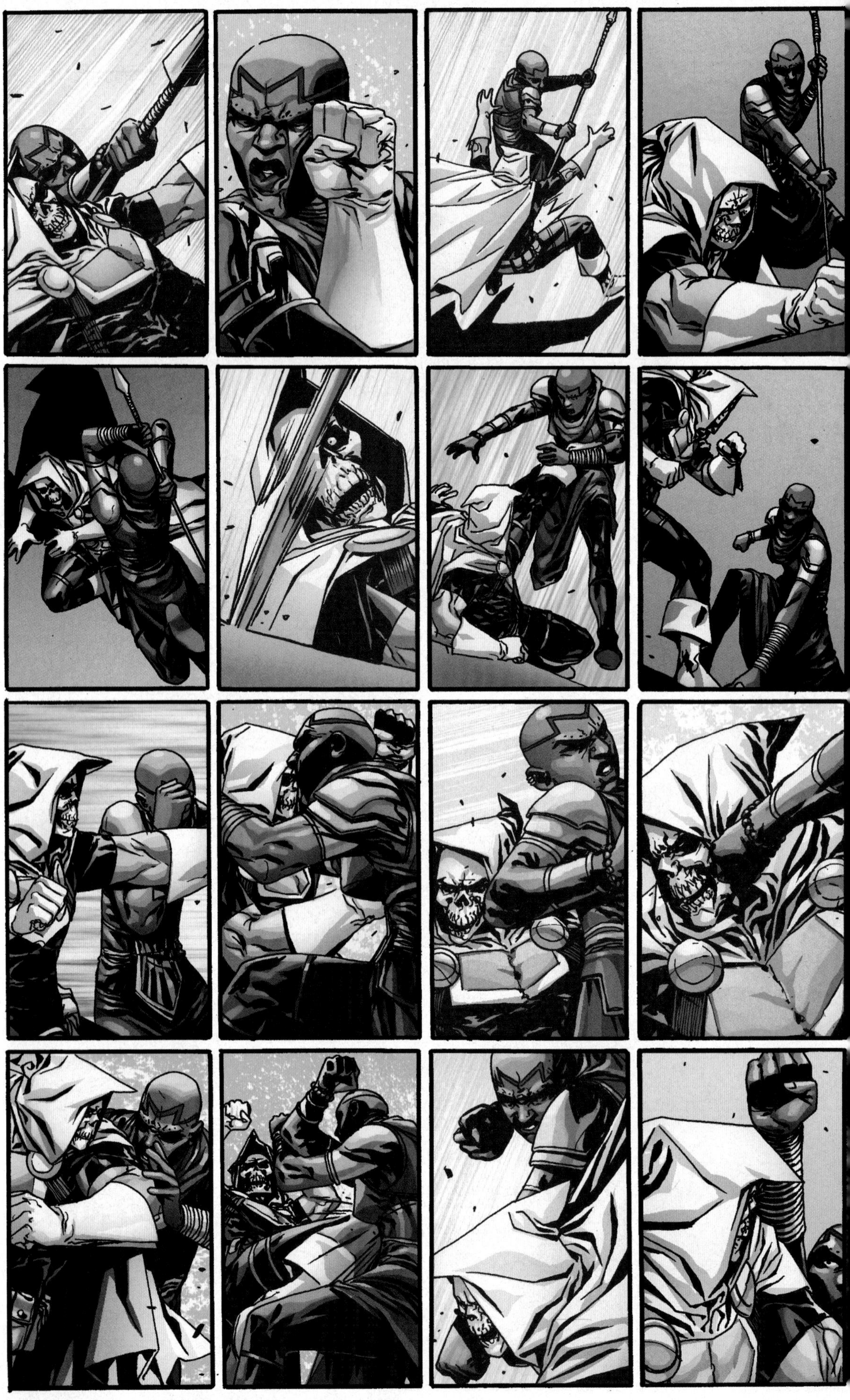

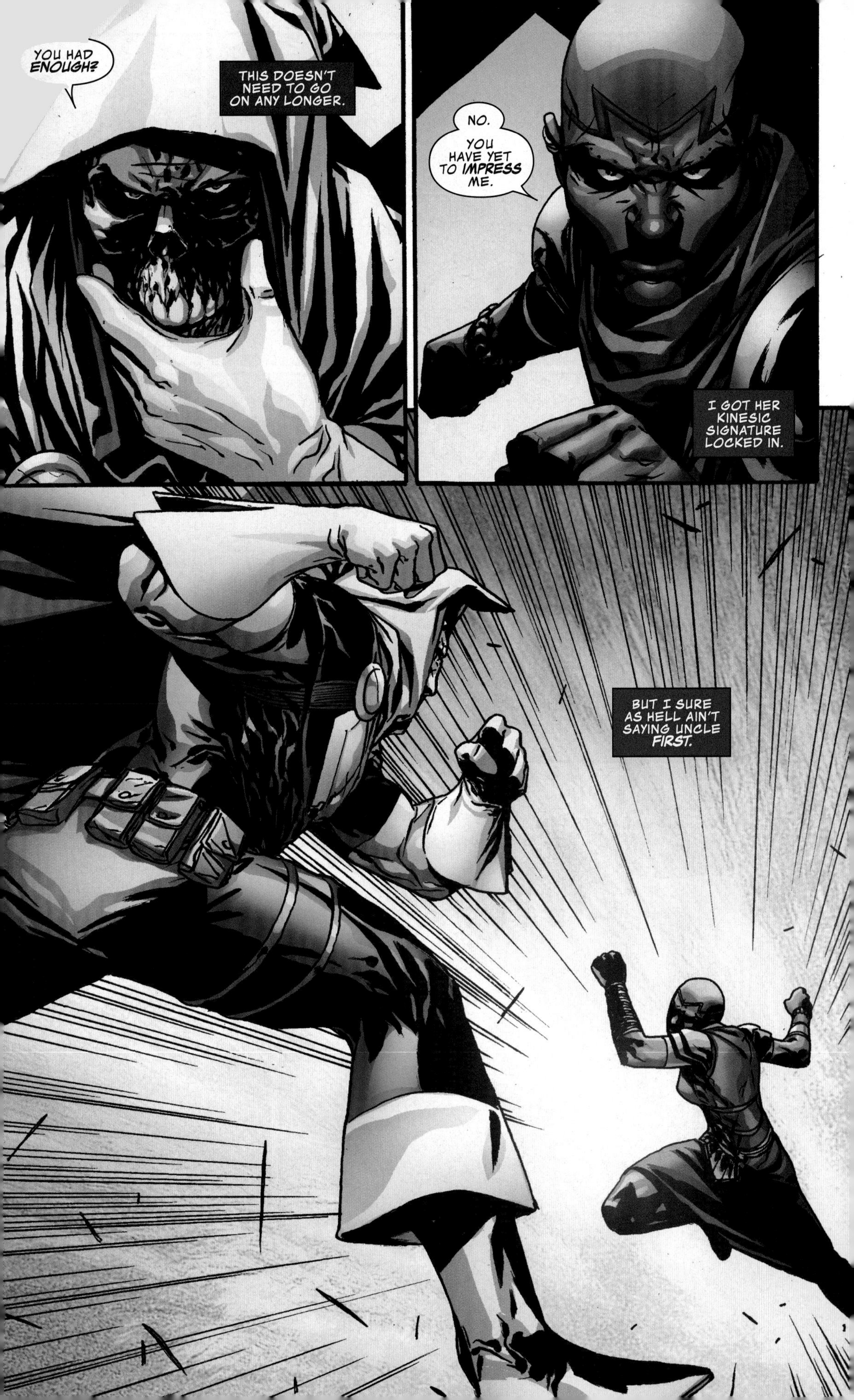
YOU HAD ENOUGH?
THIS DOESN'T NEED TO GO ON ANY LONGER.
NO.
YOU HAVE YET TO IMPRESS ME.
I GOT HER KINESIC SIGNATURE LOCKED IN.
BUT I SURE AS HELL AIN'T SAYING UNCLE FIRST.

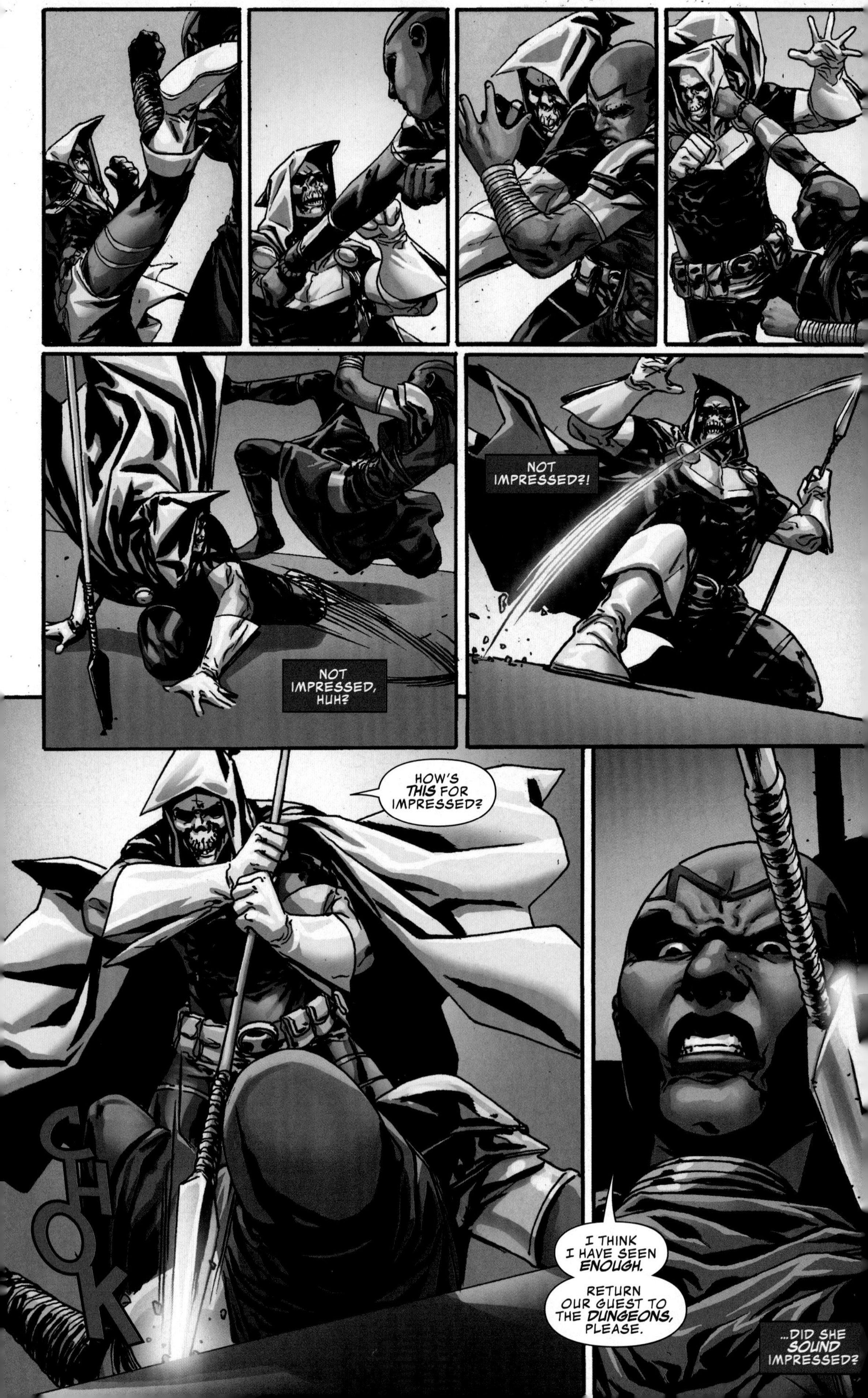
NOT IMPRESSED, HUH?
NOT IMPRESSED?!
HOW'S THIS FOR IMPRESSED?
CHOK
I THINK I HAVE SEEN ENOUGH.
RETURN OUR GUEST TO THE DUNGEONS, PLEASE.
...DID SHE SOUND IMPRESSED?

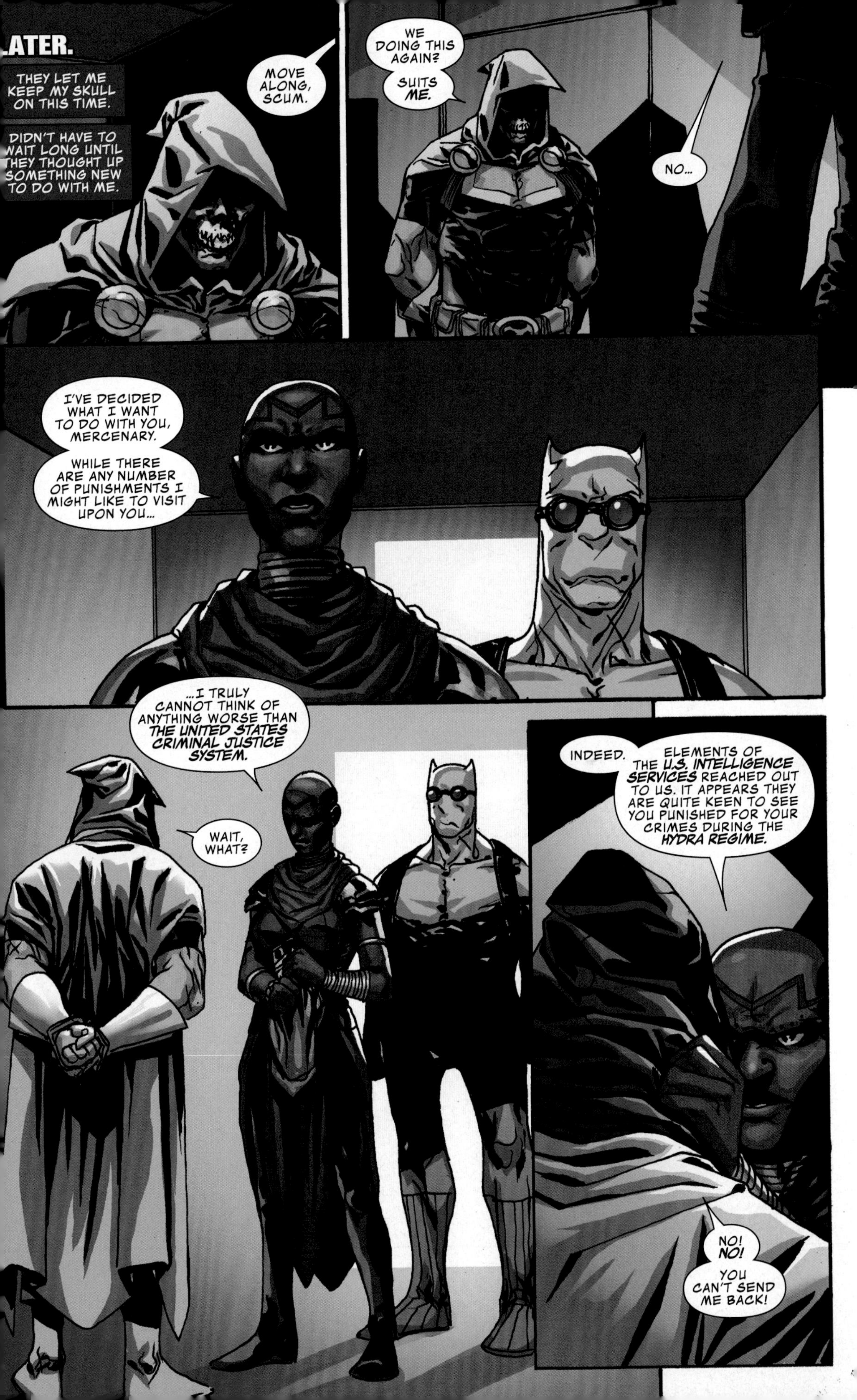
LATER.
THEY LET ME KEEP MY SKULL ON THIS TIME.
DIDN'T HAVE TO WAIT LONG UNTIL THEY THOUGHT UP SOMETHING NEW TO DO WITH ME.
MOVE ALONG, SCUM.
WE DOING THIS AGAIN?
SUITS ME.
NO...
I'VE DECIDED WHAT I WANT TO DO WITH YOU, MERCENARY.
WHILE THERE ARE ANY NUMBER OF PUNISHMENTS I MIGHT LIKE TO VISIT UPON YOU...
...I TRULY CANNOT THINK OF ANYTHING WORSE THAN THE UNITED STATES CRIMINAL JUSTICE SYSTEM.
WAIT, WHAT?
INDEED.
ELEMENTS OF THE U.S. INTELLIGENCE SERVICES REACHED OUT TO US. IT APPEARS THEY ARE QUITE KEEN TO SEE YOU PUNISHED FOR YOUR CRIMES DURING THE HYDRA REGIME.
NO! NO!
YOU CAN'T SEND ME BACK!

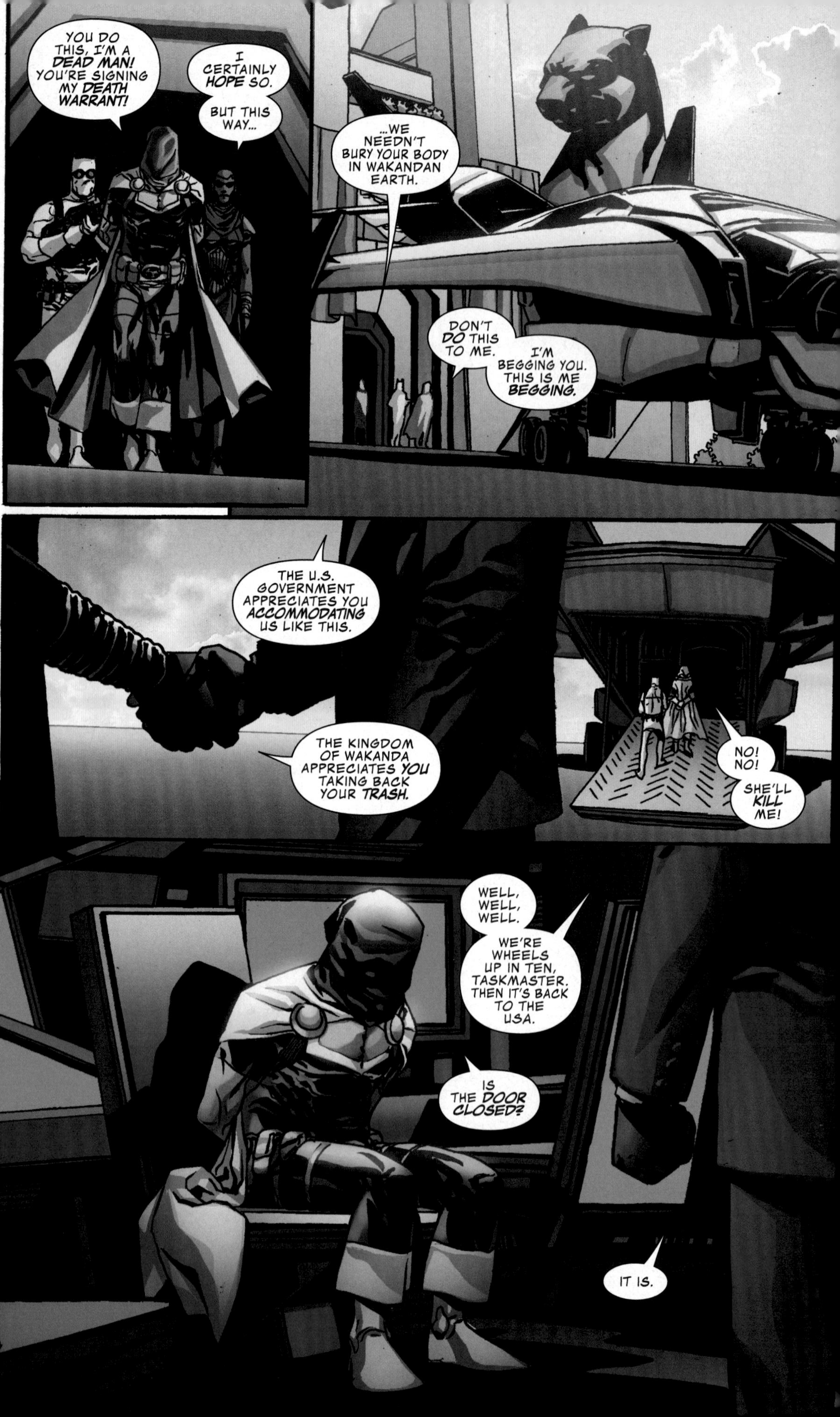
YOU DO THIS, I'M A DEAD MAN! YOU'RE SIGNING MY DEATH WARRANT!
I CERTAINLY HOPE SO.
BUT THIS WAY...
...WE NEEDN'T BURY YOUR BODY IN WAKANDAN EARTH.
DON'T DO THIS TO ME.
I'M BEGGING YOU. THIS IS ME BEGGING.
THE U.S. GOVERNMENT APPRECIATES YOU ACCOMMODATING US LIKE THIS.
THE KINGDOM OF WAKANDA APPRECIATES YOU TAKING BACK YOUR TRASH.
NO! NO!
SHE'LL KILL ME!
WELL, WELL, WELL.
WE'RE WHEELS UP IN TEN, TASKMASTER. THEN IT'S BACK TO THE USA.
IS THE DOOR CLOSED?
IT IS.

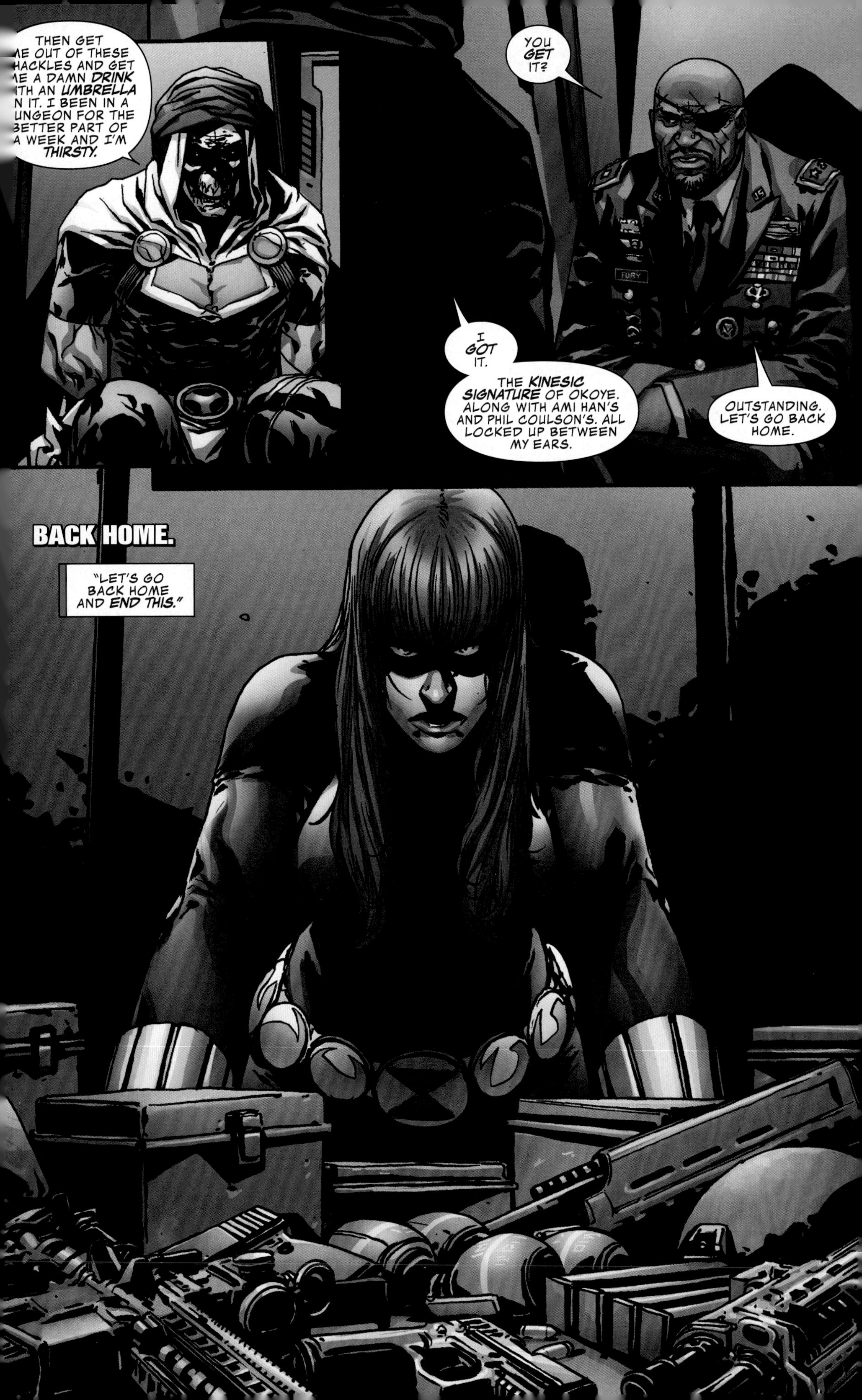
THEN GET ME OUT OF THESE HACKLES AND GET ME A DAMN DRINK ITH AN UMBRELLA N IT. I BEEN IN A UNGEON FOR THE BETTER PART OF A WEEK AND I'M THIRSTY.
YOU GET IT?
FURY
I GOT IT.
THE KINESIC SIGNATURE OF OKOYE. ALONG WITH AMI HAN'S AND PHIL COULSON'S. ALL LOCKED UP BETWEEN MY EARS.
OUTSTANDING. LET'S GO BACK HOME.
BACK HOME.
"LET'S GO BACK HOME AND END THIS."

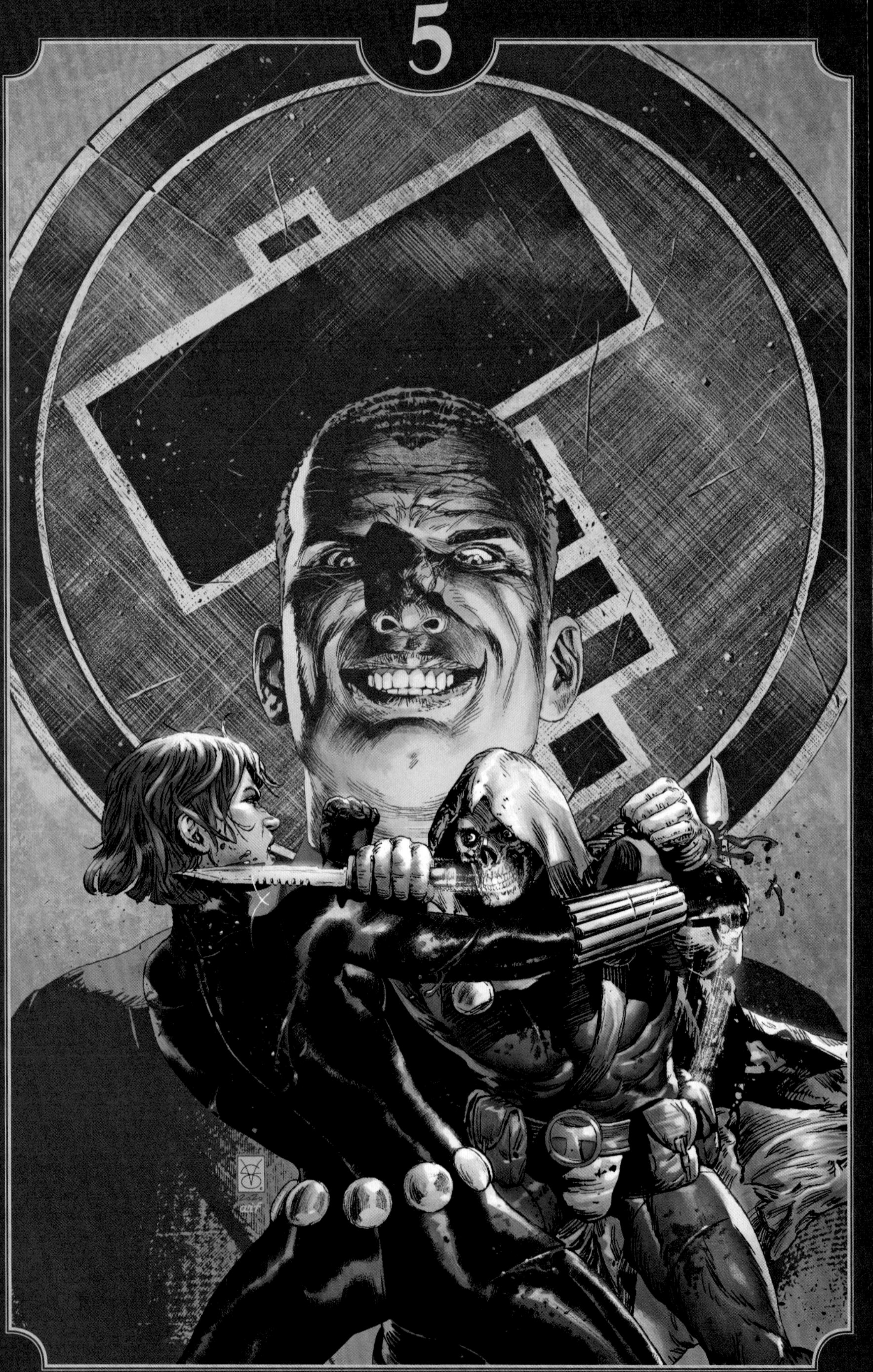
5

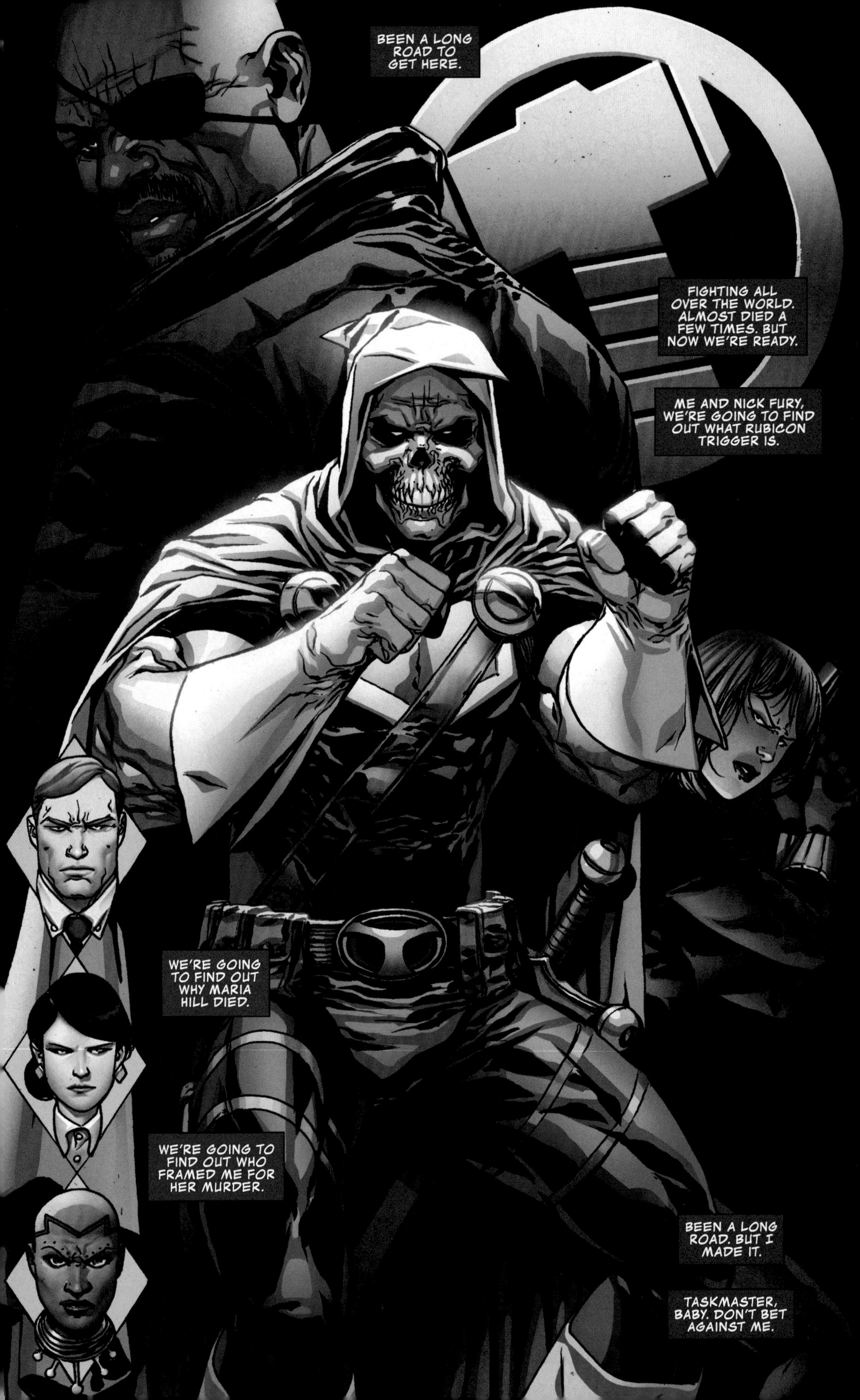
BEEN A LONG ROAD TO GET HERE.
FIGHTING ALL OVER THE WORLD. ALMOST DIED A FEW TIMES. BUT NOW WE'RE READY.
ME AND NICK FURY, WE'RE GOING TO FIND OUT WHAT RUBICON TRIGGER IS.
WE'RE GOING TO FIND OUT WHY MARIA HILL DIED.
WE'RE GOING TO FIND OUT WHO FRAMED ME FOR HER MURDER.
BEEN A LONG ROAD. BUT I MADE IT.
TASKMASTER, BABY. DON'T BET AGAINST ME.

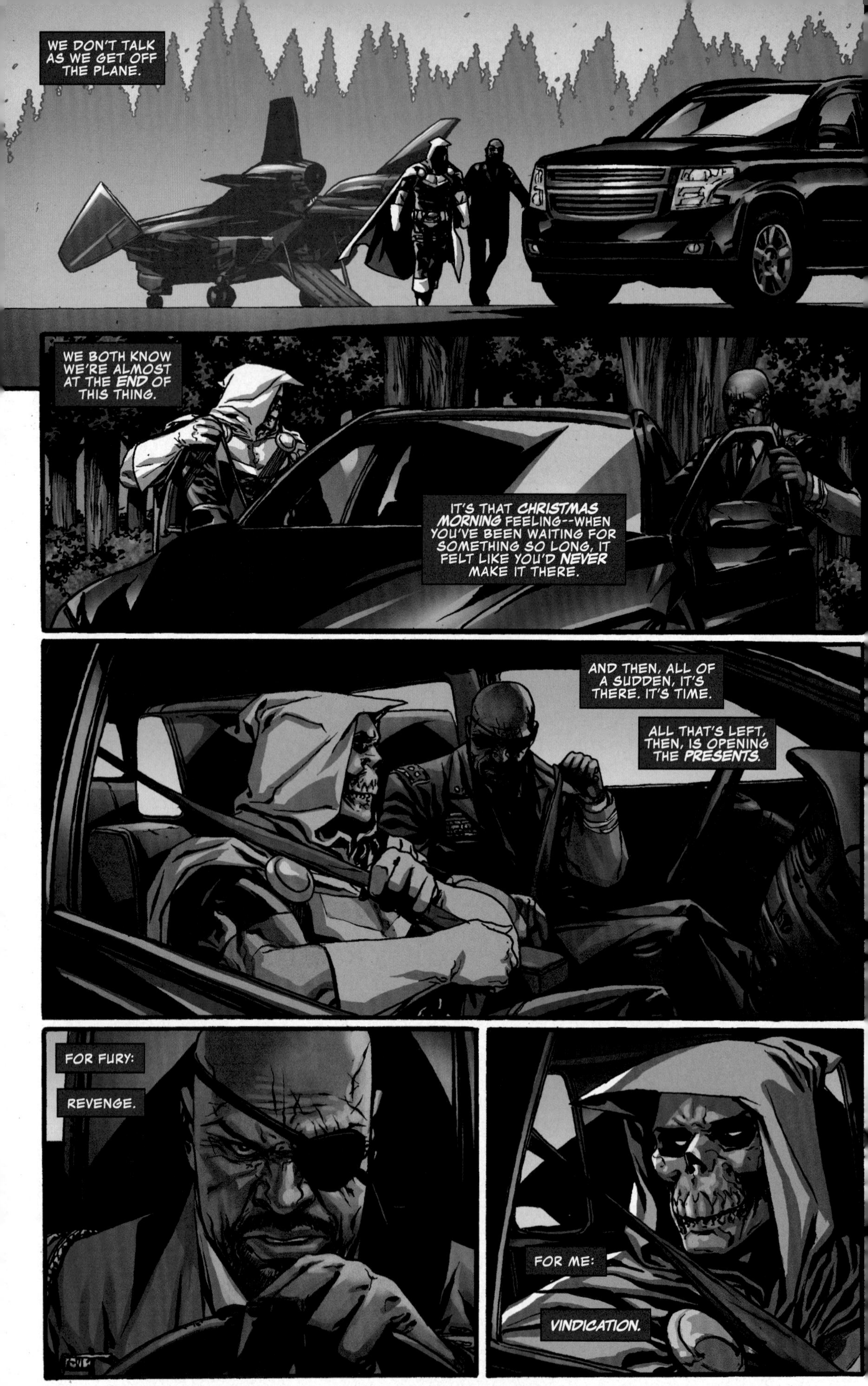
WE DON'T TALK AS WE GET OFF THE PLANE.
WE BOTH KNOW WE'RE ALMOST AT THE END OF THIS THING.
IT'S THAT CHRISTMAS MORNING FEELING--WHEN YOU'VE BEEN WAITING FOR SOMETHING SO LONG, IT FELT LIKE YOU'D NEVER MAKE IT THERE.
AND THEN, ALL OF A SUDDEN, IT'S THERE. IT'S TIME.
ALL THAT'S LEFT, THEN, IS OPENING THE PRESENTS.
FOR FURY:
REVENGE.
FOR ME:
VINDICATION.

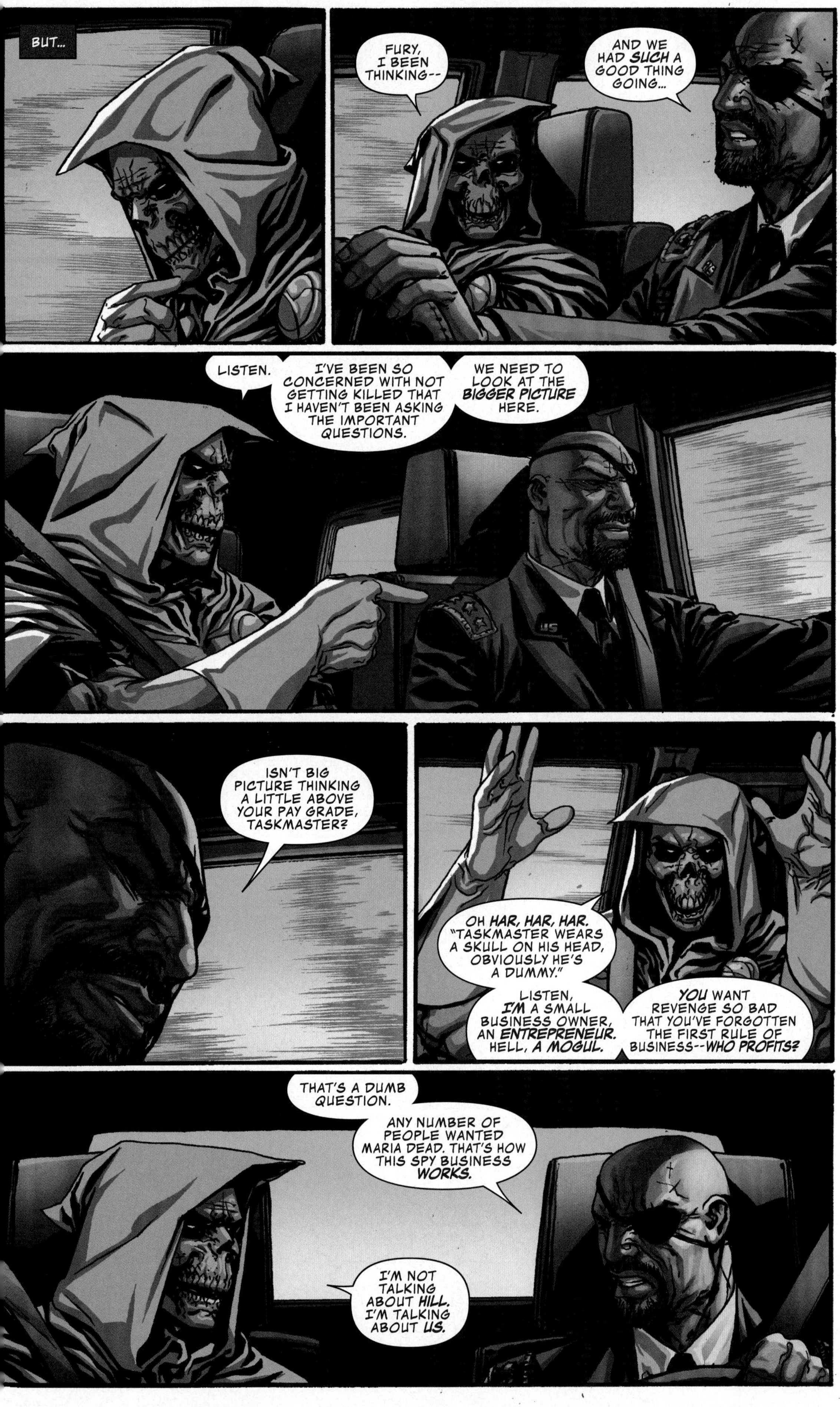
BUT...
FURY, I BEEN THINKING--
AND WE HAD SUCH A GOOD THING GOING...
LISTEN.
I'VE BEEN SO CONCERNED WITH NOT GETTING KILLED THAT I HAVEN'T BEEN ASKING THE IMPORTANT QUESTIONS.
WE NEED TO LOOK AT THE BIGGER PICTURE HERE.
ISN'T BIG PICTURE THINKING A LITTLE ABOVE YOUR PAY GRADE, TASKMASTER?
OH HAR, HAR, HAR. "TASKMASTER WEARS A SKULL ON HIS HEAD, OBVIOUSLY HE'S A DUMMY."
LISTEN, I'M A SMALL BUSINESS OWNER, AN ENTREPRENEUR. HELL, A MOGUL.
YOU WANT REVENGE SO BAD THAT YOU'VE FORGOTTEN THE FIRST RULE OF BUSINESS--WHO PROFITS?
THAT'S A DUMB QUESTION.
ANY NUMBER OF PEOPLE WANTED MARIA DEAD. THAT'S HOW THIS SPY BUSINESS WORKS.
I'M NOT TALKING ABOUT HILL. I'M TALKING ABOUT US.

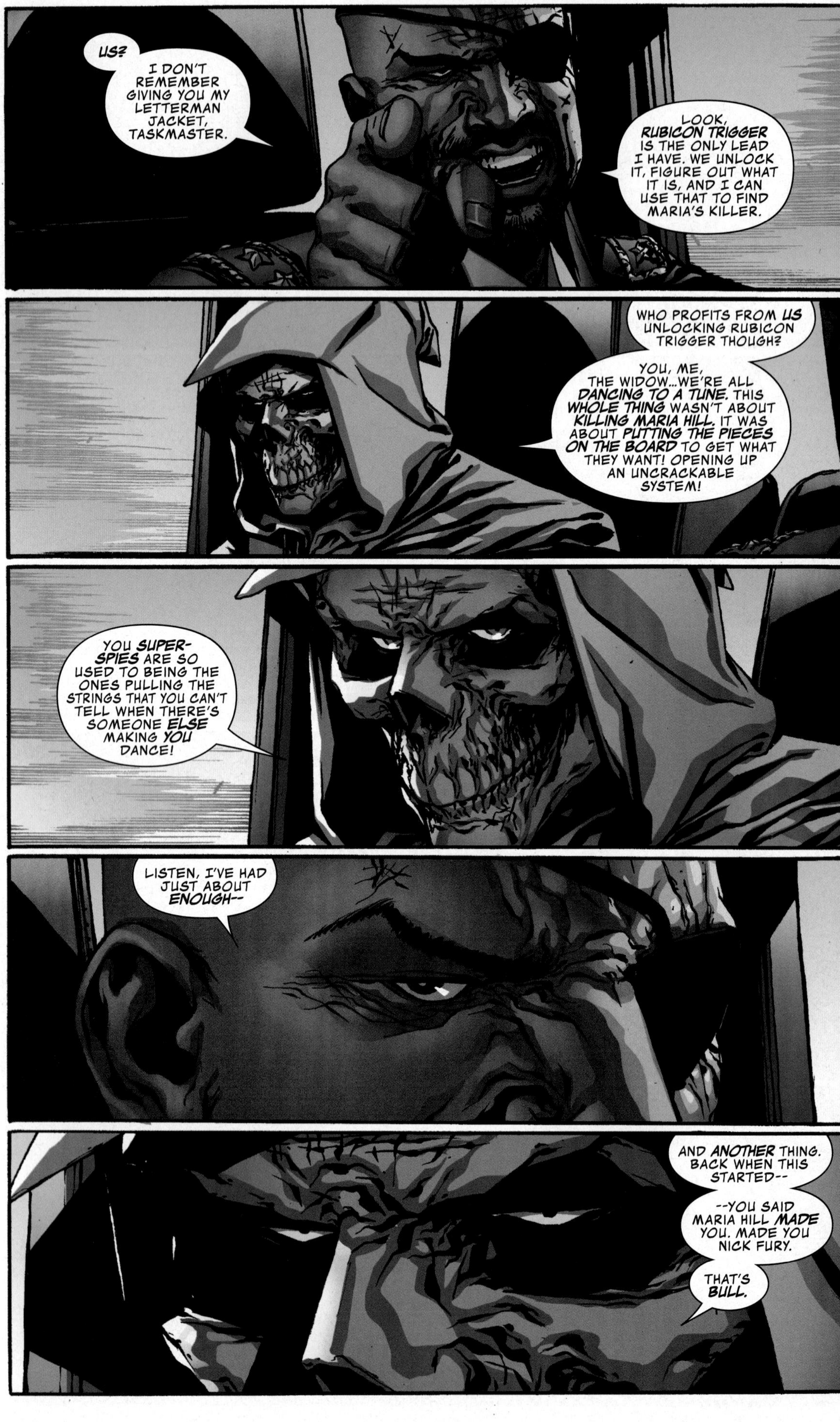
US?
I DON'T REMEMBER GIVING YOU MY LETTERMAN JACKET, TASKMASTER.
LOOK, RUBICON TRIGGER IS THE ONLY LEAD I HAVE. WE UNLOCK IT, FIGURE OUT WHAT IT IS, AND I CAN USE THAT TO FIND MARIA'S KILLER.
WHO PROFITS FROM US UNLOCKING RUBICON TRIGGER THOUGH?
YOU, ME, THE WIDOW...WE'RE ALL DANCING TO A TUNE. THIS WHOLE THING WASN'T ABOUT KILLING MARIA HILL. IT WAS ABOUT PUTTING THE PIECES ON THE BOARD TO GET WHAT THEY WANT! OPENING UP AN UNCRACKABLE SYSTEM!
YOU SUPER-SPIES ARE SO USED TO BEING THE ONES PULLING THE STRINGS THAT YOU CAN'T TELL WHEN THERE'S SOMEONE ELSE MAKING YOU DANCE!
LISTEN, I'VE HAD JUST ABOUT ENOUGH--
AND ANOTHER THING. BACK WHEN THIS STARTED--
--YOU SAID MARIA HILL MADE YOU. MADE YOU NICK FURY.
THAT'S BULL.

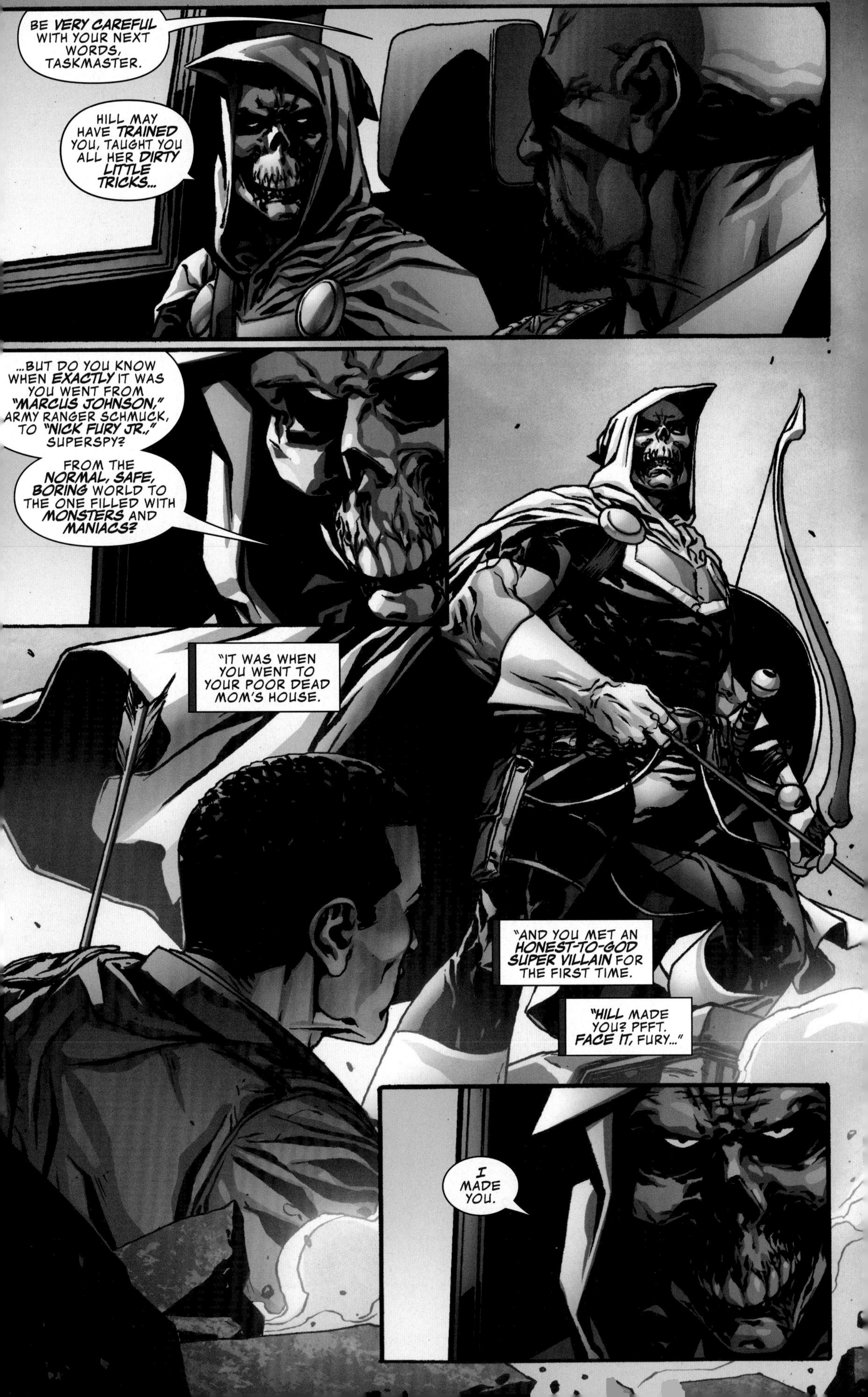
BE VERY CAREFUL WITH YOUR NEXT WORDS, TASKMASTER.
HILL MAY HAVE TRAINED YOU, TAUGHT YOU ALL HER DIRTY LITTLE TRICKS...
...BUT DO YOU KNOW WHEN EXACTLY IT WAS YOU WENT FROM "MARCUS JOHNSON," ARMY RANGER SCHMUCK, TO "NICK FURY JR.," SUPERSPY?
FROM THE NORMAL, SAFE, BORING WORLD TO THE ONE FILLED WITH MONSTERS AND MANIACS?
"IT WAS WHEN YOU WENT TO YOUR POOR DEAD MOM'S HOUSE.
"AND YOU MET AN HONEST-TO-GOD SUPER VILLAIN FOR THE FIRST TIME.
"HILL MADE YOU? PFFT. FACE IT, FURY..."
I MADE YOU.

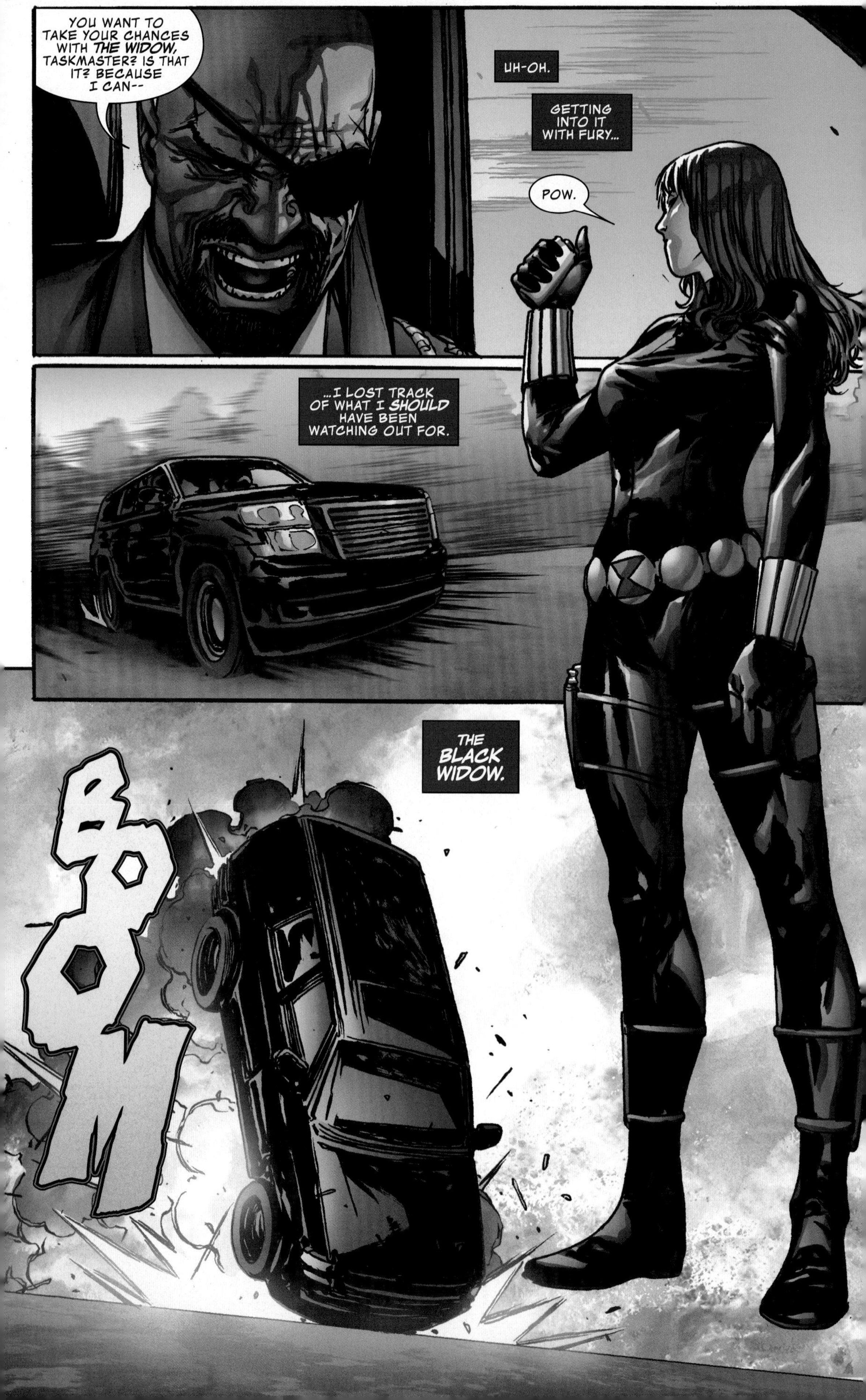
YOU WANT TO TAKE YOUR CHANCES WITH THE WIDOW, TASKMASTER? IS THAT IT? BECAUSE I CAN--
UH-OH.
GETTING INTO IT WITH FURY...
POW.
...I LOST TRACK OF WHAT I SHOULD HAVE BEEN WATCHING OUT FOR.
THE BLACK WIDOW.
BOOM

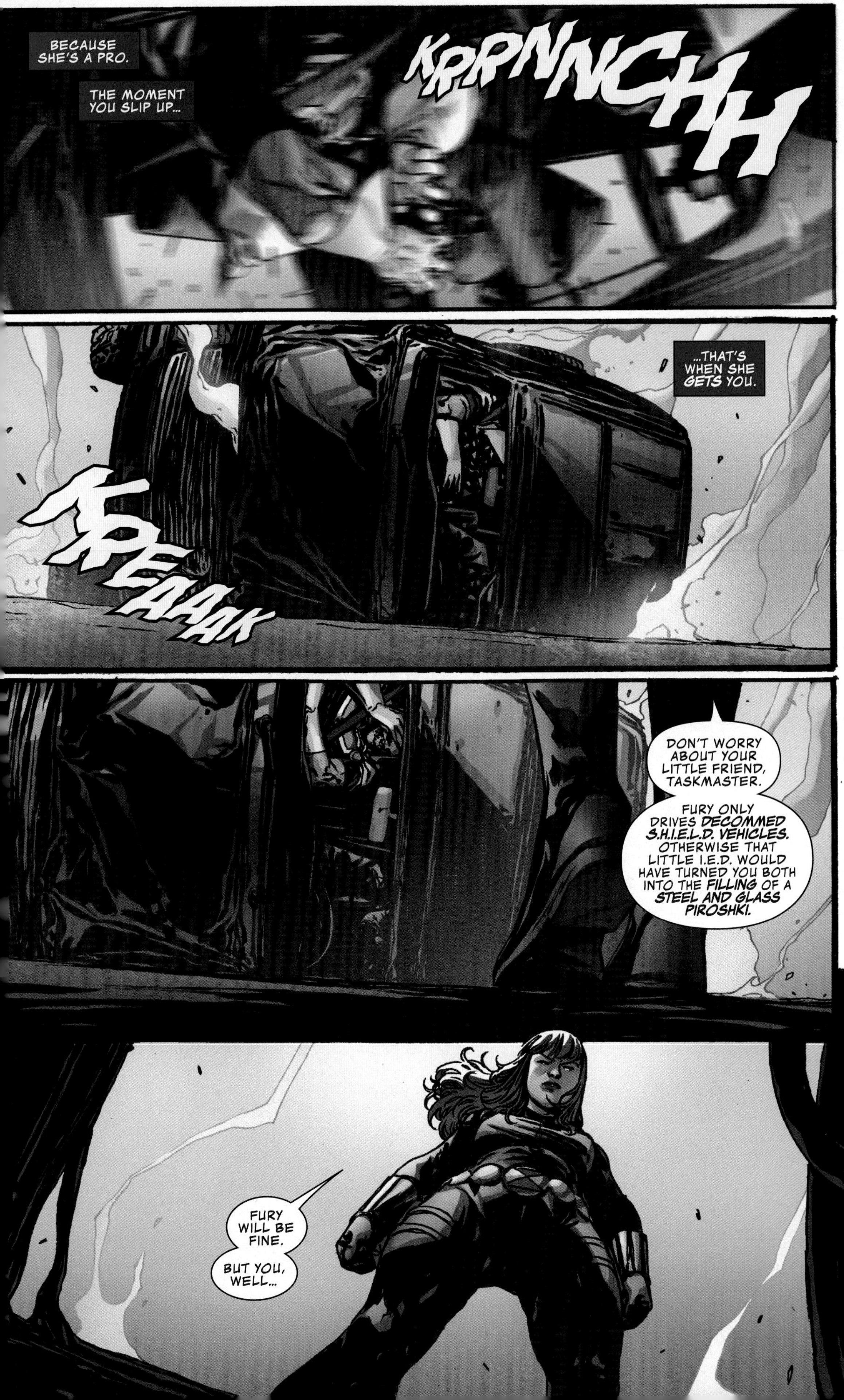

BECAUSE SHE'S A PRO.
THE MOMENT YOU SLIP UP...
KRRNNCHH
...THAT'S WHEN SHE GETS YOU.
KREAAAK
DON'T WORRY ABOUT YOUR LITTLE FRIEND, TASKMASTER.
FURY ONLY DRIVES DECOMMED S.H.I.E.L.D. VEHICLES. OTHERWISE THAT LITTLE I.E.D. WOULD HAVE TURNED YOU BOTH INTO THE FILLING OF A STEEL AND GLASS PIROSHKI.
FURY WILL BE FINE.
BUT YOU, WELL...

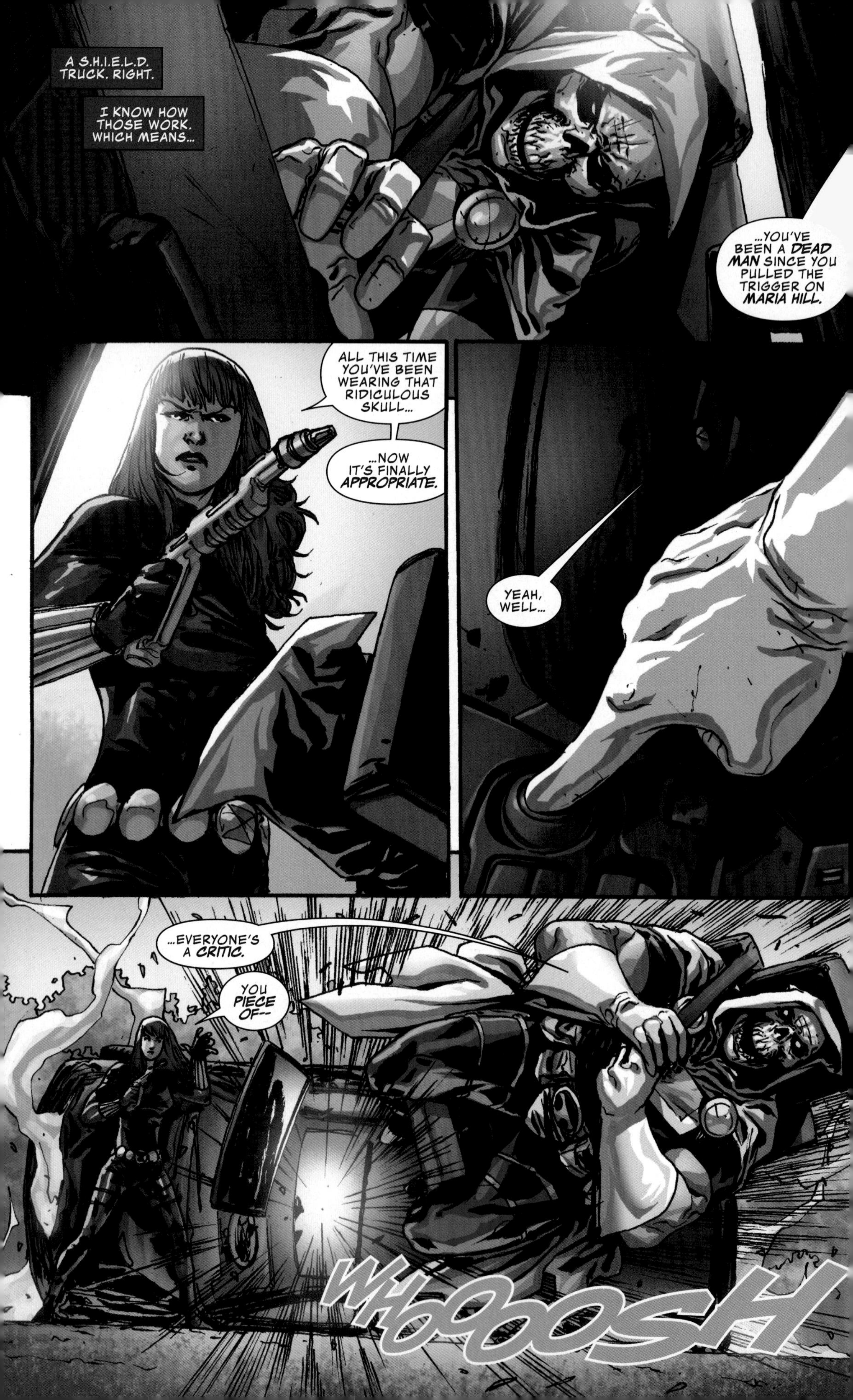
A S.H.I.E.L.D. TRUCK. RIGHT.
I KNOW HOW THOSE WORK. WHICH MEANS...
...YOU'VE BEEN A DEAD MAN SINCE YOU PULLED THE TRIGGER ON MARIA HILL.
ALL THIS TIME YOU'VE BEEN WEARING THAT RIDICULOUS SKULL...
...NOW IT'S FINALLY APPROPRIATE.
YEAH, WELL...
...EVERYONE'S A CRITIC.
YOU PIECE OF--
WHOOOOSH

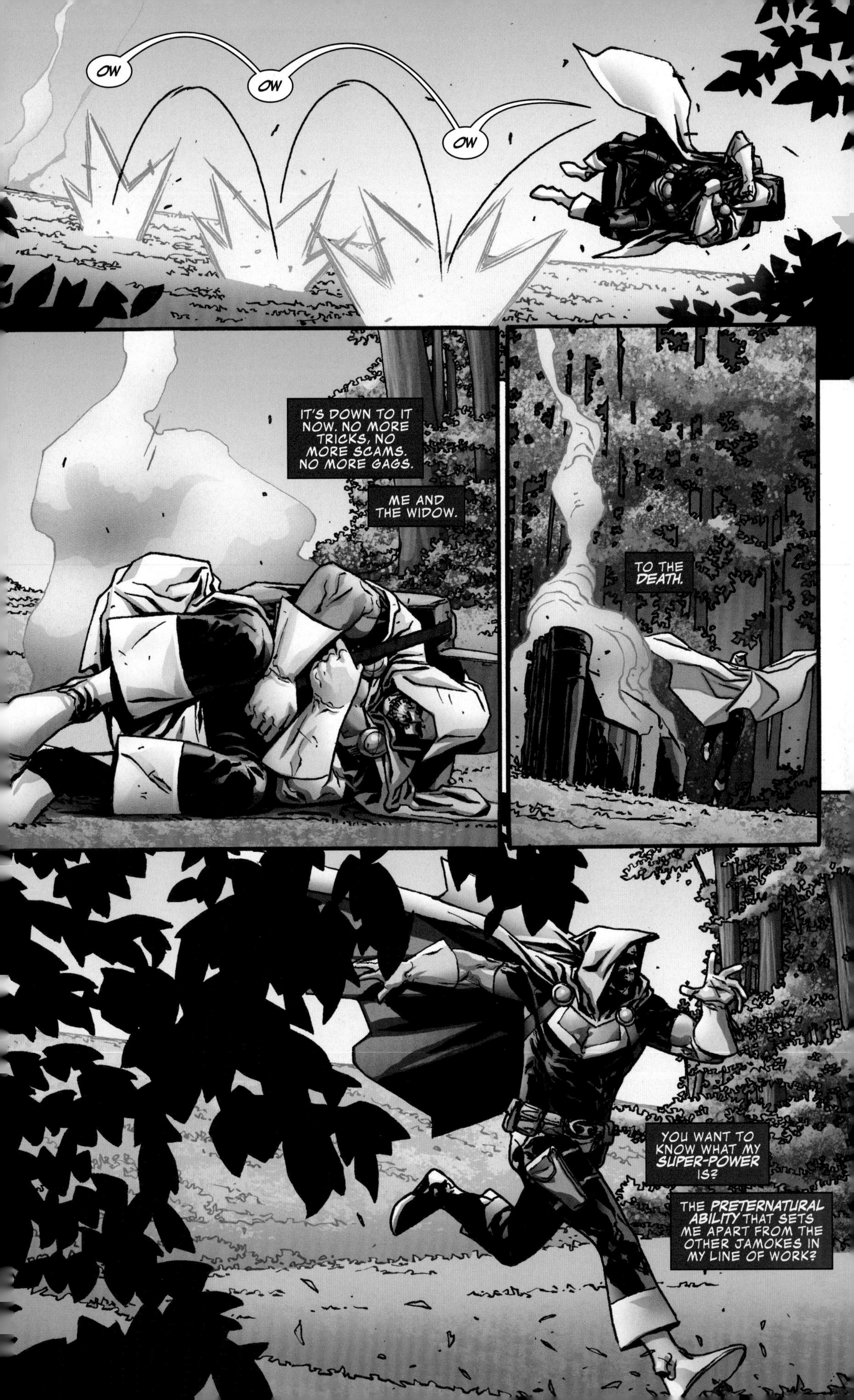
OW
OW
OW
IT'S DOWN TO IT NOW. NO MORE TRICKS, NO MORE SCAMS. NO MORE GAGS.
ME AND THE WIDOW.
TO THE DEATH.
YOU WANT TO KNOW WHAT MY SUPER-POWER IS?
THE PRETERNATURAL ABILITY THAT SETS ME APART FROM THE OTHER JAMOKES IN MY LINE OF WORK?

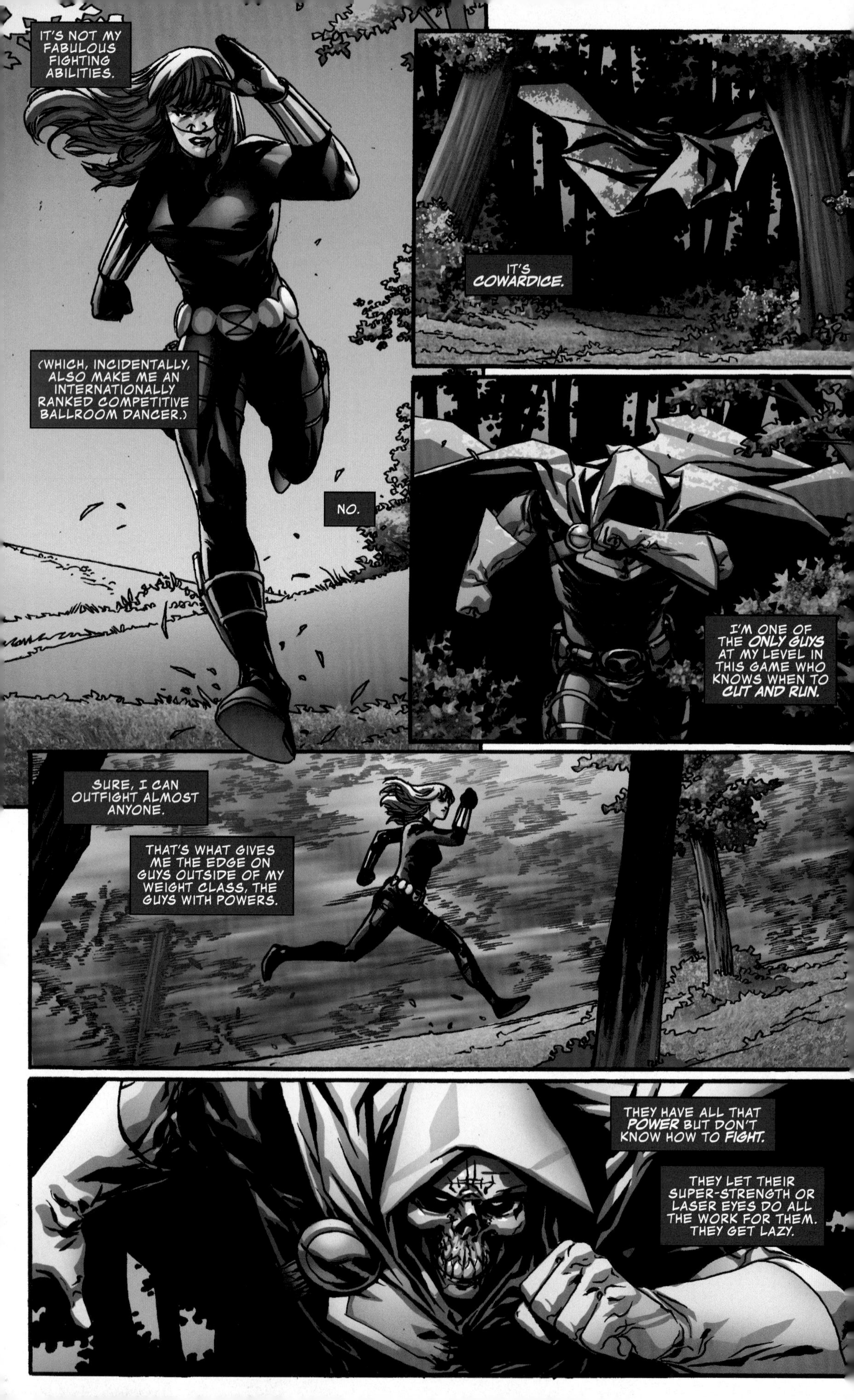
IT'S NOT MY FABULOUS FIGHTING ABILITIES.
(WHICH, INCIDENTALLY, ALSO MAKE ME AN INTERNATIONALLY RANKED COMPETITIVE BALLROOM DANCER.)
NO.
IT'S COWARDICE.
I'M ONE OF THE ONLY GUYS AT MY LEVEL IN THIS GAME WHO KNOWS WHEN TO CUT AND RUN.
SURE, I CAN OUTFIGHT ALMOST ANYONE.
THAT'S WHAT GIVES ME THE EDGE ON GUYS OUTSIDE OF MY WEIGHT CLASS, THE GUYS WITH POWERS.
THEY HAVE ALL THAT POWER BUT DON'T KNOW HOW TO FIGHT.
THEY LET THEIR SUPER-STRENGTH OR LASER EYES DO ALL THE WORK FOR THEM. THEY GET LAZY.

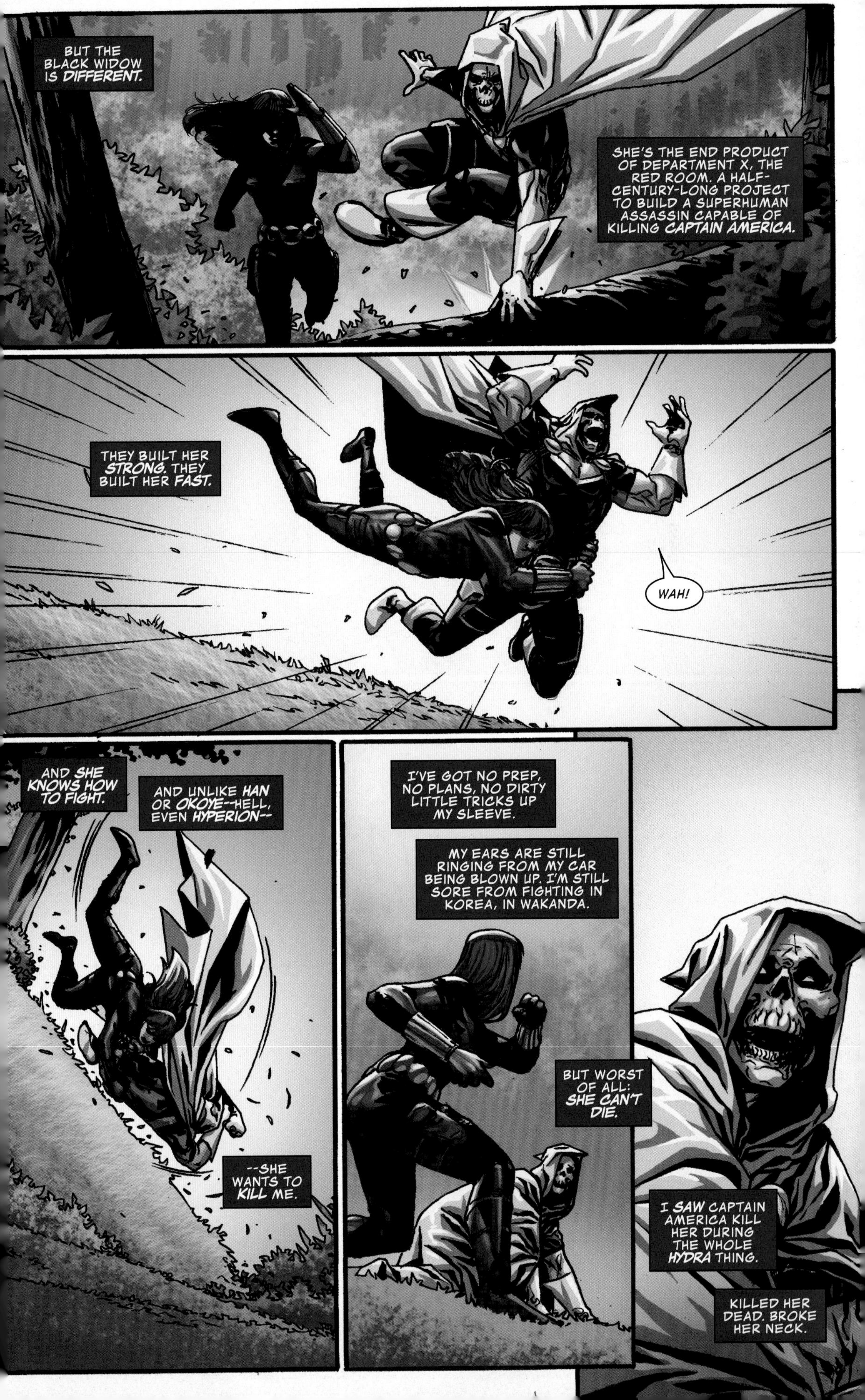
BUT THE BLACK WIDOW IS DIFFERENT.
SHE'S THE END PRODUCT OF DEPARTMENT X, THE RED ROOM. A HALF-CENTURY-LONG PROJECT TO BUILD A SUPERHUMAN ASSASSIN CAPABLE OF KILLING CAPTAIN AMERICA.
THEY BUILT HER STRONG. THEY BUILT HER FAST.
WAH!
AND SHE KNOWS HOW TO FIGHT.
AND UNLIKE HAN OR OKOYE--HELL, EVEN HYPERION--
--SHE WANTS TO KILL ME.
I'VE GOT NO PREP, NO PLANS, NO DIRTY LITTLE TRICKS UP MY SLEEVE.
MY EARS ARE STILL RINGING FROM MY CAR BEING BLOWN UP. I'M STILL SORE FROM FIGHTING IN KOREA, IN WAKANDA.
BUT WORST OF ALL: SHE CAN'T DIE.
I SAW CAPTAIN AMERICA KILL HER DURING THE WHOLE HYDRA THING.
KILLED HER DEAD. BROKE HER NECK.

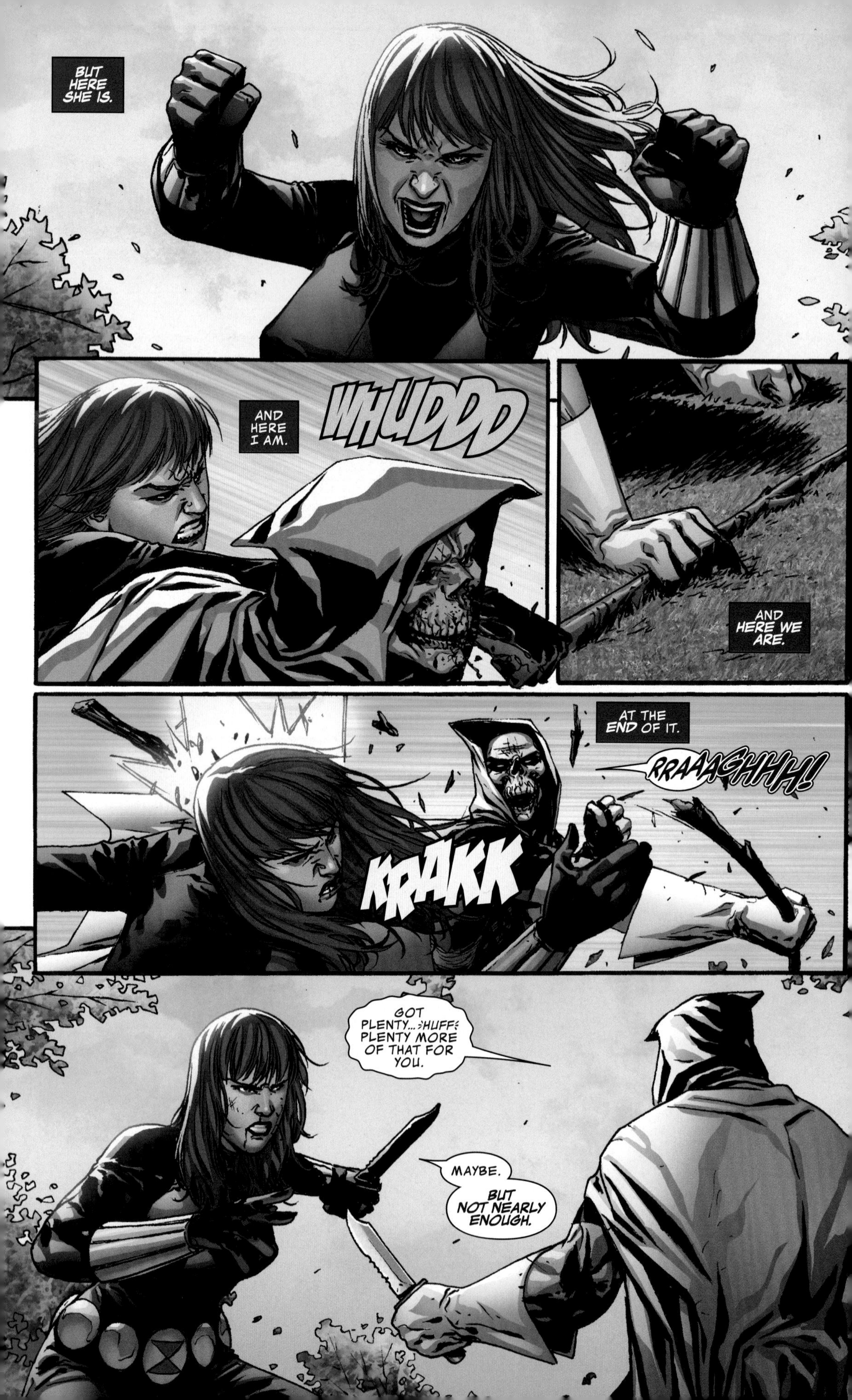
BUT HERE SHE IS.
AND HERE I AM.
WHUDDD
AND HERE WE ARE.
AT THE END OF IT.
RRAAAGHHH!
KRAKK
GOT PLENTY... ≥HUFF≤ PLENTY MORE OF THAT FOR YOU.
MAYBE.
BUT NOT NEARLY ENOUGH.

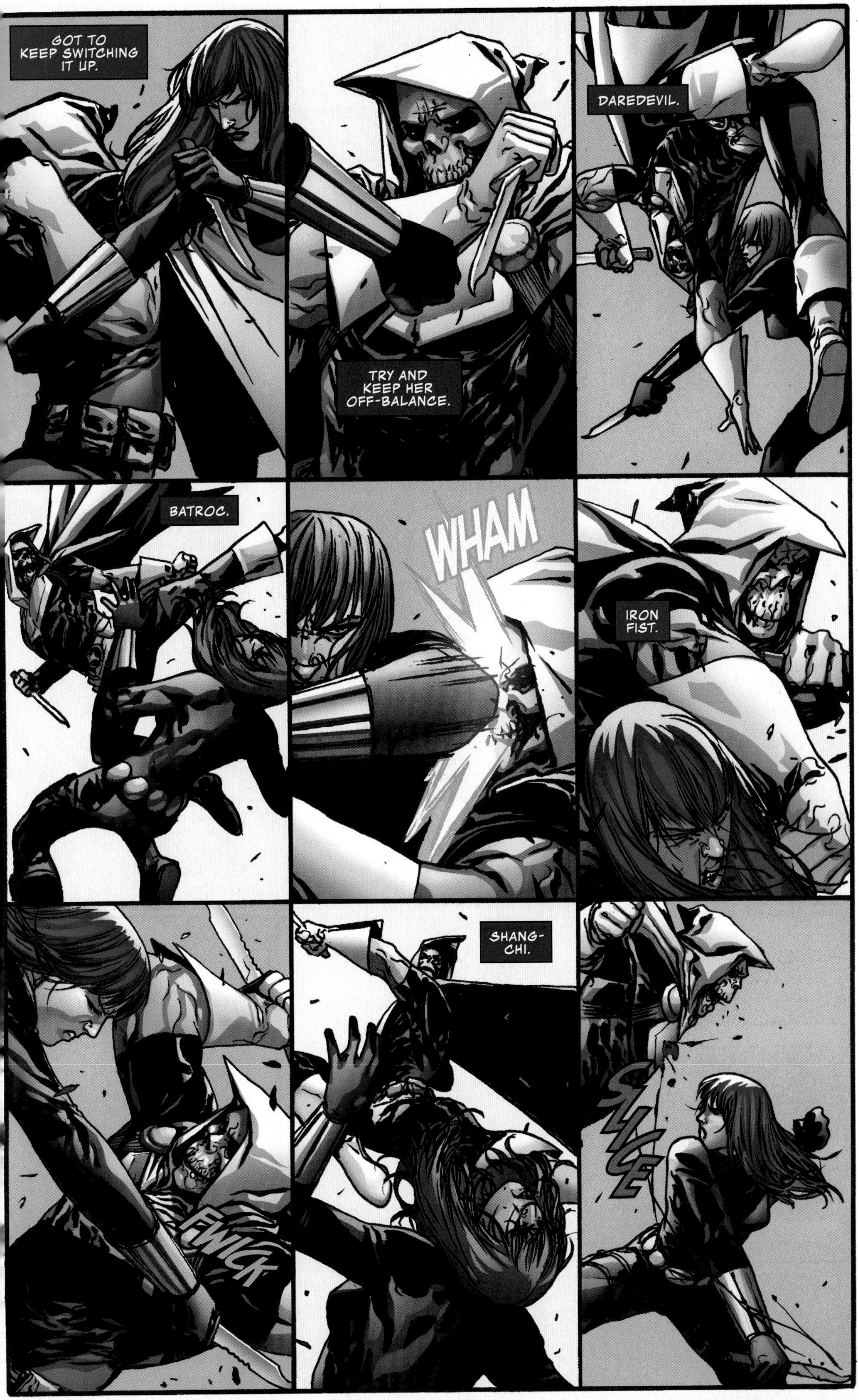
GOT TO KEEP SWITCHING IT UP.
TRY AND KEEP HER OFF-BALANCE.
DAREDEVIL.
BATROC.
WHAM
IRON FIST.
FWICK
SHANG-CHI.
SLICE

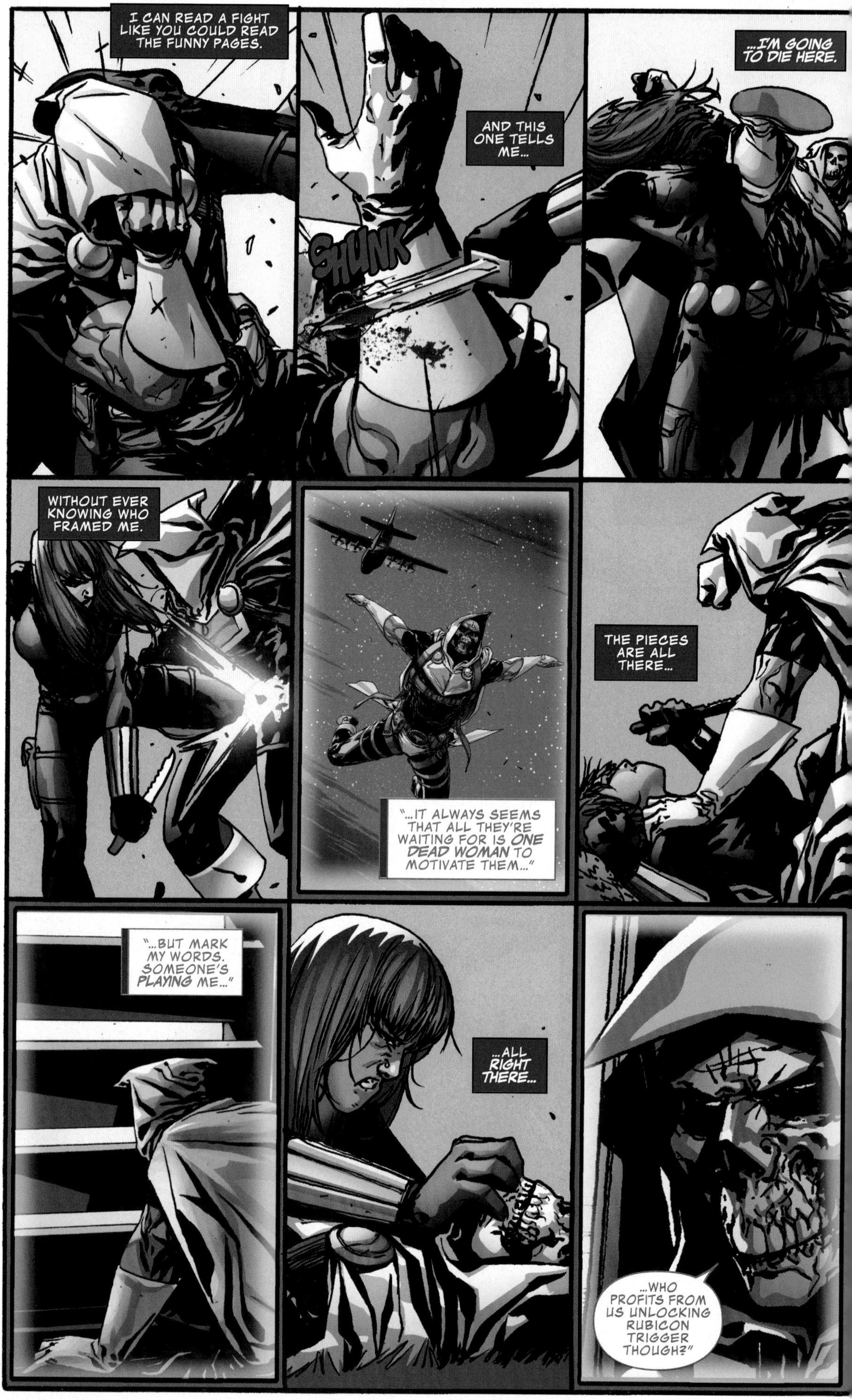
I CAN READ A FIGHT LIKE YOU COULD READ THE FUNNY PAGES.
AND THIS ONE TELLS ME...
SHUNK
...I'M GOING TO DIE HERE.
WITHOUT EVER KNOWING WHO FRAMED ME.
"...IT ALWAYS SEEMS THAT ALL THEY'RE WAITING FOR IS ONE DEAD WOMAN TO MOTIVATE THEM..."
THE PIECES ARE ALL THERE...
"...BUT MARK MY WORDS. SOMEONE'S PLAYING ME..."
...ALL RIGHT THERE...
...WHO PROFITS FROM US UNLOCKING RUBICON TRIGGER THOUGH?"

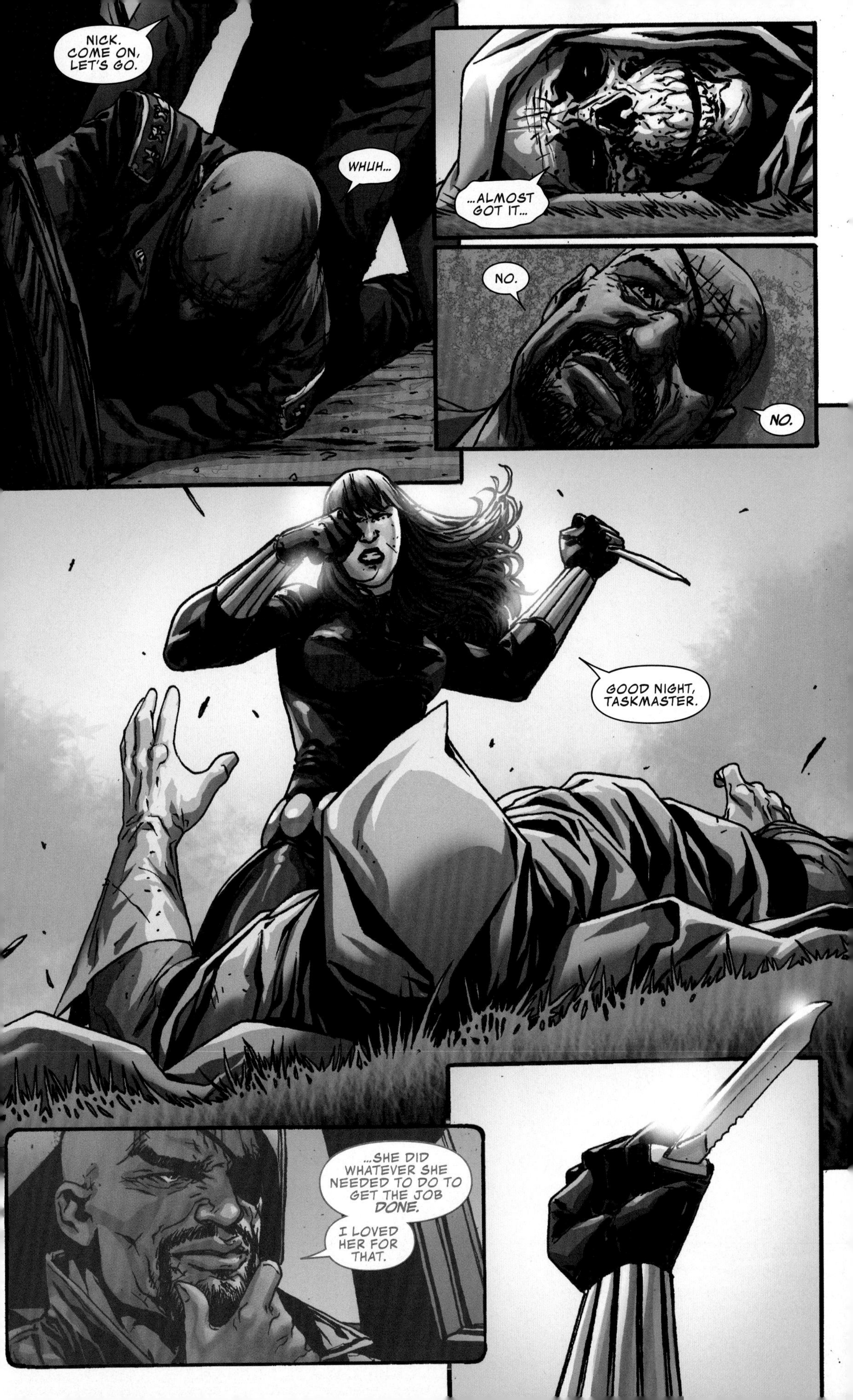
NICK. COME ON, LET'S GO.
WHUH...
...ALMOST GOT IT...
NO.
NO.
GOOD NIGHT, TASKMASTER.
...SHE DID WHATEVER SHE NEEDED TO DO TO GET THE JOB DONE.
I LOVED HER FOR THAT.

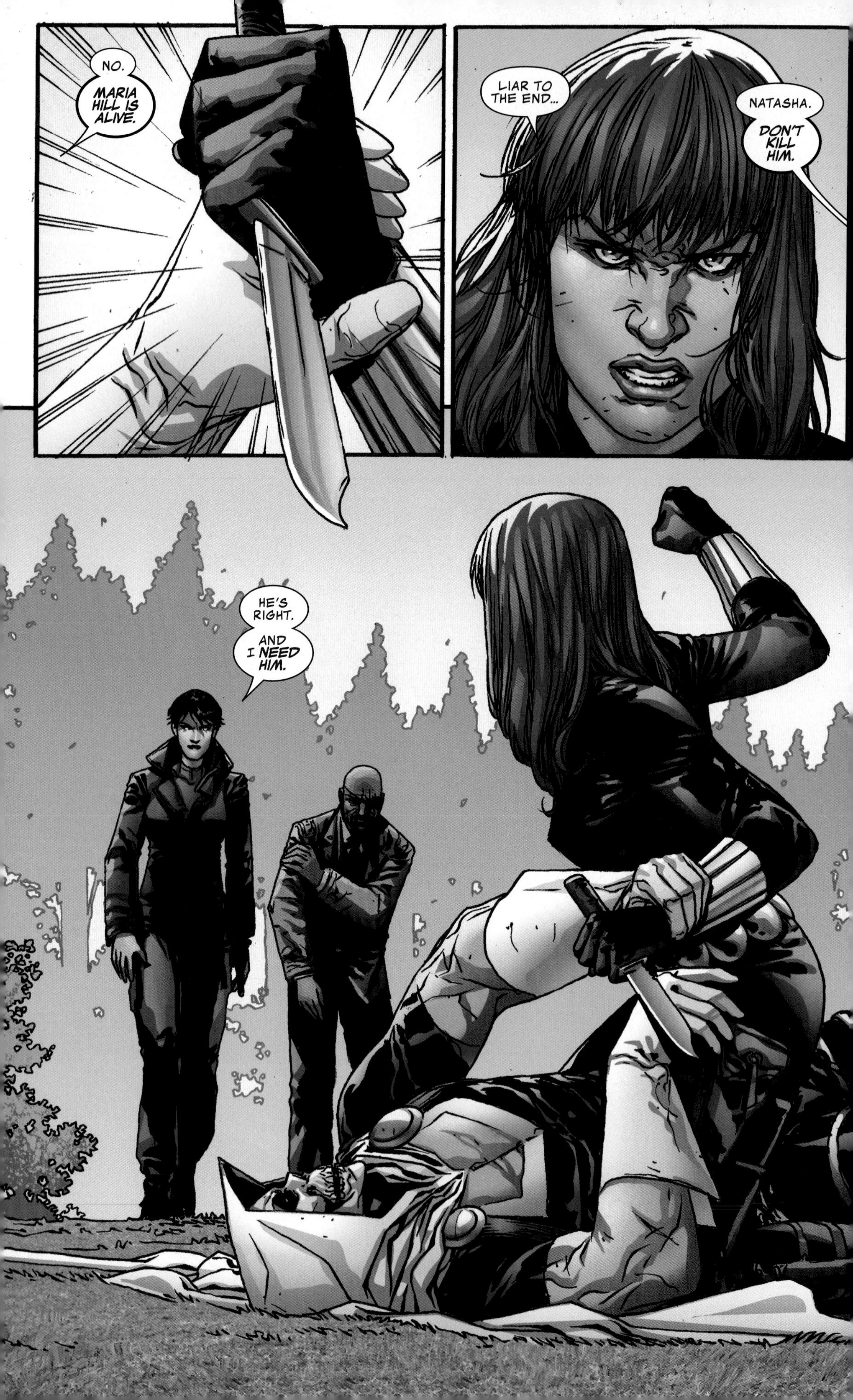
NO.
MARIA HILL IS ALIVE.
LIAR TO THE END...
NATASHA.
DON'T KILL HIM.
HE'S RIGHT.
AND I NEED HIM.

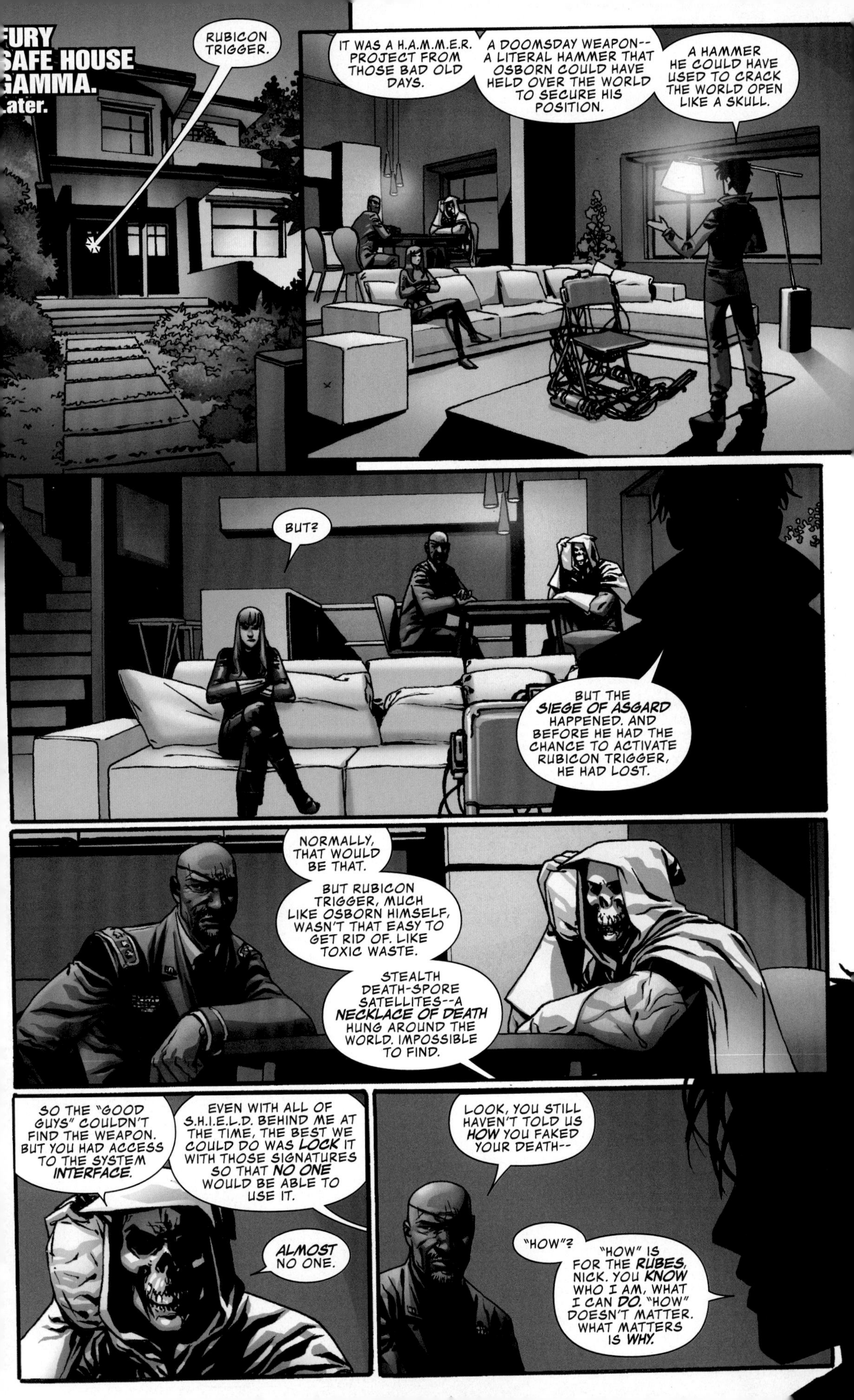

FURY
SAFE HOUSE
GAMMA.
Later.
RUBICON TRIGGER.
IT WAS A H.A.M.M.E.R. PROJECT FROM THOSE BAD OLD DAYS.
A DOOMSDAY WEAPON-- A LITERAL HAMMER THAT OSBORN COULD HAVE HELD OVER THE WORLD TO SECURE HIS POSITION.
A HAMMER HE COULD HAVE USED TO CRACK THE WORLD OPEN LIKE A SKULL.
BUT?
BUT THE SIEGE OF ASGARD HAPPENED. AND BEFORE HE HAD THE CHANCE TO ACTIVATE RUBICON TRIGGER, HE HAD LOST.
NORMALLY, THAT WOULD BE THAT.
BUT RUBICON TRIGGER, MUCH LIKE OSBORN HIMSELF, WASN'T THAT EASY TO GET RID OF. LIKE TOXIC WASTE.
STEALTH DEATH-SPORE SATELLITES--A NECKLACE OF DEATH HUNG AROUND THE WORLD. IMPOSSIBLE TO FIND.
SO THE "GOOD GUYS" COULDN'T FIND THE WEAPON. BUT YOU HAD ACCESS TO THE SYSTEM INTERFACE.
EVEN WITH ALL OF S.H.I.E.L.D. BEHIND ME AT THE TIME, THE BEST WE COULD DO WAS LOCK IT WITH THOSE SIGNATURES SO THAT NO ONE WOULD BE ABLE TO USE IT.
ALMOST NO ONE.
LOOK, YOU STILL HAVEN'T TOLD US HOW YOU FAKED YOUR DEATH--
"HOW"?
"HOW" IS FOR THE RUBES, NICK. YOU KNOW WHO I AM, WHAT I CAN DO. "HOW" DOESN'T MATTER. WHAT MATTERS IS WHY.

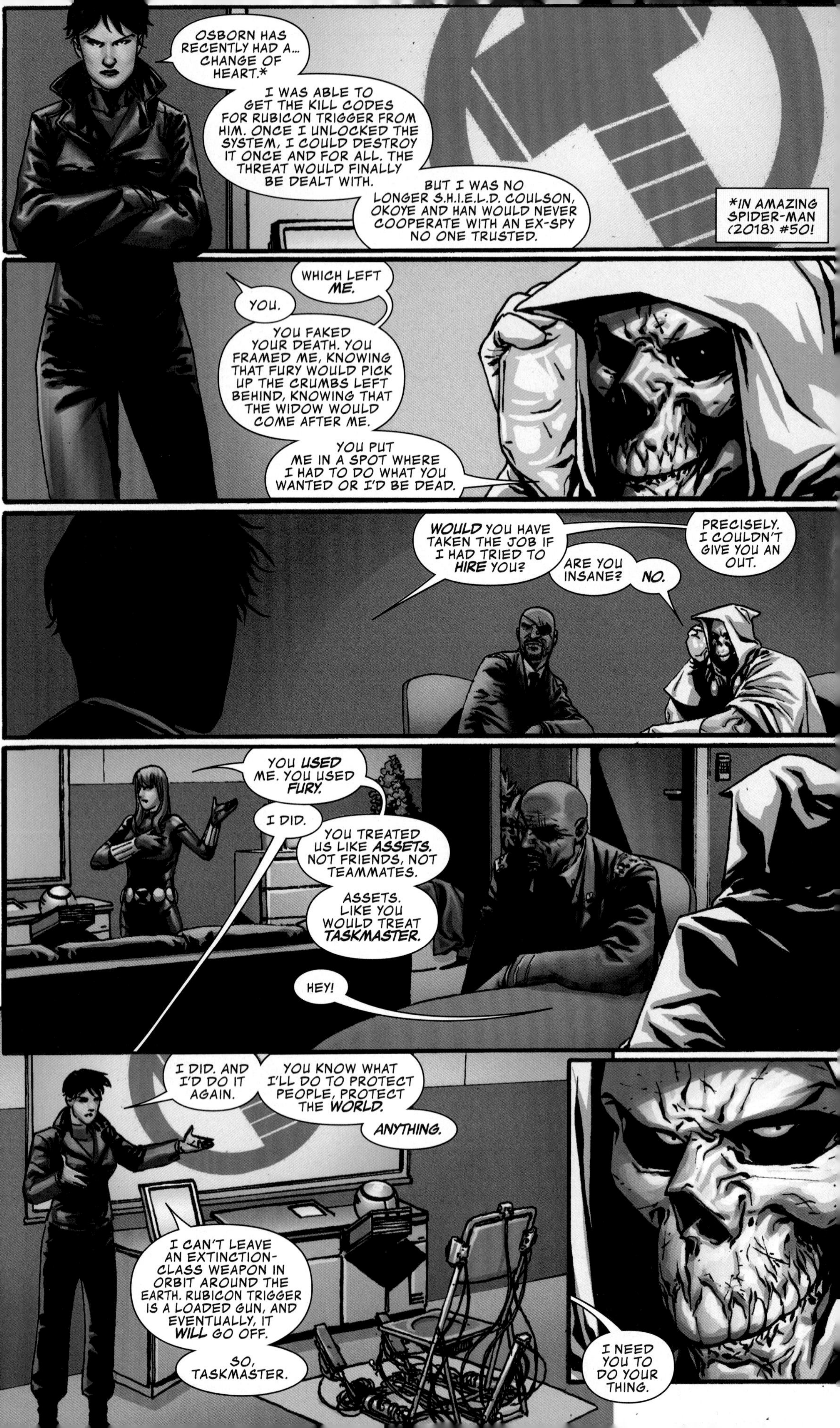
OSBORN HAS RECENTLY HAD A... CHANGE OF HEART.*
I WAS ABLE TO GET THE KILL CODES FOR RUBICON TRIGGER FROM HIM. ONCE I UNLOCKED THE SYSTEM, I COULD DESTROY IT ONCE AND FOR ALL. THE THREAT WOULD FINALLY BE DEALT WITH.
BUT I WAS NO LONGER S.H.I.E.L.D. COULSON, OKOYE AND HAN WOULD NEVER COOPERATE WITH AN EX-SPY NO ONE TRUSTED.
*IN AMAZING SPIDER-MAN (2018) #50!
YOU.
WHICH LEFT ME.
YOU FAKED YOUR DEATH. YOU FRAMED ME, KNOWING THAT FURY WOULD PICK UP THE CRUMBS LEFT BEHIND, KNOWING THAT THE WIDOW WOULD COME AFTER ME.
YOU PUT ME IN A SPOT WHERE I HAD TO DO WHAT YOU WANTED OR I'D BE DEAD.
WOULD YOU HAVE TAKEN THE JOB IF I HAD TRIED TO HIRE YOU?
ARE YOU INSANE?
NO.
PRECISELY. I COULDN'T GIVE YOU AN OUT.
YOU USED ME. YOU USED FURY.
I DID.
YOU TREATED US LIKE ASSETS. NOT FRIENDS, NOT TEAMMATES.
ASSETS. LIKE YOU WOULD TREAT TASKMASTER.
HEY!
I DID. AND I'D DO IT AGAIN.
YOU KNOW WHAT I'LL DO TO PROTECT PEOPLE, PROTECT THE WORLD.
ANYTHING.
I CAN'T LEAVE AN EXTINCTION-CLASS WEAPON IN ORBIT AROUND THE EARTH. RUBICON TRIGGER IS A LOADED GUN, AND EVENTUALLY, IT WILL GO OFF.
SO, TASKMASTER.
I NEED YOU TO DO YOUR THING.

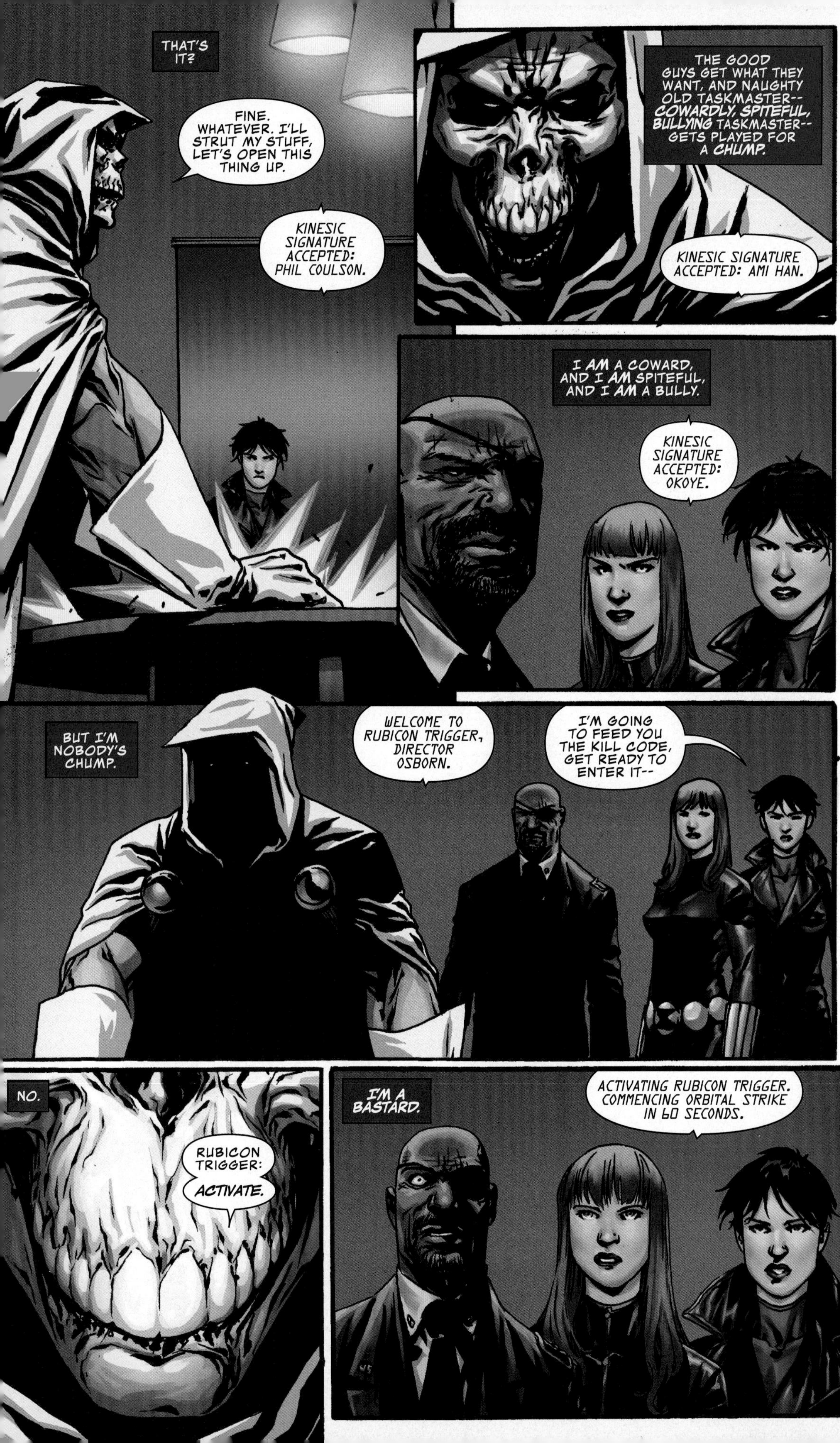
THAT'S IT?
FINE. WHATEVER. I'LL STRUT MY STUFF, LET'S OPEN THIS THING UP.
KINESIC SIGNATURE ACCEPTED: PHIL COULSON.
THE GOOD GUYS GET WHAT THEY WANT, AND NAUGHTY OLD TASKMASTER-- COWARDLY, SPITEFUL, BULLYING TASKMASTER-- GETS PLAYED FOR A CHUMP.
KINESIC SIGNATURE ACCEPTED: AMI HAN.
I AM A COWARD, AND I AM SPITEFUL, AND I AM A BULLY.
KINESIC SIGNATURE ACCEPTED: OKOYE.
BUT I'M NOBODY'S CHUMP.
WELCOME TO RUBICON TRIGGER, DIRECTOR OSBORN.
I'M GOING TO FEED YOU THE KILL CODE, GET READY TO ENTER IT--
NO.
RUBICON TRIGGER:
ACTIVATE.
I'M A BASTARD.
ACTIVATING RUBICON TRIGGER. COMMENCING ORBITAL STRIKE IN 60 SECONDS.

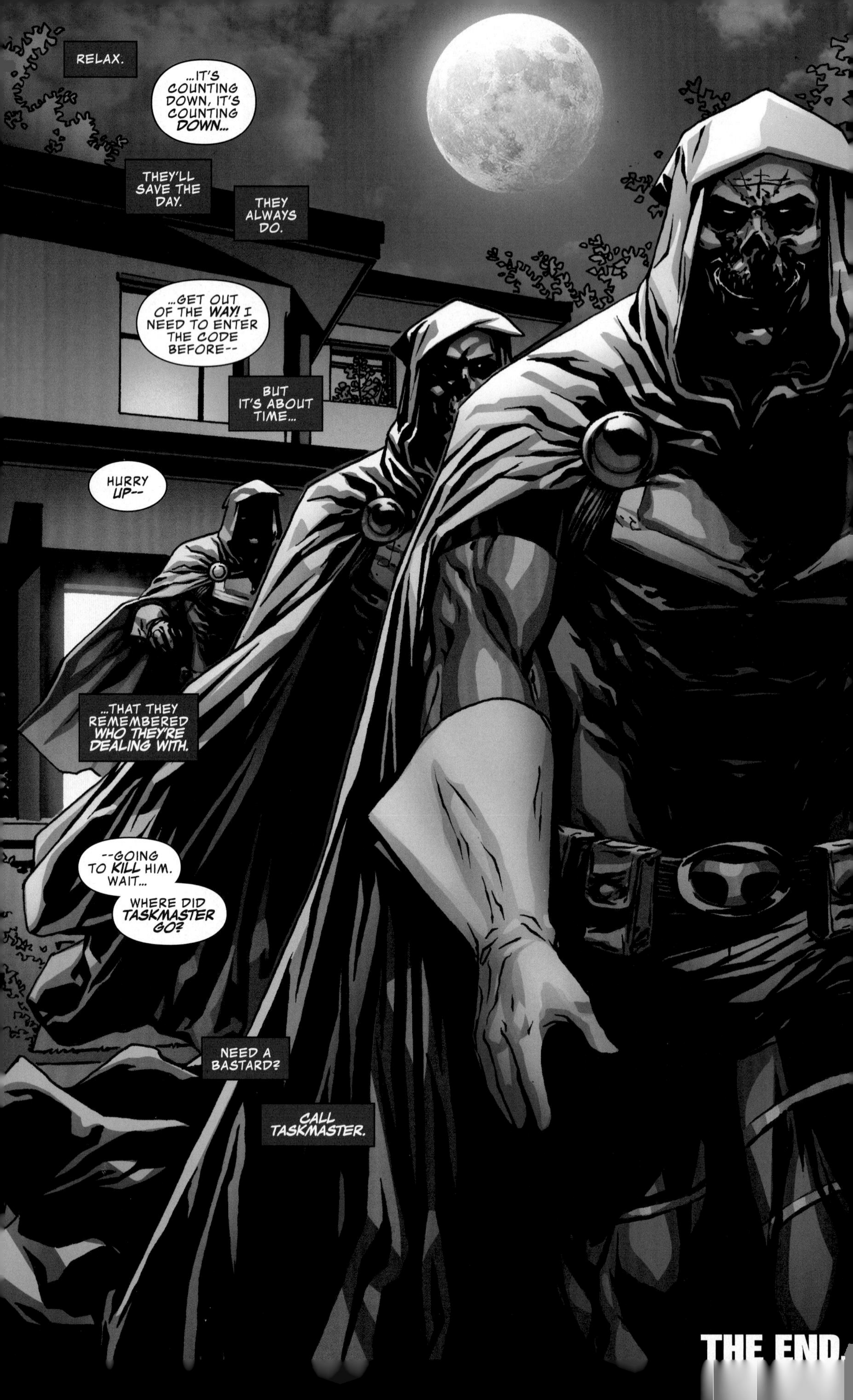
RELAX.
...IT'S COUNTING DOWN, IT'S COUNTING DOWN...
THEY'LL SAVE THE DAY.
THEY ALWAYS DO.
...GET OUT OF THE WAY! I NEED TO ENTER THE CODE BEFORE--
BUT IT'S ABOUT TIME...
HURRY UP--
...THAT THEY REMEMBERED WHO THEY'RE DEALING WITH.
--GOING TO KILL HIM. WAIT...
WHERE DID TASKMASTER GO?
NEED A BASTARD?
CALL TASKMASTER.
THE END.

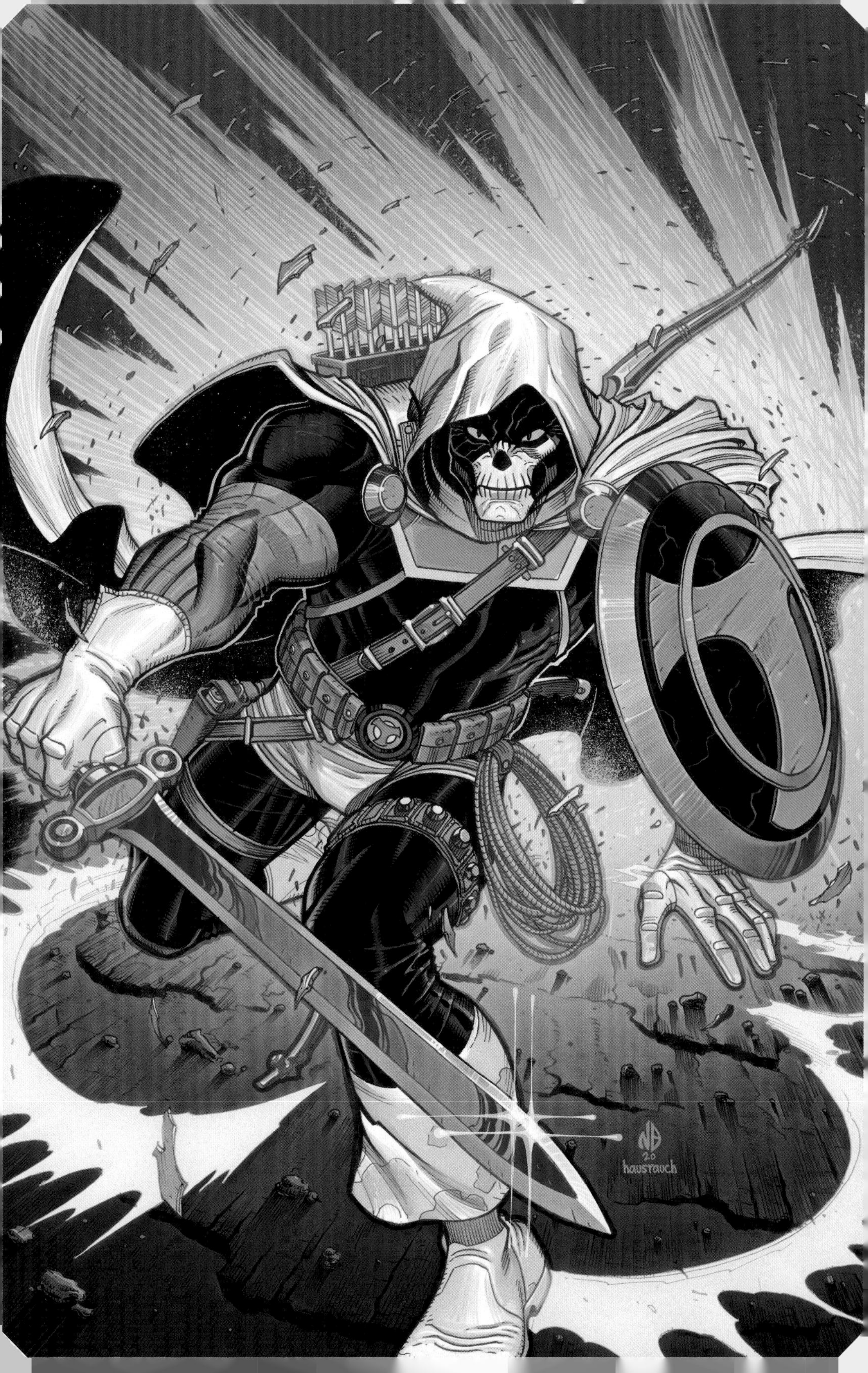
hausrauch

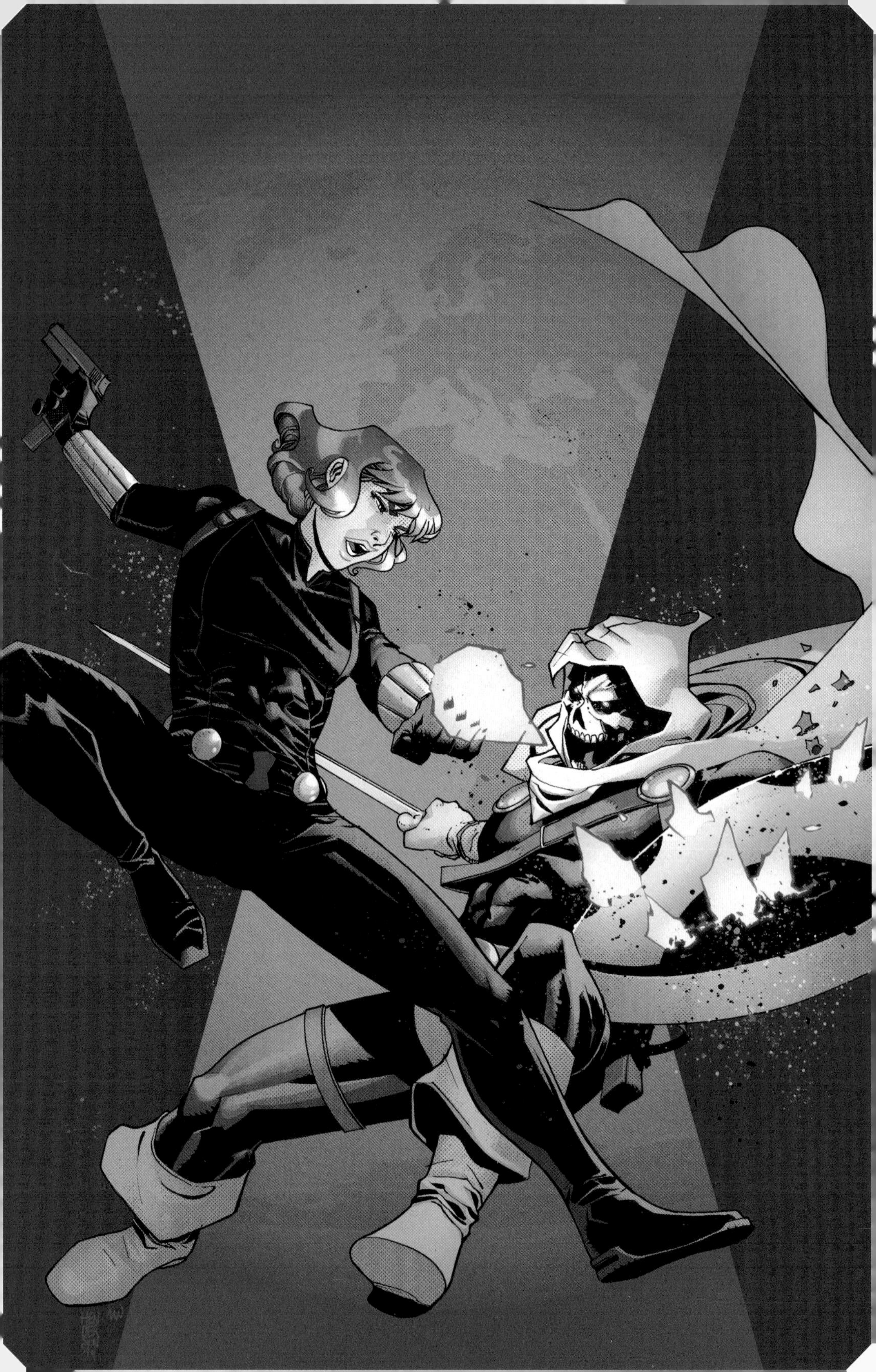

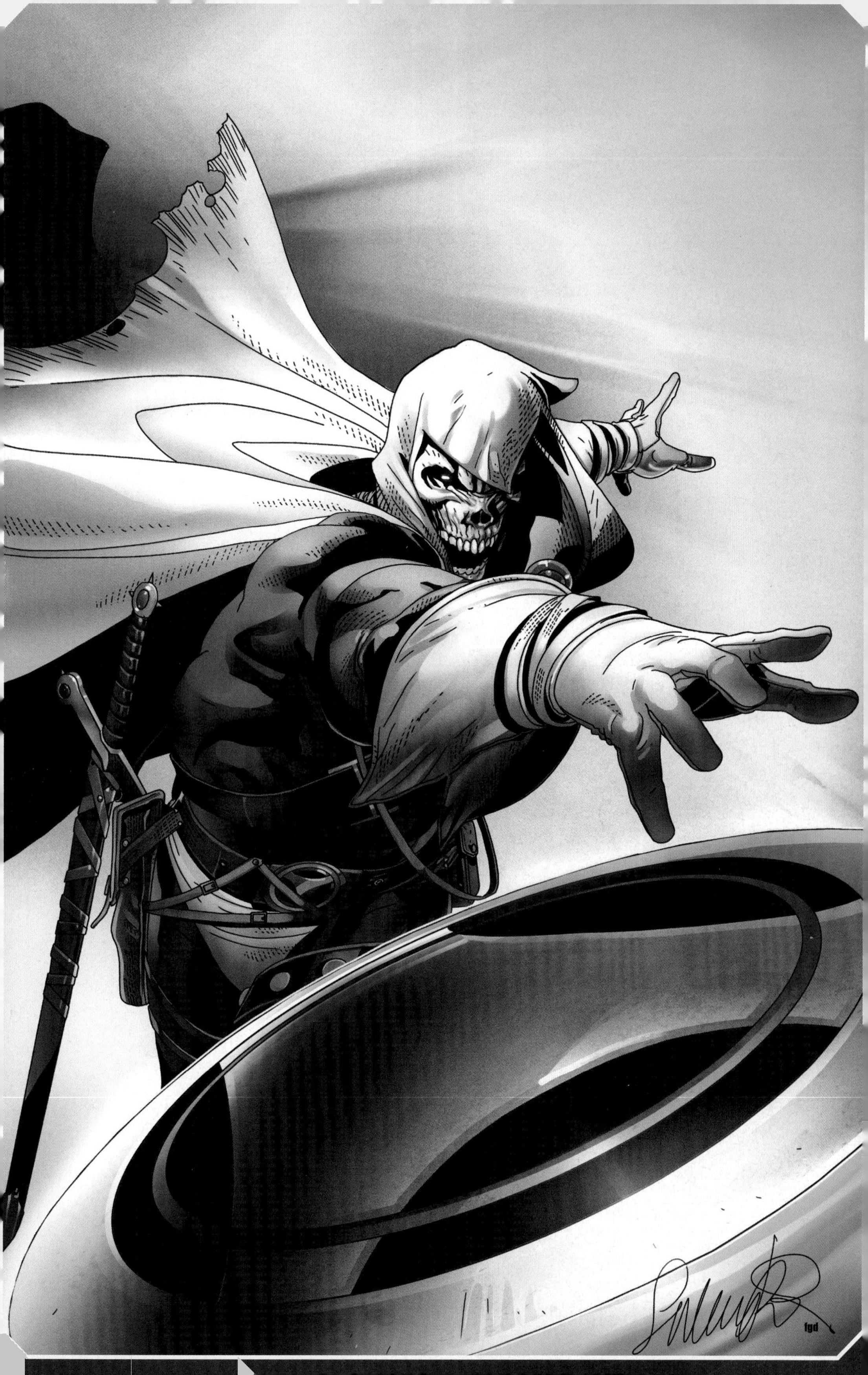

Su

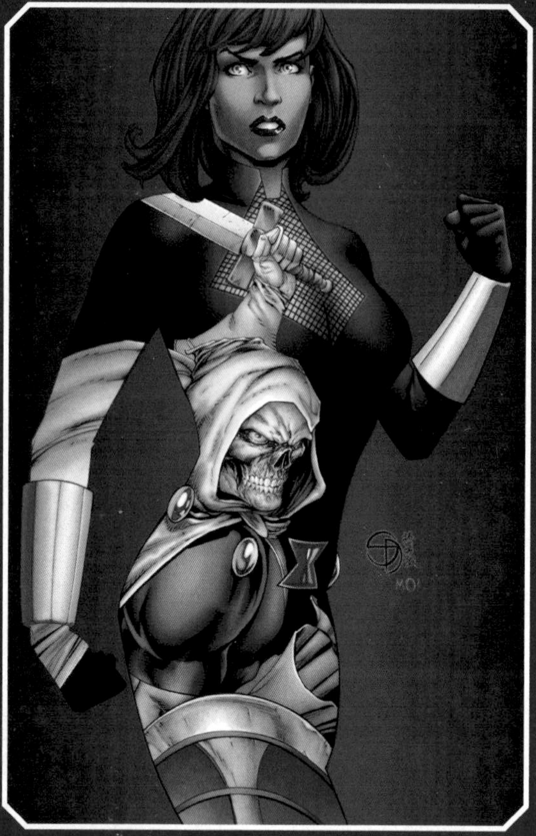

#3 VARIANT

**Shane Davis & Morry Hollowell**

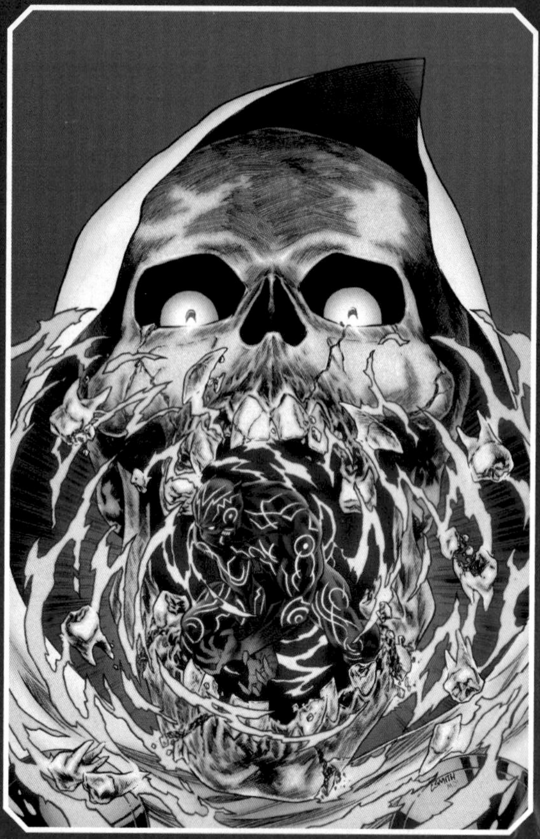

#4 VARIANT

**Cory Smith**

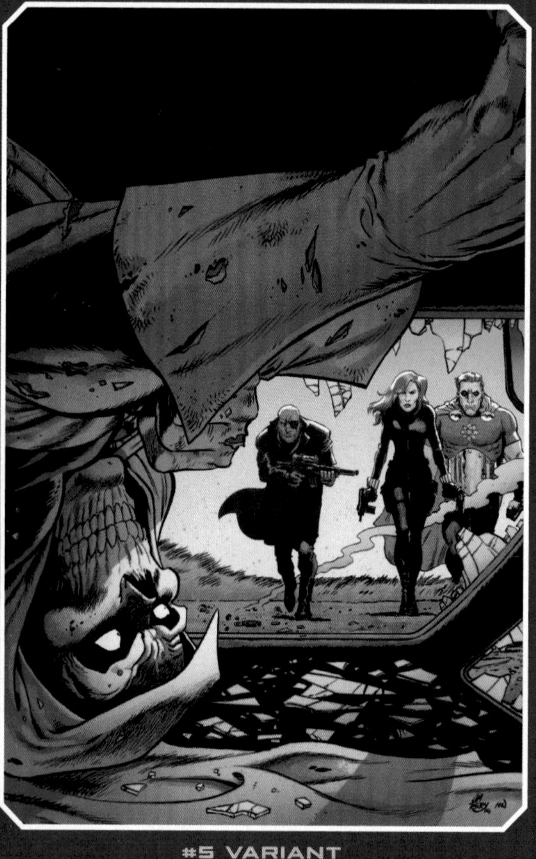

#5 VARIANT

**Jim Terry & Nolan Woodard**